HELM IDENTIFICATION GUIDES

# TERNS
## OF EUROPE AND NORTH AMERICA

Klaus Malling Olsen and Hans Larsson

CHRISTOPHER HELM

A & C Black • London

English-language edition first published 1995
by Christopher Helm (Publishers) Limited,
a subsidiary of A & C Black (Publishers) Limited,
35 Bedford Row, London WC1R 4JH
ISBN 0-7136-4056-1

A GMB Books production


Translated by David A. Christie
Design and DTP by Sandra Gardeslen
Cover: Common Tern. Photo: Karel Beylevelt

A CIP catalogue record for this book is available from the British Library


Printed and bound in Hong Kong

# Contents

# Foreword

Acknowledgements: A great many people and authorities have contributed to the end result of this book. We thank the personnel at the respective museums for access to the collections: Peter Colston and Robert Prys-Jones (BMNH), Niels Otto Preuss and Jon Fjeldså (UZM), Carl Edelstam and Göran Frisk (NRK), Per-Göran Bentz (ZMO, MN), Tore Slagsvold (ZMO), Sverker Wadén (MN), Pekka J. Nikander and Hannu Jännes (ZMH), Lennart Cederholm (ZML), René Dekker (NNH), C. J. (Kees) Roselaar (ZMA) and Phil Angle (NMNH).

For the loan of photographs, fruitful discussions, suggestions for the outline plan and other good advice, I warmly thank a large number of people. These are: Jan Abromovitz, Jonathan Alderfer, Per Alström, Jens Frimer Andersen, Peter Arctander, Ferje Axelsen, Arnoud B. van den Berg, Karel Beyleveld, Bertil Breife, Jens B. Bruun, Mads Jensen Bunch, Steen Christensen, Arthur Christiansen, Erik Christopherson, Peter Colston, John Damgård-Nielsen, Rolf Danielsen, Lars Dinesen, Henrik Dissing, Paul Doherty, Ola Elleström, Erik Enevoldsen, Patrik Engström, Hanne & Jens Eriksen, Knud Falk, Dick Forsman, Michael J. Gallagher, Hans Gebuis, Mats Gothnier, Iver Gram, Jan Hägg, Per Schiermacher Hansen, Björn Hillarp, Erik Hirschfeld, Markku Huhta-Koivisto, Stig Jensen, Hjalte B. Johansen, Thomas W. Johansen, Mikael Jonahsson, Lars Jonsson, Henrik Kisbye, Nils Kjellén, Arie de Knijff, Peter de Knijff, Peter Kock, Ko de Korte, John Larsen, Knud Larsen, Mikkel Lausten, Henry Lehto, Harry J. Lehto, Ton Lindroos, Johan Lorentzon, Jesper Madsen, Stig Toft Madsen, Ingvar Martinsson, Ger Meesters, Dick Meijer, Åse Mielow, Dirk Moerbeek, Killian Mullarney, Kurt Møller Nielsen, Pekka J. Nikander, Lars Nilsson, Lars-Erik Nygren, Knud Pedersen, René Pop, Richard F. Porter, Robert Prys-Jones, Hans Roersma, Hadoram Shirihai, Uffe Gjøl Sørensen, Thorsten Stegmann, Briand Strack, Rasmus Strack, Peter Sunesen, Ola Svensson, Vibeke Tofte, Anders Tvevad, Magnus Ullman, Thure Wikberg, Claudia Wilds, Anders Wirdheim and Alan Wormington.

The book is dedicated to the memory of two field ornithologists, each a giant in his own domain [sphere]: Peter J. Grant and Svend Christoffersen ('Stoffer').

# Introduction

### The format of the species accounts

The species are dealt with in the following manner. First there is a section on identification in the field. Here, the most important structural characters, behaviour, flight action, and the distinguishing features of the various plumages are mentioned. The intention of this is to enable anybody directly to identify to species the majority of terns. A section on moult follows. The data are taken from a large number of field notes supplemented with studies of skins and photographs and discussions with a number of ornithologists. They have been supplemented with data from the literature, mainly from Cramp (1985) and Glutz von Blotzheim & Bauer (1982). For each plumage a detailed description follows, which is intended mostly for those who are eager to know more about the minor details of plumage.

Geographical variation is dealt with briefly. The species account ends with data on measurements and weight from museum skins, supplemented with information from the literature.

The following museum collections have been examined: *BMNH* British Museum (Natural History), Tring, England [now known as the Natural History Museum, Tring]. *UZM* Universitetets Zoologiske Museum, Copenhagen, Denmark. *MN* Malmö Naturmuseum, Malmö, Sweden. *NRK* Naturhistoriska Riksmuseet, Stockholm, Sweden. *ZML* Zoologisk Museum, Lund, Sweden. *ZMU* Zoologisk Museum, Uppsala, Sweden. *ZMH* Zoological Museum, University of Helsinki, Finland. *ZMO* Zoologisk Museum, Universitetet i Oslo, Norway. *NNH* Nationaal Natuurhistorisch Museum, Leiden, Netherlands. *ZMA* Zoölogisch Museum (Instituut voor Taxonomische Zoölogie), Amsterdam, Netherlands. *NMNH* National Museum of Natural History, Smithsonian Institute, Washington, D.C., USA.

There is also a key listing point by point the most important species characters.

### Different light conditions produce different impressions

The terns are predominantly pale birds (apart from the *Chlidonias* species, Sooty and Bridled Terns and the noddies). How a tern appears is much influenced by light conditions. Against the light, the silhouette and any translucency of the wing are the most important characters, while the colours are difficult to perceive and sometimes misleading. Strong sunlight often causes the outermost elongated tail feathers to 'disappear'. In direct light one quicky sees colour contrasts, bill colour and elongated outermost tail feathers, while silhouette and proportions are often poorly observed.

Strong sunlight has an appreciable influence on the perception of colours. In particular, tropical sunlight can even make dark upperparts become pale, important to be aware of if attempting to assess colour differences on the upperparts in a mixed flock of terns at midday on an Indian Ocean shore. Strong sunlight also impairs our perception of the contrast between back and rump/tail, and normally grey areas can become white. In low sunlight the birds become greyer and a certain reddening of the plumage can occur.

Dull, cloudy weather causes grey colour tones to stand out more obviously, and in this light details such as a white rump and tail are seen clearly. A certain browning can also occur. Small finer differences between closely related species are of great value in direct comparison.

One should also note that backlighting can cause the Black Tern's wing to appear pale and shining, almost as on White-winged Black Tern.

Closer observations, however, reveal that the colour never comes up to the quality of the snow-white front edge of the wing of White-winged Black.

In photos, plumage contrasts often stand out more strongly than in real life. A sunlit nape or rump against a part of the plumage in shadow produces false contrasts. Hard printing produces false, strong dark/light contrast (see photo of Black Tern in Alström 1989) which is not evident in the field.

## Judging size and proportions

Size is of course best assessed in direct comparison with other terns, but comparison with gulls or other coastal birds is also useful. Terns often appear in mixed flocks with gulls. Only the Caspian Tern and the Little Tern are so different that they are immediately distinguished by size alone. On the other hand, the individual species each have their own jizz, which, with practice, becomes of great value for the experienced observer. Slight differences, in combination, are of great identification value and often what one immediately reacts to. In the USA, knowledge of jizz has been of very great help in separating Royal Terns from Caspian Terns, but with a lone Royal Tern in West Europe one must of course supplement this with as many details of plumage as possible.

## The various plumages

Generally speaking, terns are observed in the Northern Hemisphere only in two plumages: the **adult summer plumage** and **juvenile plumage**. Occasionally, subadult (2nd-3rd calendar-year) terns are seen, especially during summer, but they always represent a minority in areas of breeding sites.

**Adult summer plumage** is worn from late winter until autumn. The plumage is characterised by a black cap, or a black head and underparts (the smaller *Chlidonias* terns). In spring, all the primaries are fairly uniformly coloured, but normally with a slight contrast between the older outer feathers and the fresher inner ones (up to 5-6). Fresh primaries are initially covered with a silver-grey dusting, which is gradually worn away. In summer and autumn, the outer primaries therefore gradually darken, and normally become distinctly darker against pale inner ones on autumn migration. The prominent dark wing wedge on e.g. Sandwich Tern and Common Tern then emerges, and on perched birds the outer wing becomes darker, as only exposed parts of the wing darken under the influence of light, in flight, parts of the wing which were protected by overlying feathers and which are therefore paler are also revealed. Long outermost tail feathers are at their longest during the spring, and in summer can be worn away or broken off. Bill and leg colours are at their brightest in the breeding period.

Normally, only small parts of the head and body are moulted in late summer, but a few species (e.g. Royal, Sandwich and Forster's Terns) moult the head after the breeding season and acquire the winter head during the autumn. In general, the sort-distance migrants moult more of the plumage than the long-distance migrants. The Arctic Tern wears its winter plumage only in the winter quarters.

**Adult winter plumage** shows a white forehead and crown and black 'half-mask'. Many species acquire darker lesser coverts which form a dark band at

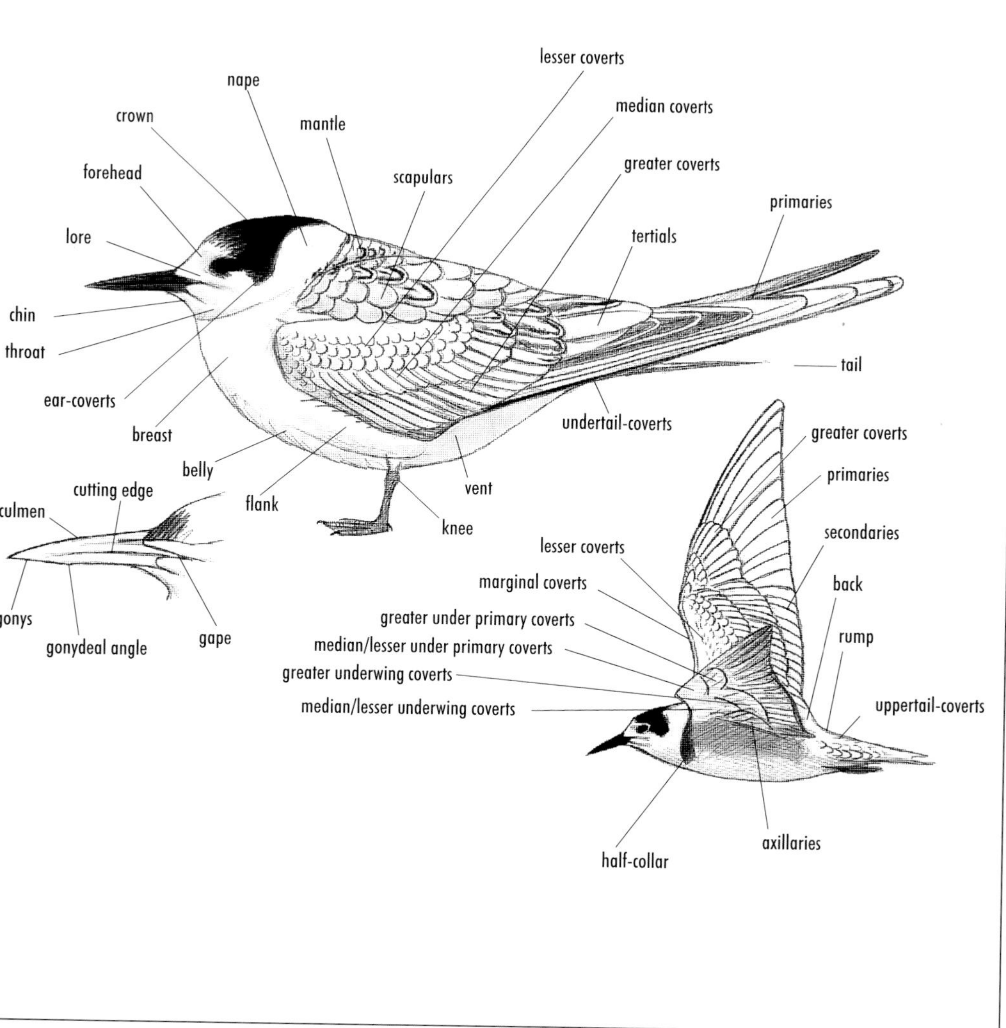


***FIGURE 1*** Tern topography.

the leading edge of the wing. The outer primaries become darker during the autumn and contrast well with the inner ones. This plumage is adopted after the breeding season (see above), but with most species mainly in the winter quarters. Black Tern and White-winged Black tern moult the head and body feathers gradually during the autumn, and in late summer have a mottled plumage. Bill and legs become duller. Many species acquire a black bill in winter.

**Juvenile plumage** recalls that of adult winter, but newly fledged birds have a yellowish-brown to brown tinge on the head and the back feathers. Most have scaly upperparts, dark bands across the lesser coverts and secondaries, and a darker tail with shorter streamers than adults. In the weeks following fledging they are more compact than adults, as the outermost primaries are still growing. Wing, tail streamers, bill and legs are shorter than those of the adults.

Only Roseate Tern, Sandwich Tern, *albifrons*-group and Forster's Tern moult parts of the plumage before the southward migration.

**First-winter/first-summer plumage** recalls adult winter plumage. The plumage is worn in the first summer, so birds in 'winter plumage' during the summer are about one year old. Parts of the plumage (up to five outer primaries, their coverts, and outer tail feathers) are juvenile, and are replaced late in the second winter. Outer juvenile primaries usually appear at some time in the third calendar-year.

**Second-summer plumage** is like adult summer plumage, but often has some subadult elements such as pale feathers in the forehead or the cap. Tertials and primary coverts are often darker than those of adults. The larger crested terns often have a few dark-marked tail feathers. The outer primaries usually differ from those of the adults in being darker.

With the Common Tern, it has been established for certain that very old birds can have 'subadult features' such as white forehead, dark secondary bar and white-spotted underparts (Austin 1938). It may be supposed that other species, too, can show such features, which is why exact ageing in the field cannot be recommended. Third-calender-year birds of known age have also, however, shown the characters mentioned, but many (most?) are identical to adult summer.

It must also be pointed out that subadult and winter plumages of some species are still poorly known. We are therefore very interested in further information concerning this for any subsequent editions of this book. Be extra careful, therefore, with terns in unusual plumages, and examine closely terns in the winter quarters: among all the exotic species one encounters in the tropics, there is much to do there concerning our own native species even if it seems more interesting to scrutinise bee-eaters than terns in West Africa.

The species which breed around or south of the Equator have different breeding seasons from northern populations, and are therefore in summer plumage at other times. See the various species.

## General points concerning moult

Moult differs somewhat among the species (see particular sections under the individual species).

In general, **adults** moult to **summer plumage** in late winter and spring, when the cap is acquired (as, e.g., with the 'hooded gulls' such as Black-headed Gull *Larus ridibundus*). At this time, the previous summer's remex moult is completed, and on arrival at the breeding grounds the plumage is fairly uniform. Some species replace up to four or five inner primaries, which are then paler than the outermost. Primary moult is suspended before the breeding period, but is resumed again after it, when the central and outermost feathers are usually darker and contrast with the inner ones. This is most obvious with those birds which have had the longest pause in their moult. The moult of the tail begins with t1 after the breeding season. At the same time the moult of the head, body and coverts to winter plumage begins. During the early part of the autumn migration the majority of terns are still in predominantly summer plumage (apart from Sandwich, Royal and Forster's Terns, which moult into winter plumage from as early as midsummer).

The moult to **winter plumage** takes place after the breeding season until well into the winter. The outer unmoulted primaries are moulted in the middle of winter, and at the same time a new moult wave begins with the inner primaries. The secondaries are normally moulted in two waves in autumn and winter. The tail moult is completed at the same time. A few acquire a new tail during the winter.

**Juveniles** normally moult to **first-winter plumage** in the winter quarters, but some species moult the head and upperparts in their first autumn. The median and greater coverts are normally moulted during winter, whereas the lesser coverts and secondaries are retained in the first summer. Head and body are normally in winter plumage in the first summer, but a few new feathers may be grown in head and body. Moult of tail and primaries commences around the new year. Up to the first summer t1-t3(4) and four to five inner primaries are moulted. The contrast between the retained juvenile outer primaries (and their coverts) and new inner ones is obvious in the first summer, as the juvenile primaries are abraded relatively more quickly than those of adults and in addition are or poorer quality. Birds which are already completing the primary moult in late summer have outer primaries paler and fresher than the innermost ones (contrast the opposite in adults), but this is thought to be rare (even the exception?) in northern Europe.

Birds which in their **second winter** have not yet managed to complete the primary moult have almost blackish worn outer primaries contrasting with paler inner ones (may be seen up to late in second winter, in third calendar-year). In the first summer juvenile lesser coverts and outer tail feathers are usually still present. They are moulted in the following autumn.

The moult to **second-summer plumage** is similar to that of the adults, but may differ somewhat. Thus, the primary moult does not follow such a stringent pattern as in adults. They (i.e. the primaries) are moulted in two different places (innermost and outermost in the outer wing), and not uncommonly a few odd feathers may be 'leapfrogged', so that an 'extra wedge' can be seen, surrounded by fresh new primaries.

## Wear

The terns are not thought to be subject to heavy wear in the same way as gulls. One exception is provided by some second-calendar-year birds, which can be extremely worn in their first summer. For primary wear, see above.

## Aberrants

Colour variations such as leucism and albinism are extremely rare among the terns. I do not know any instances of colour aberrations in terns. This contrasts with gulls, in which one sometimes sees aberrant individuals. The fact that so few terns are seen in aberrant plumages may perhaps be explained by their 'tougher' and specialised lifestyle making it more difficult for terns to survive with abnormal plumage than is the case with the opportunistic gulls. A few claims exist, however, of abnormally dark Common and

Forster's Terns having sooty-grey plumage, and thus recalling White-cheeked Tern (C. Wilds *in litt.*).

## Hybrids

Hybrids among terns are rare. Hybrid pairings between Roseate Tern and Common Tern are known from Britain and the Netherlands (Alström *et al.* 1992), and hybrid parents have produced young in North America (Hays 1975). Hays (1975) suggests hybridisation between Common and Arctic Terns, Gull-billed and Forster's Terns (older observations). In the text of this book, reference is made to hybridisation between Sandwich and Lesser Crested Terns, Roseate and Common Terns, and Black and White-winged Black Terns which has been noted in Europe.

## Abbreviations, symbols and descriptions

**Ad** term used to describe plumage worn by a bird during reproductive or nuptial period, but not necessarily the plumage of a bird actively engaged in reproduction

**Imm** immature, a non-adult bird

**Juv** term used to refer to the plumage at point of fledging

**p** primaries

**s** secondaries

**t** tail (rectrices)

♂ male

♀ female

**cal-yr** calendar-year. From when the bird hatches until 31 December of same year is 1st cal-yr. 2nd cal-yr is from 1 January to 31 December of following year, etc.

*Maps:*

**Black** breeding areas

**Grey** distribution range

# Gull-billed Tern

*Gelochelidon nilotica*

Photos **1-9**

### Identification in the field

The Gull-billed Tern is a powerful, gull-like tern. It is the size of Sandwich Tern, but appears distinctly 'tougher', with broader bill, heavier and rounded head and longer legs. The uniform grey upperparts (including rump and tail) of summer plumage are an important feature compared with Sandwich Tern. In flight, the broad head and bill merge evenly into each other and into the elliptical body, which is deepest and broadest across the breast. Sometimes has more pendulous belly and 'drawn-in' lower breast. Combination of powerful bill, broad nape and broad breast gives a characteristic front-heavy and aggressive anterior emphasis. The tail projection beyond the wing is equal to the breadth of the wing at its base.

The Gull-billed Tern has a gull-like flight, steady and composed with slow and stiff, sometimes even 'frozen' wingbeats. In flight, the body does not move up and down as with smaller terns, which reinforces the gull-like impression. Its foraging is also different: the Gull-billed Tern does not plunge-dive, but makes gentle dips towards the surface like a giant swallow or a Black Tern in slow motion.

When perched, the Gull-billed Tern appears aggressive. The broad black bill is heavy and powerful with curved upper mandible and a marked gonydeal angle. The bill is equal in length to about 60-75% of the length of the cap in summer plumage. It runs directly into the heavy, rounded head, the highest point of which lies immediately behind the eye. Broad round nape lacks Sandwich Tern's crest. The black legs are long, about the same length as the bill, with obvious 'knee' on the upper third to quarter.

The uniform grey upperparts (including rump and tail) are slightly darker than on Sandwich. The primary tips are dark, but a dark 'Sandwich Tern wedge' on the upperside of the primaries is lacking or at best poorly marked (on worn birds in late summer and autumn).

The underwing is white with dark tips to 5-6 outermost primaries, gradually broadening towards outermost primary (Vinicombe 1989). Exceptionally, the darkest-marked individuals have as much dark on the underside of the primaries as Caspian Tern. Against the light, secondaries and innermost primaries are only slightly translucent.

Gull-billed Tern is most often confused with the equally large Sandwich Tern. Confusion, however, is due mostly to lack of knowledge. Gull-billed is a powerful, broad-billed bird with a self-assured, almost aggressive air about it. Sandwich is a typically slender and elegant tern with longer, thinner and more characterless bill than Gull-billed, a mawkish nape crest and white tail/rump contrasting with paler grey back. The bill is like a thin peg fitted on, not like a broad protraction of the cap as in Gull-billed. In flight, Sandwich is distinctly lighter, with more front-heavy fore area, narrower and more angled wings (with more obviously translucent secondaries and inner primaries), and after the breeding season shows a pronounced contrast above between innermost pale and outermost dark primaries. It most often reveals itself by the characteristic grating 'krree-ik'.

**Adult in summer plumage** has shiny black cap, which merges into the broad black bill. Bill and cap form a black helmet, as forehead and bill base are fairly uniform in width. This is obvious, for example, when the bird is seen directly head-on. From late summer the head is moulted, and in late summer to early autumn the cap is peppered white; the cap is moulted uniformly throughout its length, not from bill base backwards as with Sandwich Tern. A white forehead with dark cap is therefore uncommon, and more usually a black patch develops over the ear-coverts and contrasts against the gradually whiter surroundings. Many retain the summer cap longer into the autumn than Sandwich Tern. It is commonly present at the end of August, when it is more the exception on Sandwich.

**Adult winter plumage** shows white head with black 'highwayman's mask'. The head is the palest among the larger terns (note that Forster's Tern has similar head). The mask varies. The palest individuals have only a weak dirty-grey patch behind the eye, and the head then recalls that of winter-plumaged Mediterranean Gull *Larus melanocephalus*. On most, however, eye and mask merge together, creating a 'mascara effect'. The crown may have grey spots, but at a distance always becomes pale against the distinct black mask.

The winter plumage is otherwise like summer plumage, but the upperparts can be paler grey, and a slight contrast between new innermost primaries and unmoulted outermost can occur, most obviously in late autumn. The remiges, however, suffer less wear than in other terns and a dark 'Sandwich Tern wedge' in the outer wing is decidedly uncommon, more usual being a weak grey wedge in the outermost wing.

**Juvenile** recalls adult winter plumage, and is normally more weakly dark-marked than other young terns. The dark mask is normally greyer and more poorly defined than that of the adults, and the crown has narrow black streaks. Newly fledged young have a yellowish-brown tinge on forehead, crown and mantle. The upperparts are grey, with variable dark, narrow V marks on the back, tertials and inner coverts. Most, however, lack distinct dark spots, and have the upperparts very adult-like (but tinged sandy in late summer and early autumn). The tail is pale grey with a faint darker terminal band. The wing is similar to that of adults, but has a weak dark grey secondary bar (clearest on inner secondaries) and dark grey greater primary coverts. The bill is black, with yellowish-grey base on recently fledged young. The legs are dark red-brown.

Juvenile plumage varies. The palest and least marked are rather like adults, while others have heavier black markings above. Such birds differ from Sandwich Tern in shape, weaker markings, shorter and thicker bill, and characteristic white head with dark oval or round patch behind eye; Sandwich has narrow, but invariably black stripe from eye to eye.

**First-winter plumage** is much as adult winter plumage, but the pale overall im-

***PLATE 1***

**Gull-billed Tern *Gelochelidon nilotica***

Similar in size to Sandwich Tern, but heavier, with rounded head, shorter and heavier black bill and grey rump and tail. In summer plumage, black cap and bill give helmet-like appearance; in all other plumages, white-headed with a dark mask restricted to dark spot behind eye. Dark trailing edge to primaries broader than on Sandwich Tern (appearing intermediate between Sandwich and Caspian Tern). Does not normally plunge-dive. Flight attitude similar to gull.

1 **Juvenile.** Typical individual in fresh plumage. Note slightly sandy tinge to head and mantle (soon disappearing through wear).

2 **Juvenile moulting to first-winter.** A well-marked individual, showing unusually heavily patterned retained juvenile scapulars and tertials.

3 **Adult winter.** Note black 'bandit's mask' (often heavier than on individual illustrated).

4 **Adult summer plumage.**

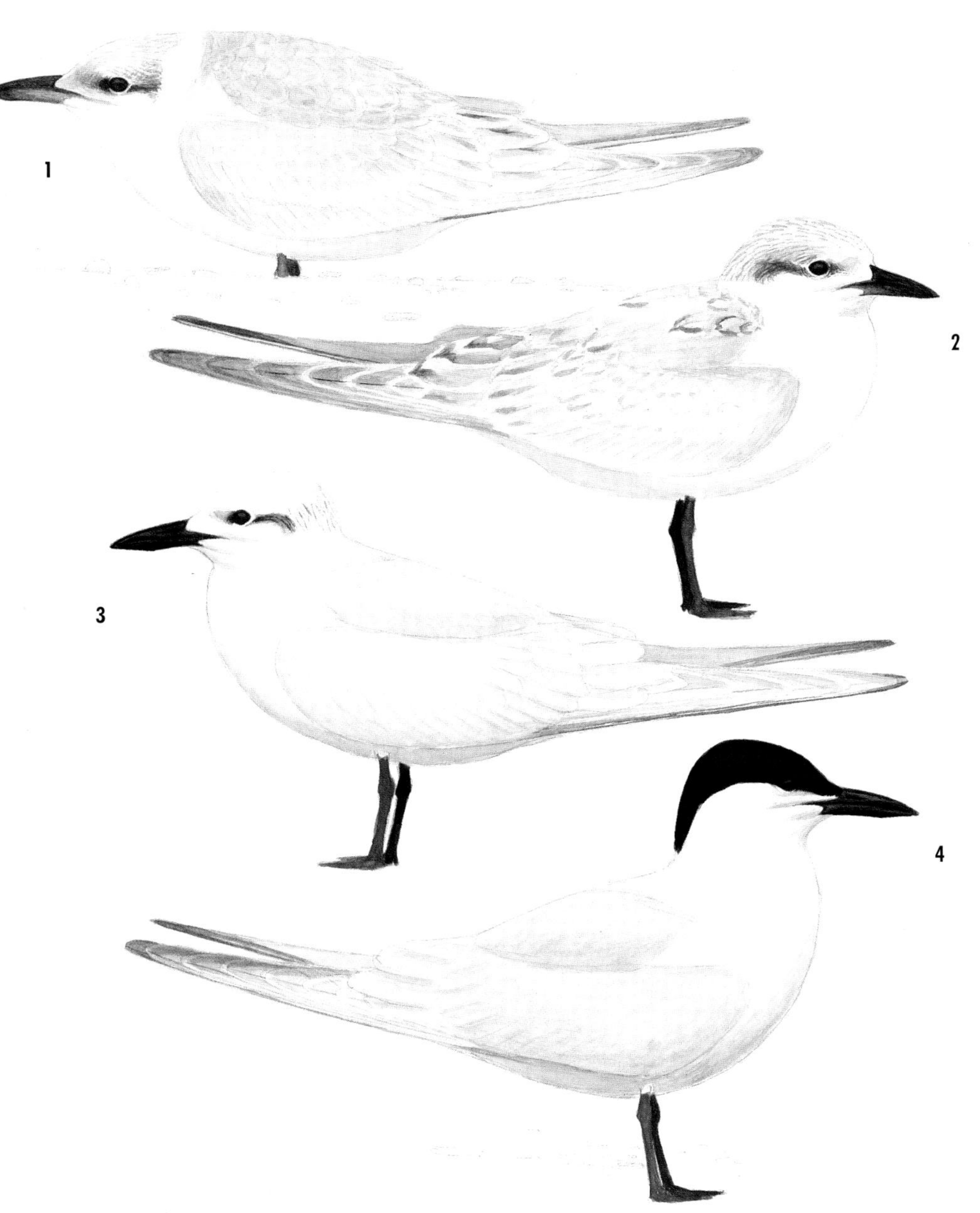
1
2
3
4

***FIGURE 2*** Gull-billed Tern. Development of head from summer to winter plumage. Note that crown becomes white-peppered during middle stages of moult. Full summer hood is retained well into population.

pression is modified by retained juvenile tertials, greater primary coverts and worn dark primaries (most obvious in late autumn).

**First-summer plumage** is similar to adult winter plumage, but with very worn and dark juvenile outer primaries and primary coverts, together with vestiges of dark secondary bar. The head is as in winter plumage, but broad black drop-shaped spots may spread over the crown and nape.

### Voice

Normally rather silent. Adult's call is a deep, two-note, somewhat guttural and laughing staccato, *gek-gek-gek* or *gir-vit*. Juvenile's call is a soft *pe-eep* or a rapid *pe-pe-eep*, rather like that of juvenile Sandwich Tern.

### Moult

**Adult** has complete moult to **winter plumage**. Primary moult starts with inner feathers in mid June to mid July (Glutz *et al.* 1982) at or near the nesting site. The moult is broken off before migration, with 2-5 innermost primaries replaced; in November, the majority have renewed 4-6 inner primaries, and a few per cent have moulted outer primaries as early as early December. Primary moult is suspended during autumn migration. It is resumed after arrival in the winter quarters, and is completed in February-March (rarely mid December).

Moult of head and body begins with the crown in late July, and is followed by the forehead in mid August. About 50% (West Europe) have 75-100% of the summer cap in mid August (compare Sandwich Tern). Head moult is completed at end August to mid October. Up to the end of September, most have 50% of summer cap. In October-December the majority have a 'winter head'. From Bahrain, Hirschfeld (1991) gives 27 out of 347 with 100% cap in November-December.

The tail moult begins with t1 in early July to mid August, and is followed by t2, t3 and t6 (Cramp 1985); t4-5 are normally moulted last. The moult is suspended during the migration, but resumed again from November. The whole tail may be moulted in winter quarters.

The moult to **adult summer plumage** is partial. It starts with inner primaries at end December to end February (immediately after earlier moult series have stopped), and is broken off in January-March with inner 2-3 (4-6) primaries replaced (race *nilotica*; inner 3-5 (6) in *arenae* and *affinis*). 30-35% of European *nilotica* do not renew any inner primaries (Cramp 1985). The tail is moulted end January to April, beginning with t1-2; occasionally t4-6 are not moulted, and then appear worn during spring and summer. Head moult commences in (end December) February-March; in March, some still have a few winter feathers in the crown. Body and a few back feathers and scapulars are moulted in February-March.

**Juvenile** has a complete moult to **first-winter plumage** from end August to end

September. The head and some back feathers are moulted earliest, and are followed at end September to November by body, parts of back and scapulars, and lesser and median coverts. Tertials and greater coverts are moulted December-February, but a few tertials may be retained until at least April. The tail is moulted in October-February. Primary moult commences end December, and is broken off at end of March, with up to 8 inner primaries replaced. Primary coverts are moulted in association with their respective primaries. Odd remiges may be missed: a May individual had primaries 1-4 and 8-10 new, but 5-7 worn.

The first moult series is completed in July to early September of second calendar-year, when head and body are moulted to **second-winter plumage**. New moult series commences simultaneously in primaries and tail. The subsequent moults are as in adult; retained primaries are generally more worn than the corresponding ones of adults.

**GULL-BILLED TERN** QUICK KEY TO IDENTIFICATION

1. **Sturdy elliptical body with short, broad head and thick black bill gives species an aggressive expression which lacks the usual 'tern elegance'.**
2. **Upperparts uniform grey, lacking contrast between back and rump/tail.**
3. **Flight heavy and gull-like, composed and relaxed. Does not plunge-dive, but snatches food items from the ground or the water surface.**
4. **When perched, heavy and with short and broad bill, rounded head and long black legs.**
5. **In summer plumage, bill and cap merge into one another, like a black helmet.**
6. **In winter and immature plumages, white-headed with dark mask through ear-coverts. Combination of head markings and broad bill diagnostic.**
7. **Only the tips of the primaries are dark, with slightly broader dark tip below. A distinct dark wing wedge like Sandwich Tern's is at best weakly suggested (autumn).**
8. **Juvenile poorly marked, almost as adult, but with darker tail tip and secondary bar.**
9. **Juvenile's upperparts vary, but are only exceptionally as heavily marked as on juvenile Sandwich Tern.**
10. **Low call is never conspicuous.**

**Detailed description** *Gelochelidon nilotica nilotica* (Europe, North Africa, Middle East to Kazakhstan, Manchuria and Pakistan)

Length: 35-38 cm, wingspan 100-115 cm.

**Adult summer plumage:** Cap black, in fresh plumage glossy blue-black. The cap is broadly rounded against white nape. White area between gape and cap 3-4 mm broad. Upperparts and tail pale blue-grey; fresh feathers can be silver-grey with narrow pale tips. Outer tail feathers often paler. Primary tips and outer web of outer primary dark grey. Secondaries and inner primaries have narrow pale edges.

Underparts white, sometimes with faint grey tinge on belly (especially males). Dark tips to outermost 5-6 primaries form dark trailing edge to outer part of hand, broadest towards wingtip (including above). From midsummer the primaries' silver-grey tint is worn off and outer 5-6 primaries become darker (during autumn dull black, apart from white on inner webs which have been protected by neighbouring feathers). New remiges pale grey. In worn plumage, cap becomes duller and upperparts darker.

Bill black, with curved upper mandible and distinct gonydeal angle in centre of lower mandible. Gonys length 15-19 mm. Extreme tip of bill sometimes pale (visible only in the hand). Mouth orange. Legs black, occasionally with reddish-brown tinge, rarely with pale patches (subadults?).

**Adult winter plumage:** As summer plumage apart from following. Head white. Crown and nape have variable grey tinge or narrow dull black streaks (sometimes on lores). Dull black to mid-grey mask from eye to ear-coverts can be restricted to a few dark spots on ear-coverts.

Underparts white. Upperparts often paler than in summer plumage. Contrast between innermost and outermost primaries depends on stage of moult; most obvious during autumn, when may show darker wedge (rarely as distinct as on Sandwich Tern).

**Juvenile:** Head much as adult winter plumage, but in fresh plumage has pale yellowish-brown tinge, and dark mask normally more diffuse. Upperparts a shade darker than on adult. Upperpart feathers are tinged brown at base and have variable dark spots and pale tips. The most heavily dark-marked birds have dark V marks on upperparts (especially mantle), scapulars, tertials, inner wing-coverts and primary coverts. Commoner types have faint grey-brown subterminal spots on a few tertials, scapulars and central tail feathers. The palest juveniles have adult-like upperparts, but with faint sandy-coloured feather edges until mid autumn. Tertials most heavily marked: birds with heavy V marks on tertials have at least a few similarly marked upperpart and tail feathers. The palest birds, however, have unmarked tertials. Tail pale with grey terminal band and white tips (up to 3-4 mm, broadest on birds lacking dark markings above). Underparts white.

1
2
3
4
7
8
5
6
9

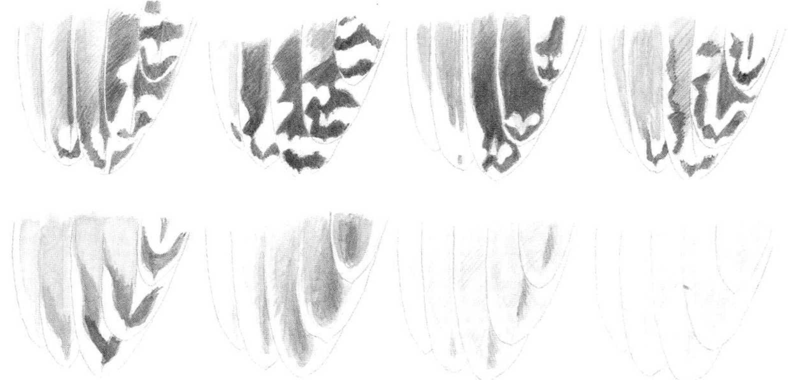

Wing feathers dark grey with faint trace of silvery-grey. Primaries have narrow white tips and dark silvery-grey outer webs.

Bill black, on recently fledged young pale orange with black tip. Gonys length 9.5-13 mm. Upper mandible black from August, base of lower mandible normally has orange or olive-brown coloration until September (up to 50% of inner part). Legs greyish-yellow to greyish-red, blacker in autumn. May retain pale areas in tarsus into first winter.

**First-winter plumage:** As adult winter plumage, but retained primaries and their coverts juvenile (grey-brown with pale edges; pale grey on adults). A few secondaries and tail feathers as well as tertials are retained until May-June of second calendar-year.

**Second-winter plumage:** Is assumed late in the first summer (second calendar-year). Much as adult winter plumage, but some have black spots on nape and crown. This plumage is acquired end August to September, about two months before adults. Retained old feathers are darker and more worn than those of adults.

**Second summer:** As adult summer but may show narrow white feather edges in the hood and a slight dark wedge in median to outer primaries.

Subsequent plumages probably cannot be distinguished with certainty from adult winter plumage. Birds in summer plumage with narrow white feather edges in the cap are possibly in second-summer plumage (Cramp 1985).

**PLATE 3**

Variation in juvenile tertials in nominate Sandwich Tern *Sterna sandvicensis sandvicensis* and Gull-billed Tern *Gelochelidon nilotica.* The heavily marked Gull-billed are rarely seen. Note that Nearctic race of Sandwich Tern (*acuflavida* and Cayenne Tern *S. (s) eurygnatha*) show solid dark centres to tertials and rather narrow pale fringes (similar to juvenile tertials of Lesser Black-backed Gull *Larus fuscus*).

## Geographical variation

Slight. Races *affinis* (East Asia) and *aranea* (eastern North America to West Indies) are smaller than *nilotica*. Race *aranea* has ground coloration as *nilotica*, but shorter wings and legs. Race *affinis* has whitish-grey tail; t1-t2 darker, but normally paler

**PLATE 2**

**Gull-billed Tern *Gelochelidon nilotica***

1 **Juvenile Wholly fresh and heavily marked individual.**
2 **Juvenile (in flight).** Note broad dark trailing edge to outer primaries.
3 **First-winter.** A typical bird in December-January, which has not yet started primary moult.
4 **First-summer.** Similar to adult winter, but with darker, heavily worn outer primaries and traces of dark secondary bar.
5 **Adult summer (fresh spring plumage).** Note uniform grey mantle, rump and tail.
6 **Adult moulting from summer to winter plumage (August).** Note white-peppered cap. Some birds acquire darker outer primaries and may show dark primary wedge similar to Sandwich Tern (although rarely as marked as on typical Sandwich).
7 **Adult winter (late autumn: outer primary unmoulted).** Note typical head pattern.
8 **Adult winter.**
9 **Second-summer.** As adult summer, but note darker outer primaries. Many birds at this age show some white spotting in cap.

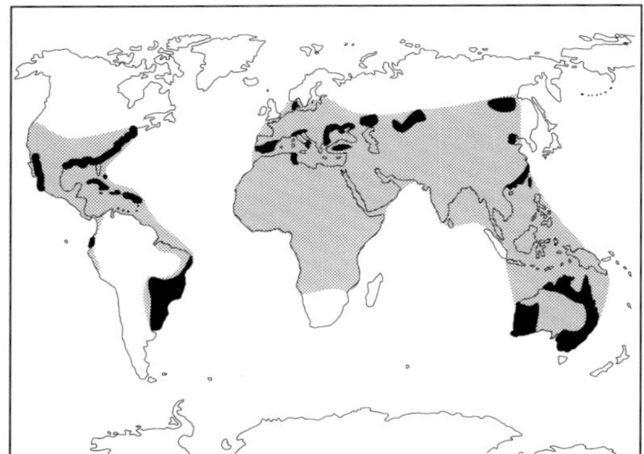

***MAP 1*** Distribution of Gull-billed Tern *Gelochelidon nilotica.*

than rump and back; white area between gape and bill 2-3 mm. Races from South America and Australia have paler grey upperparts than *nilotica*, white rump and tail, as well as white outer webs to primaries. Outside region, several subspecies; *macrotarsa* (Australia) is biggest and palest (as pale as Sandwich Tern).

### Measurements

In mm. Own measurements, NMNH, NNH, ZMA, UZM, NRK, ZML, ZMU, MN. Race *nilotica* (Europe to Central Asia) and aranea (North America). Adults May-August; juveniles August-September. Weight according to Glutz (1982) and Cramp (1985).

**WING LENGTH**

| | | | |
|---|---|---|---|
| *nilotica* | | | |
| Ad ♂ | 300-352 | (321.7) | n = 33 |
| Ad ♀ | 293-335 | (315.6) | n = 29 |
| Juv | 287-317 | (299.6) | n = 25 |
| *aranea* | | | |
| Ad ♂ | 285-313 | (298.6) | n = 35 |
| Ad ♀ | 282-305 | (294.2) | n = 20 |

• Glutz *et al.* (1982): ♂♂: Central Asia 294-337 (315.2; n = 18), Mongolia 298-326 (313; n = 5).
• Race *affinis* (Java, Bali): ad ♂ 290-323 (303.4; n = 30), ad ♀ 280-310 (290.8; n = 14) (NNH).

**TAIL FORK**

| | | | |
|---|---|---|---|
| Ad ♂ | 24-51 | (39.3) | n = 54 |
| Ad ♀ | 24-48 | (38.1) | n = 34 |
| Juv | 17-30 | (22.7) | n = 15 |

• In winter plumage, adult has tail fork 30-45 mm.

**BILL**

| | | | |
|---|---|---|---|
| *nilotica* | | | |
| Ad ♂ | 35.5-43.7 | (39.7) | n = 54 |
| Ad ♀ | 34.5-41.1 | (38.2) | n = 34 |
| Juv | 34.8-40.3 | (37.6) | n = 15 |
| *aranea* | | | |
| Ad ♂ | 36.2-40.3 | (37.7) | n = 35 |
| Ad ♀ | 33.5-38.8 | (36.0) | n = 20 |
| Juv | 33.1-36.5 | (34.9) | n = 10 |

• Race *affinis*: ad ♂ 32-5-40.2 (38.1; n = 28), ad ♀ 32.5-38.9 (35.4; n = 14) (ZMA, NNH).

**BILL DEPTH AT GONYS**

| | | | |
|---|---|---|---|
| Ad | 8.1-11.5 | (9.7) | n = 84 |
| Juv | 7.7-10.5 | (8.8) | n = 20 |

• Average for ♂♂ and ♀♀ the same.

**BILL DEPTH AT NOSTRILS**

| | | | |
|---|---|---|---|
| Ad | 9.2-13.5 | (11.8) | n = 84 |
| Juv | 9.2-13.3 | (10.7) | n = 20 |

**TARSUS**

| | | | |
|---|---|---|---|
| *nilotica* | | | |
| Ad ♂ | 29.7-36.5 | (33.0) | n = 57 |
| Ad ♀ | 29.5-34.3 | (32.3) | n = 33 |
| Juv | 28.9-37.4 | (31.9) | n = 14 |
| *aranea* | | | |
| Ad ♂ | 28.7-33.5 | (31.0) | n = 35 |
| Ad ♀ | 28.0-31.7 | (29.8) | n = 20 |

**WEIGHT** (in grams)

| | | | |
|---|---|---|---|
| Central Asia, May-June | | | |
| Ad ♂ | 170-230 | (197.0) | n = 7 |
| Ad ♀ | 180-199 | (189.6) | n = 5 |
| Netherlands, August | | | |
| Ad ♂ | 204-245 | (227.8) | n = 6 |
| Ad ♀ | 189-292 | (247.5) | n = 4 |
| Juv ♂ | 220-243 | (230.7) | n = 3 |

• Glutz mentions a third-calendar-year bird, emaciated but still alive, weighing 155 g.

# Caspian Tern

*Sterna caspia*

Photos **10-19**

### Identification in the field

The Caspian Tern is the largest tern. It is bulky and almost the size of a large gull, with pointed wings and characteristic dark gannet-like underside to primaries contrasting with all-pale upperside of primaries. In flight, these flash black and white and create an impression quite unlike that of other terns, all of which have pale at base of primaries below. The big red bill dominates the fore parts and, together with the angular head, gives a heavy, powerful 'macho impression'.

The Caspian Tern has a purposeful and self-confident, almost majestic flight with slow, stiff and shallow wingbeats. In flight it is front-heavy, with powerful neck and head and large red bill the dominant features. The body is elliptical, with deep, somewhat 'cut-off' belly. The tail is relatively shorter than on other terns and has only a slight fork. The flight silhouette is not unlike that of a gannet – an impression which is of course reinforced by the stiff flight and the black underside of the primaries (which, in association with the pointed tern wings, also recalls Lesser Black-backed Gull *L. f. fuscus*). The dominant head/bill and short rear end make the Caspian Tern, in terms of proportions, the 'sea eagle of the terns'! It often draws attention by its heron-like call, which is audible at long range; on such occasions, the observer can see the bird open its bill, the call being heard a couple of seconds later!

The Caspian Tern forages by diving almost vertically from 5-20 m for fish of up to 20 cm. Here, too, the similarity to a gannet is obvious. It scans coasts purposefully and suddenly stops to turn around and dive, not unlike hunting harriers. It often breaks off the dive near the water surface. Less dramatic is its foraging over lakes.

Perched birds are powerful and broad-shouldered: when among the smaller terns, comparable with a jumbo aircraft on an airfield! The red, dagger-shaped bill, as long as the head, is obvious at surprisingly long range. Flat crown and 90°-angled nape, together with the bill, give an angry and aggressive look: like a broad-billed and red-billed, hefty Sandwich Tern, but twice the size. The long and strong legs make it stand still taller above other terns.

**Adult in summer plumage** has a black cap and short crest (shorter than on other crested terns), producing a 'cropped', angular nape. The bill is blood-red with a narrow dark ring around the tip. The upperparts are pale grey with contrasting white rump and tail; but some tail feathers can be pale grey and the outer 3-4 primaries slightly darker. The underparts are white.

Summer plumage is acquired early and moulted late. From as early as February most have the summer cap, which generally is retained during the autumn migration. At most a few odd white feathers may be seen in the forehead and crown by September. Note that Royal Tern has a 'summer cap' only for a short period early in the breeding season.

**Adult in winter plumage** is similar to summer plumage, but forehead, lores and crown are paler, with dark spots – as a neat freckled pattern, but which at a distance becomes uniform grey. The black mask is broader than on other crested terns, and at a distance can give the impression of a washed-out 'summer head'; it covers the eyes and ear-coverts;

the eye normally does not stand out. Only rarely is a white area visible around the eye or on the forehead, but always in association with a dark-spotted crown.

The bill may be duller than in summer, and has a broader black ring up to a couple of centimetres wide around the tip. Rarely, the entire bill tip is black. The outer primaries are often darker through wear at the end of the year.

**Juvenile** recalls winter-plumaged adult, but the dark-spotted forehead and crown merge together with dark, brown-toned mask and form a dark cap, which at a distance can almost appear complete. The mask continues behind the eye farther down onto the neck sides than on adults. Some have a paler grey forehead and crown, so that the head becomes tricoloured. Juvenile Caspian Tern has a narrow pale eye-ring, unlike adult.

The orange-red bill is shorter than that of adults, and with a broader black band which may cover the entire tip.

The upperparts are much more poorly marked than those of larger crested terns. The palest birds are almost like adults, but normally show a trace of light brown on the back. Back and, especially, scapulars usually have dark V-shaped markings, and at a distance become dark-spotted. The upperwing is pale grey with faint darker bars across lesser coverts and secondaries, sometimes so faint that the bird appears uniformly pale above. The bars become more and more clear, however, in late autumn and winter. The primaries show the adults' 'gannet patch' below. The tail is grey-white with dark terminal band. The legs are initially pale but rapidly become blacker as autumn approaches; the majority have black legs from early August.

**First-winter plumage** is much as adult winter plumage, but the cap is darker, the tail dark-tipped and the wing has dark bars across lesser coverts and secondaries. Retained juvenile primaries and their coverts are blackish. Dark areas show increasing contrast in late winter and spring with faded, whitish greater coverts. During primary moult, there is a clear contrast between new pale inner and old dark outer feathers. In April-May the inner half of the primaries have been renewed, and dark bars on secondaries and tail are obvious.

**First-summer plumage** has a 'winter head'. Dark secondary bar is retained (at least on central secondaries) and the outer, unmoulted juvenile primaries and their coverts are dark. The tail has an incomplete dark terminal band. The bill is red, generally with broader black band than on adult.

**Second-winter plumage** is much as adult winter plumage, but tail tips may still be dark. Primaries possibly more worn, and in certain situations a dark grey tinge may be evident on the secondaries.

---

***PLATE 4***

**Caspian Tern *Sterna caspia***

Largest tern, in size similar to Herring Gull *Larus argentatus*, but with narrower and more slender wings. Huge, coral-red bill, flat head and short crest give fierce impression, strengthened by the hoarse, heron-like call. In flight, compact and front-heavy with dominating head and bill and relatively shorter tail than other terns. Wholly dark undersurface to primaries, together with lazy, slow flight, gives gannet-impression. Dark eye is covered by dark mask; in most plumages appears dark-hooded (see Royal Tern).

1 **Juvenile (fresh plumage, July-August).**
2 **First-winter (spring).** Similar to adult winter, but note darker and more worn outer primaries. The bird illustrated is an unusually white-fronted individual; most look similar to 3. See also plate 5 (3).
3 **Adult winter.** Note dark-spotted forehead and complete dark surround to eye, creating almost full cap at distance (see Royal Tern).
4 **Adult summer.** A typical individual. Note: Second-summer (not illustrated) is similar, but can in many cases be identified by combination of a few white spots in cap and darker outer primaries.

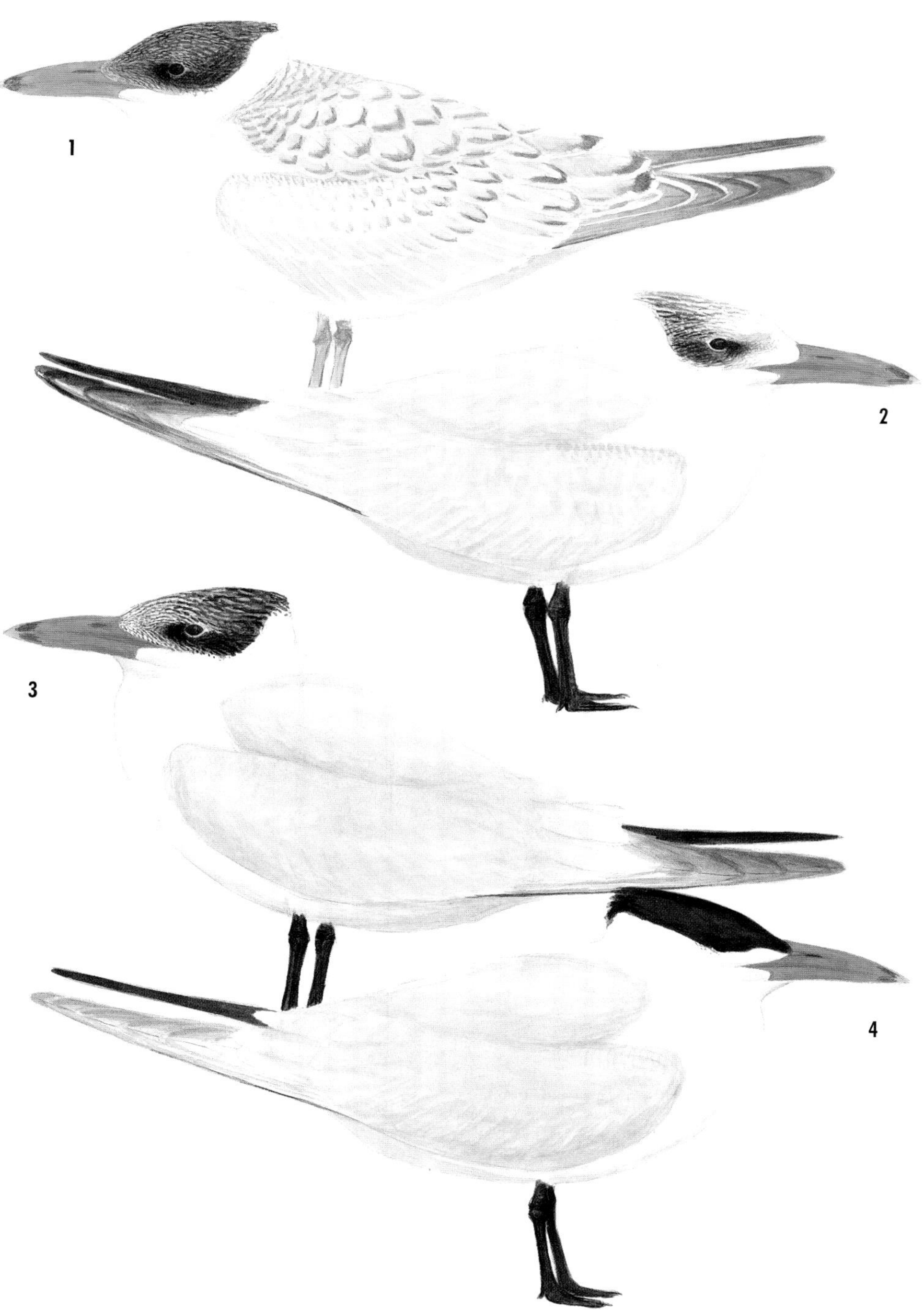
1
2
3
4

**CASPIAN TERN** QUICK KEY TO IDENTIFICATION

1. **Strikingly big and heavy tern recalling Lesser Black-backed Gull, with front-heavy appearance, short tail and steady flight.**
2. **Large red bill very conspicuous even at distance.**
3. **Underside of primaries forms dark patch, like adult Gannet's, contrasting well with whitish upperside.**
4. **Head in winter and juvenile plumages predominantly dark, forehead and crown 'freckled'.**
5. **Juveniles indistinctly marked, with scaly pattern on back and faint dark leading and trailing edges to secondaries.**
6. **In first summer resembles adult, but with elements of white in cap and dark secondary and tail bands.**
7. **Call far-carrying and raucous, like Grey Heron's.**

**Second-summer plumage** is much as adult summer plumage, but sometimes has a pale-spotted cap and a faint darker secondary bar. The outer 4-6 primaries are darker and contrast with the innermost pale grey ones. The outer primary coverts may be dark grey with white edges. The tail is white, but a few tail feathers (especially t3 and t5) may be darker.

## Voice

The adult's call is a far-carrying, hoarse and loud *krääå*, recalling that of Grey Heron *Ardea cinerea*. Juvenile's call is weaker and more squeaky. A wigeon-like call has been heard (Walker 1981).

## Moult

**Adult** has a complete moult to **winter plumage**. The moult starts from late July to late September, but only to a limited extent near the breeding sites. Forehead and crown are moulted first, but up to early September only minor areas are moulted. From October-November the head is normally winter-plumaged, but a few retain the summer cap longer. Primary moult can begin at the end of July to late September when (1) 2-3 (4-5) inner primaries are shed, but is usually delayed until after arrival in winter quarters. In December-January the majority have moulted 6-8 inner primaries (pers. obs., North Africa). The moult is completed in January-February, but primaries normally in March to early April. The tail is moulted from late summer, beginning with t1; an individual in early August had replaced t1 and t3.

Moult to **adult summer plumage** is partial. It includes head, parts of the body and the inner 2-4 primaries, which are moulted in February-March, immediately after the autumn primary moult is completed. The tail moult is complete or partial. Over 80% from West Africa in early to mid February had a summer head (photos from Senegal), but white feathers can be present in forehead and forecrown up to the end of March.

Moult of wing and tail feathers is suspended before the spring migration, and resumed after the breeding season. Individuals with delayed moult migrate north with old, worn flight feathers.

**Juveniles** have a complete moult to **first-winter plumage** in the winter quarters. The moult begins in September-December and is completed March-May. Head, back and most coverts are moulted first, followed by tertials, primary coverts and remiges. The primary moult begins in October-November. In December-February 1-4 inner primaries have been changed, in March-April 6-7 inner ones. The moult can, however, be completed in May-June, but normally not until August-October (Gantlett & Harris 1987; pers. studies). The moult is usually suspended in summer.

The next primary moult may begin with inner primaries in March-April, which means that three different generations of primaries can be present.

Subsequent moults are similar to those of adults, but moult of remiges is generally slower, starting earlier and finishing later (e.g. March-April to October; three birds in their second summer had replaced the innermost 3-5 primaries in August). Old remiges are relatively more worn than those of adults.

## Detailed description

Length 47-54 cm, wingspan 130-145 cm.

**Adult summer plumage:** Cap black, with metallic green gloss when fresh. Nuchal crest short. Rearmost part of nape and underparts white. Cheeks rarely have small black freckles beneath eye, and underparts can have faint greyish tinge. Upperparts light grey, back and rump paler. Lower rump to tail white, tail occasionally with faint tinge of grey (especially t3-5). Outer 5-6 primaries have blackish-grey tips and inner webs. As on other terns, fresh feathers are coated with a silver-grey powder, which is gradually worn away. That part of the feather which is concealed beneath the adjacent feathers retains a silvery coloration longer than exposed parts. With wear, the upperparts become darker grey.

Underwing is white with outer 5-6 primaries blackish-grey, the latter forming a solid dark area on the underside of the hand (sometimes slightly paler on inner part and outermost primaries, very rarely reduced to broad black tips on 5-6 outer primaries).

Bill coral-red to carmine-red with narrow yellowish tip, and with blackish-grey or brown ring just before tip; ring often only hinted at, sometimes lacking, especially during period when feeding young (possibly to larger degree among southern breeding populations). Legs and feet black with orange to pink soles.

**Adult winter plumage:** Much as adult summer plumage apart from following differences. Forehead, upper lores and crown white with blackish-grey or black spots or streaks. In worn plumage, dark predominates over white. Black mask from rear edge of lores over ear-coverts to nape has elements of white in it. Underparts white. Worn, unmoulted remiges darker than new, silvery-grey ones. Worn tail feathers brownish-grey; tail sometimes grey and contrasting with white uppertail-coverts.

Bill orange-red, with incomplete dark ring 1-3 (3) cm broad inside tip (can cover entire tip). Legs black, rarely red-brown or bright red (van Aalst 1989; Koppejan 1990).

**Juvenile:** Forehead, lores, crown and nape densely spotted blackish-brown and greyish-white/pale sandy. Mask from eye to lower ear-coverts dull black. Narrow white eye-ring. At a distance, the head on darkest individuals appears similar to adult summer plumage. Forehead and crown become paler with wear. Underparts as adult, but sometimes with black patch at leading edge of carpal.

Upperparts pale grey, on fresh birds with cinnamon-brown, yellow-brown or white feather tips. Mid-grey lesser coverts and secondaries form two

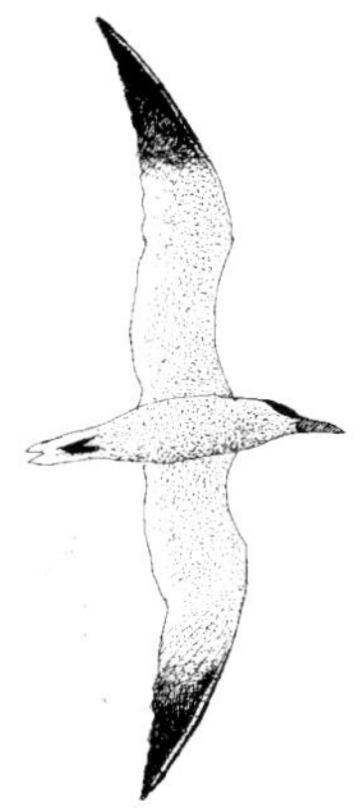

faint dark wingbars, most pronounced near body. A few back feathers have distinct dull black to grey-brown triangular 'scale-like markings'. Others have faintly dark-patterned back, upper scapulars and tertials. Uppertail-coverts whitish-grey with variable dark dots.

Tail feathers pale grey to white with broad white edges along tips and inner webs. The tail has a dark terminal band. Some have greyish-black tips to the central 1-3 rectrices, others a broader and more complete dark terminal band. Remiges dark, with white inner webs and tips to outer 5-7 primaries and greater primary coverts.

Bill orange to red with black ring near tip. Legs greyish-yellow to dark red-brown when just fledged, but black in late summer and early autumn.

**First-winter plumage:** Much as adult winter plumage, but with faint dark leading edge to wing and dark secondary bar, dark-tipped tail and dark worn juvenile primaries (and their coverts). From winter on, worn remiges show strong contrast with fresh pale ones. Wing moult 'delayed' compared with adults' (see above).

During spring and summer of second calendar-year moults directly into **second-winter plumage**, which is rather like adult winter plumage apart from retained juvenile greater primary coverts, remiges and rectrices. See Moult.

**Second-summer plumage:** Similar to adult summer plumage apart from following differences. Cap may have white spots and streaks. Black spots may be present below front edge of cap. Secondaries and outer primary coverts often dark grey with pale edges. 4-5 outer primaries dark, contrasting with pale grey inner ones. Tail white with odd grey feathers (especially t3-5). The bill generally

1
2
3
4
5
6
7
8

has broader black tip. 'Adults' with forehead and crown spotted or streaked white in spring and summer are presumably third- or fourth-calendar-year individuals (Cramp 1985).

Primary moult active or arrested; 5-9 inner primaries exchanged April-August.

**PLATE 5**

**Caspian Tern *Sterna caspia***

1 **Juvenile (fresh plumage, July-August).** Heavily marked individual: compare weakly marked bird (2).
2 **Juvenile.** Weakly marked individual, looking similar to adult winter. Note shorter, orange bill and darker-centred secondaries and tail.
3 **Juvenile.**
4 **First-winter (March-April).** Distinguished from adult winter by dark secondary bar, dark tail feathers and dark primary coverts. Note much-worn outer primaries. First-summer similar.
5 **Second-summer.** Similar to adult summer, but with darker outer primaries and normally some grey in tail. This individual shows darker-centred secondaries (others show adult-like pale secondaries). Many birds at this age show a few white spots in cap.
6 **Adult winter (December-January).**
7 **Adult summer (March-September).**
8 **Adult summer.**

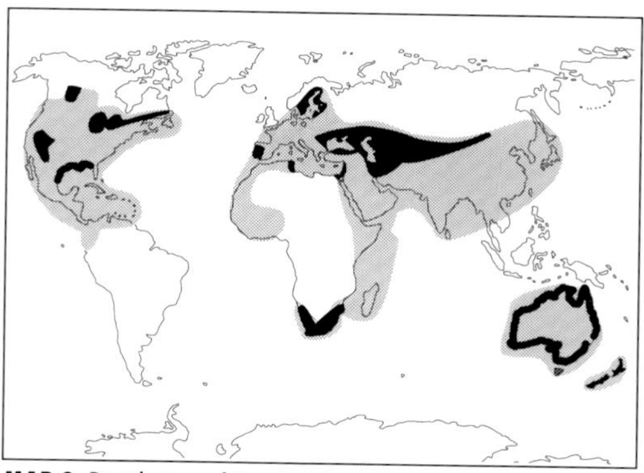

***MAP 2*** Distribution of Caspian Tern *Sterna caspia.*

## Geographical variation

The species is monotypic. Birds from North America, the Red Sea and the Persian Gulf are somewhat smaller than European ones, while birds from South America and Australia average larger. These differences, however, are so small that they are of no value in the field. A large number of birds studied in Europe, Central Asia, tropical Africa, North, Central and South America, and Australia have all looked typical 'Caspian Tern-sized'. Only a few birds from the Red Sea have appeared a trifle smaller.

## Measurements

In mm. Own measurements, UZM, NNH, MN, ZML, NRK, ZMU, ZMH, ZMO (Europe, Central Asia and Africa). Weight according to Glutz (1982).

WING LENGTH

| | | | |
|---|---|---|---|
| Ad ♂ | 404-442 | (421.6) | n = 20 |
| Ad ♀ | 387-436 | (411.4) | n = 25 |

TAIL FORK

| | | | |
|---|---|---|---|
| Ad | 25-47 | (37.6) | n = 29 |
| Juv | 20-29 | (26.0) | n = 11 |

BILL

| | | | |
|---|---|---|---|
| Ad ♂ | 67.8-79.0 | (71.4) | n = 30 |
| Ad ♀ | 61.9-73.0 | (67.6) | n = 39 |
| Juv | 54.2-70.6 | (63.3) | n = 14 |

• Two ads from New Zealand 64 and 66.6 mm (skins, NNH).

BILL DEPTH AT REAR EDGE OF NOSTRILS

| | | | |
|---|---|---|---|
| Ad | 18.0-22.4 | (20.6) | n = 33 |

TARSUS

| | | | |
|---|---|---|---|
| Ad | 38.0-50.0 | (44.1) | n = 68 |

• Average ad ♂ 44.7 (n = 24), ♀ 43.0 (n = 13). Juv 44.9-48.2 (n = 6).

WEIGHT (in grams)

| | | | |
|---|---|---|---|
| Ad ♂ | 600-700 | (675) | n = 8* |
| Ad ♀ | 500-640 | (618) | n = 7 |

* Max. weight given as 860 g (Glutz). ♀ from Denmark, August, weighed 670 g (UZM).

# Royal Tern

Photos **20-31**

*Sterna maxima*

### Identification in the field

The Royal Tern is the size of a Common Gull *Larus canus*, has a red bill, and is a 'toned-down', smaller, slimmer and pale-winged version of the Caspian Tern. It is well proportioned and combines lightness with power. Compared with Caspian, it is slimmer and obviously more lightweight, with narrower wings, longer tail and more slender, orange bill. An important point is that the underside of the primaries is white with black trailing edge (tips of 5-6 outer primaries), as for example on Crested, Lesser Crested and Sandwich Terns. The upperparts are the palest grey of all the crested terns. The usual call resembles that of Sandwich Tern, quite unlike Caspian's heron-like call.

The Royal Tern occurs in two races. The American *maxima* is bigger, with a heavier bill which is reminiscent of a pale dagger-shaped Caspian bill with its downward-curved tip to upper mandible and prominent gonydeal angle. The bill is reddish-orange to orange, usually yellower in winter (see below). The West African *albididorsalis* (rare vagrant in northwest Africa and Spain) is somewhat smaller and paler, with a slimmer bill (in shape recalling that of Crested and Lesser Crested), with less well-marked gonydeal angle than on *maxima*. The bill is orange, generally yellower than that of *maxima*.

The race *albididorsalis* can be confused with Lesser Crested Tern, but in direct comparison is bigger and heavier, with deeper chest, broader bill, longer legs, slightly paler upperparts and white rump and tail. Lesser Crested is only Sandwich Tern-sized, with narrower bill and darker grey upperparts on which rump and tail are almost concolorous with the back. Note, however, that tropical sunlight can make it difficult to determine the colour differences even in direct comparison.

Occurring in western America (within *maxima's* range) is Elegant Tern, which is only the size of Lesser Crested. It is slimmer than Royal, with narrower and relatively longer bill which may have a red base and distinctly translucent yellow distal part. The bill clearly droops at the tip, but the lower mandible is straighter, with less well-marked gonydeal angle. In winter plumage, Elegant Tern has a broader black facial mask than Royal Tern.

Royal Tern in active flight has thrusting, slow wingbeats and can then recall a slim Caspian Tern with Lesser Crested/Crested Tern proportions. The silhouette is long and narrow, with centre of gravity around the breast. It forages elegantly with direct lunges towards the water surface or with oblique to vertical plunges from several metres' height. It also snatches food items from the water surface, feeds like a skimmer or even parasitises smaller terns.

When perched, it recalls a small slim Caspian Tern with narrower and shorter legs. The wings fall level with the tail or project a couple of centimetres beyond it (always project clearly beyond tail on Caspian). The bill is paler and slimmer than Caspian's, with translucent, pale tip when seen against the light. It is often held slightly upwards, producing a snub-nosed appearance.

Adult in summer plumage has a black cap for only a short period early in the breeding season; as early as June the majority have a white forehead. A few retain the summer cap for slightly longer (presumably failed breeders: Davenport & Hollyer 1982). The border of the cap in front of the eye is straight (slightly down-curved on Caspian). The shaggy nuchal crest is longer and more obvious than Caspian Tern's. The legs are black.

**Adult in winter plumage** has a white head with narrow U-shaped black band from behind eye to the nape. A broad white eye-ring surrounds the eye, which stands out as a large black spot, accentuated by a black loral spot in front of the eye. The crown is white, sometimes with a few scattered dark streaks. Some have a diffuse, dark and incomplete neck band from rear edge of ear-coverts to the middle of the neck sides (at least *maxima*).

Nominate *maxima* has a reddish-orange to orange, more rarely orange-red or warm yellow, bill. Race *albididorsalis* has a warm orange-yellow to pale yellow bill, sometimes with a greenish or brownish tinge, but at best pale orange.

With wear, the outermost primaries become darker and contrast well with the rest of the wing.

**Juvenile** has head much as adult winter plumage, but the black mask is broader, the crown more heavily dark-marked and the hint of a 'neck-collar' more frequent. White eye-ring may be narrower than the adult's.

In very fresh plumage, the grey mantle/back is tinged yellowish-brown. Three dark bars on the wing across lesser and greater coverts and also secondaries contrast well with pale grey median coverts, giving the wing the character of a young gull. The tail is pale grey with dark terminal band, the rump a shade paler. The tail projections are shorter than on adults. Primary coverts and remiges are dark: perched birds show a dark U-shaped frame to the inner wing. The underwing is white with dark trailing edge to all feathers (most obvious on inner wing) and sometimes pale grey lesser coverts.

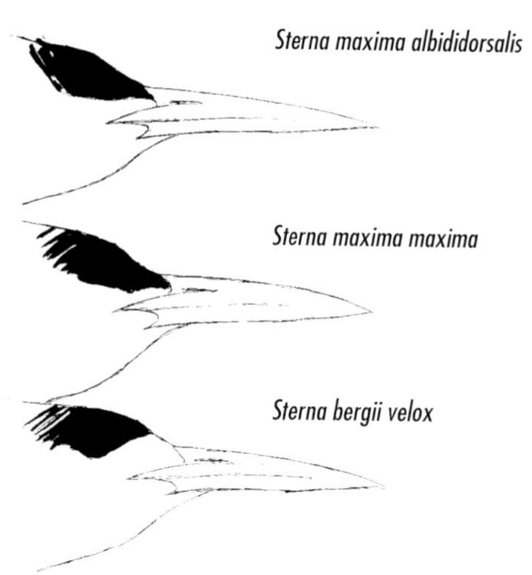


***FIGURE 3*** Differences in bill shape between Royal Tern *albididorsalis* , Royal Tern *maxima* and Crested Tern *velox*. The *maxima* shown is of the most typical kind (American west coast), whereas eastern populations have bill more similar in shape to *albididorsalis*, although still with clearly angled outer part of upper mandible.

The bill is orange-yellow to (more rarely) greyish-yellow. The legs are initially greyish-yellow to orange, but 'blacken' during the autumn. Some retain pale legs until the second winter (*albididorsalis*: Dubois 1991).

**First-winter plumage** is acquired in October-November. It resembles juvenile plumage, but the upperparts are uniform grey. Dark covert bars are sometimes broken during autumn and can be worn away during winter, but dark secondary bar is retained. In the sharp sunlight in which Royal Tern for the most part winters, juvenile feathers are rapidly bleached. In late winter and spring, the plumage appears pale and untidy. The juvenile remiges are bleached brown, and the central part of the wing is almost whitish. An obvious pale panel is thereby formed on the upperwing, and this can

1
2
3
4

**PLATE 6**

**Royal Tern *Sterna maxima***
Large, orange-billed tern, in size similar to Common Gull *Larus canus* or Ring-billed Gull *L. delawarensis.* Almost as large as Caspian Tern, but slender and in shape more of a giant Sandwich Tern, showing typical tern proportions such as slender head and wings, and clearly elongated outer tail feathers. Bill orange (not coral-red with darker tip) and undersurface of primaries pale with dark trailing edge similar to Sandwich Tern (and other large terns). Out of summer plumage, head is white with a dark line behind the eye and across the nape. Dark eye appears staring, surrounded by broad white eye-ring.

1 **Juvenile moulting to first-winter.**
2 **First-summer (March-April).** Retains winter head in first-summer. In later first-summer, coverts are much worn. Note: Bill of this individual shows the typical dagger-shape of West African subspecies *albididorsalis* (see text).
3 **Adult winter.** Note broad white eye-ring isolating dark eye. This head plumage is present most of the year. Note: Bill shape of this individual is heavier, typical of Nearctic subspecies *maxima.*
4 **Adult summer (March-May).** Note that summer hood is present for only a few months. Bill coloration is strongest when full hood is present.

be translucent and stand out very prominently against dark secondaries (as on second-calendar-year Common Gull in late spring and summer). The tail has an obvious dark terminal band.

**First-summer plumage** resembles adult winter plumage, but the mask is generally broader, and the dark secondary bar may be retained until at least autumn of second calendar-year (sometimes until summer of third calendar-year). Unmoulted juvenile outer primaries and their coverts are dark grey-brown, contrasting with fresh pale inner primaries. Three generations of primaries can be present; the middle ones are the most worn, and dark tips are also more evident on the upperparts. Dark bar across lesser coverts may be lacking, but some retain this until second-summer plumage (Urban *et al.* 1986). The tail has some dark-tipped central to outer rectrices.

**Second-winter plumage** is much as adult winter plumage, but has darker and relatively more worn outer (juvenile) primaries and primary coverts and a dark secondary bar (latter is gradually reduced; last to be moulted are the middle secondaries). The tail is white with shorter projections than on adult and often has an element of dark spotting or streaking on the outer rectrices.

**Second-summer plumage** is much as adult summer plumage, but white-tipped feathers may be present in the cap. Some still have a suggestion of a dark secondary bar (rarely, also of lesser-covert bar). The tail is white, but often with some darker or dark-spotted feathers.

## Voice

Recalls a coarse, lower-pitched and monotone Sandwich Tern call: *kree-it, kerriup* or *drrree* (pers. obs., USA). It has been described as musical (Lewington *et al.* 1991). On the breeding grounds harsher calls are heard, like a very high-pitched Caspian Tern. Juvenile has distinctly higher calls than adult.

## Moult (*maxima; albididorsalis* similar)

**Adult** has a complete moult to **winter plumage** which begins with the forehead in late May-June. The head feathers may be completely renewed from late June to early July (c. 1% in late August to early September have a summer head). Black spots can be present in forehead and crown until end of September. The upperparts are moulted in July-August, but some coverts later (as late as February). The tail moult begins at the end of August and finishes in November-December; t1 is moulted first, and the moult sequence is t1-t2-t3-t5-t6-t4, but with considerable individual variation (Cramp 1985). Primaries are moulted from July-early August. The inner (3) 5-7 primaries are changed in September to early October, 7-9 inners have been renewed by November/January, and primary moult is usually completed in late January to early March.

**Adult** moults to **summer plumage** in a partial moult, which begins in early February with head and some body feathers. The odd individual has a summer cap from late January. Feathers around bill base and lores are the last to be acquired. By the end of March the majority have a 'summer head'.

A new primary moult series is begun in November-December. The majority of those examined in February-March had renewed up to 5 inner primaries. The moult is suspended in April, with 4-6 inner primaries renewed (before breeding).

**Juvenile** has a complete moult to **first-winter plumage**. The moult begins with head, mantle and back, greater coverts, scapulars and central tail feathers in late September-November. The majority of those studied in eastern USA had, by early October, not started on the moult apart from t1.

Body and covert moult is largely complete in January-February, but a few greater and lesser coverts together with the tertials are renewed later. The tail is moulted from late September (t1 first; t1-3 are changed by December), and is finished in April-May. Primary moult normally begins in late November-January, but a few moult inner primaries as soon as early October (pers. obs., eastern USA). The innermost 1-4 primaries have been changed by late February-March (pers. obs., Costa Rica). In May-June, 5-7 (8) inner primaries have been replaced. Race *albididorsalis* is said to moult later than *maxima*: birds in January-February had changed only t1 plus inner primaries (skins, BMNH).

Moult to **second-winter plumage** is complete. It begins in April-May with head and remaining primary and tail feathers. The moult proceeds slowly: in September-October the majority have exchanged 3-4 (5) inner primaries, but some only 1-2 (Cramp 1985; pers. obs., USA); 1-5 outer primaries may still be old in November-December (skins, NMNH, NNH). At the same time, remaining juvenile outer primaries are moulted, so three different generations of primaries can be seen from summer to autumn. The second primary moult series ends in February-March. Tail moult is completed in December-January; t5-6 are normally growing in September-October, but the sequence varies, and some retain these until the following spring.

Subsequent moults are as for adults. Tail and wing moults are started in December-January, often interrupted in summer and completed around September.

### Detailed description

Length 45-50 cm, wingspan 125-135 cm (*maxima*).

**Adult summer plumage:** Cap black. White area between cap and gape 5.5-7 mm wide. Sides of head, hindneck and underparts white. Upperparts pale grey. Tertials and secondaries have white edges. Rump pale whitish-grey, sometimes greyer in centre (Moon 1983). Tail-coverts and tail white with faint grey tinge. Outer web and tips of rectrices are white to brownish-grey; 6-8 cm of outer part of t4-6 may be dark-tinted. Underwing-coverts white, sometimes with pale grey tinge on lesser coverts. Primaries pale grey above, white below with dark grey tips to 5-6 outer primaries and narrow pale edges; primaries 7-9 have broadest dark tips. Worn outer primaries may have paler grey tips. Birds in moult show distinct contrast between pale inner and darker outer primaries.

Bill (*maxima*) heavy, with dowcurved upper mandible and prominent gonydeal angle; orange to orange-red, paler and yellower from July. West American population in general has a stronger bill. Race *albididorsalis* has a narrower dagger-shaped bill with less prominent gonydeal angle; bill averages yellower (yellow-orange to orange) than on *maxima*.

Legs black; soles ochre-yellow, light red or yellow-orange, sometimes black.

**Adult winter plumage:** Forehead, lores and crown white, sometimes with short and narrow black streaks or spots, especially at junction between crown and black mask from behind eye through nape. Mask may be narrow – as a black line behind eye, uniform in width with latter. Black triangular loral patch. Broad white area around eye mostly isolates the eye, which stands out as a large black spot; on some the mask reaches the eye, which 'fuses with' black ear-coverts. Suggestion of a dark, incomplete band from rear edge of ear-coverts to middle of neck sides may be present (at least on *maxima*).

Otherwise as summer plumage, but unmoulted wing and tail feathers dark and worn. Bill: *maxima* has orange-red to orange bill, on a few per cent chrome-yellow (pers. obs., USA, Costa Rica and Venezuela, September-March); *albididorsalis* has orange-yellow to yellow or greyish-yellow bill, sometimes tinged green or brown.

**Juvenile:** Head much as adult winter plumage, but dark mask is broader, especially over crown, and incomplete neck band from rear edge of ear-coverts to neck sides is more common (though only a few per cent). Eye-ring narrower than on adults.

Underparts much as adult, but lesser coverts more commonly pale grey. Mantle white with variable grey to yellow-brown spots. Scapulars and tertials grey with white fringes and yellow-brown to grey-brown subterminal spots. Back, rump and uppertail-coverts grey with white tips, latter broadest at tail base and on rump sides. Tail feathers grey with broad white edges (sometimes tinted yellowish-brown) and dark tips. Bases of outer webs pale grey.

Remiges pale grey with broad white tips and narrow white edges on secondaries and inner 8 primaries, becoming gradually smaller towards outers. Primaries have silvery-grey outer webs. Lesser upper primary coverts dark grey. Longest lesser and all median coverts white, contrasting with rest of wing. Greater coverts dark grey with faint brown tinge. Primary coverts dark grey with pale edges.

Grey feathers wear to grey-brown or black (especially primaries, tail and centres of secondaries and tertials). On worn birds, the dark secondary bar appears as a row of dark spots rather than a solid bar.

Bill: *maxima* reddish-yellow, yellow-orange or (more rarely) banana-yellow; *albididorsalis* yellow, often tinged brown or green.

Legs initially yellow-ochre to orange-toned, from October spotted black (Moon 1983). Of 900 juvenile *maxima*, 80% had uniformly coloured legs (of which 56% black, 26% orange and 15% pink) and 20% pale-spotted legs (Chamberlain 1939). Of 201 juvenile *albididorsalis* (Senegal), 51% had orange to ochre-orange legs, two had legs spotted black and orange and the rest had black legs (Dubois 1991). Race *maxima* is said to acquire black legs more rapidly.

**First-winter plumage:** Resembles adult winter plumage, but with grey bar across lesser coverts (weaker than on juvenile, but in spring obvious against faded median coverts), dark secondary bar and dark-tipped tail feathers. Unmoulted primaries and primary coverts dark.

Worn birds in late winter and spring have faded juvenile primaries (up to 7). The secondaries have grey-brown centres, and the median and greater wing-coverts are whitish from wear.

**First-summer plumage:** Much as first-winter plumage. Dark bar across secondaries is present until at least October, when it is darkest on the middle secondaries. Tail white with variable dark areas on especially outer part of t5-6. Retained juvenile tail feathers have grey-brown outer part; t5-6 have up to 8 mm of pale colour at tips. Any remaining juvenile primaries faded, with reduced blackish-grey tips on underside.

**Second-winter plumage:** Much as adult winter plumage, but the majority retain dark secondary bar. Can show remnants of dark lesser-covert bar. Aged by different moult cycle from adults: in autumn moults the 5 innermost primaries, whereas adults moult the 5 outermost. Birds studied in USA in September/October had 1-4 fresh inner primaries and 1-3 juvenile outer primaries. Legs black, sometimes with a touch of yellow.

**Second-summer plumage:** Much as adult summer plumage, but normally with white-spotted crown and forehead; some have a winter head. A few have indistinct dark bar across lesser coverts. Often has two active moult series in primaries; worn outermost primaries clearly darker than the rest. See Cramp (1985).

**ROYAL TERN** QUICK KEY TO IDENTIFICATION

1. **Size of Common Gull, like a slim, pale-winged Caspian Tern with more slender orange bill.**
2. **Combination of orange bill and just a dark trailing edge to outer wing distinguishes this species from Caspian Tern.**
3. **Bigger and longer-legged with longer bill and heavier fore area than Lesser Crested Tern, which is only the size of Sandwich Tern.**
4. **Differs further from Lesser Crested in paler upperparts with white rump and tail.**
5. **In winter plumage has narrow black mask behind eye, latter surrounded by broad white eye-ring. Wears winter plumage for most of the year.**
6. **Upperwing of juveniles and younger immatures has three dark bars across inner part, so that upperwing has contrasting gull-like pattern.**
7. **Call resembles that of Sandwich Tern.**

1
2
3
4
5
6
7
8

**PLATE 7**

**Royal Tern *Sterna maxima***

1 **Juvenile.**
2 **Juvenile.**
3 **First-winter (March).** Aged by winter hood, dark secondary bar and darker, worn outer primaries and primary coverts. In spring often looks extremely bleached. Often retains darker lesser coverts well into second winter.
4 **Second-winter (September-October).** Separated from adult winter by traces of dark bars on lesser coverts and secondaries, as well as some grey in tail.
5 **Adult winter (early autumn).** Compare with 4, and notice uniform grey inner wing and wholly white tail.
6 **Second-summer.** As adult summer, but with darker primaries (and sometimes, as shown, dark secondary bar).
7 **Adult summer (March-May).**
8 **Adult moulting into winter plumage.**

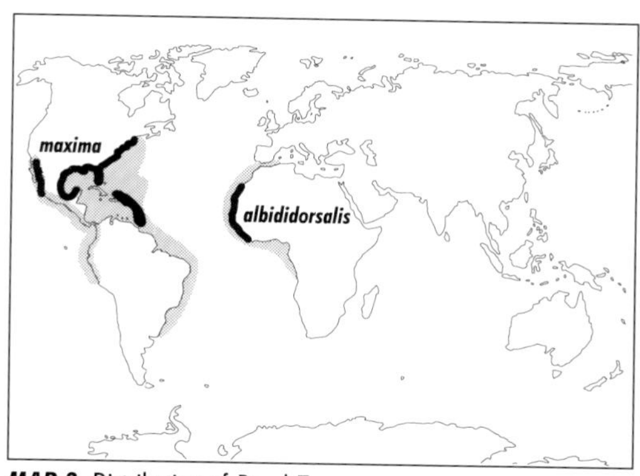


***MAP 3*** Distribution of Royal Tern *Sterna maxima.*

## Geographical variation

Race *albididorsalis* (West Africa) is smaller and slimmer than *maxima*. Its more slender, dagger-shaped bill is somewhat like Crested Tern's in shape, with less-marked gonydeal angle than *maxima* (Wheeler 1989). The bill is yellow to orange-yellow outside the breeding season (see above). Upperparts are generally paler than on *maxima*, and tail extensions generally shorter.

Pacific populations of *maxima* have an orange bill during the breeding season, yellow to yellow-orange in winter, and slightly longer wings than others of the race. Populations from South Africa have a bill like that of *albididorsalis*.

### Measurements

In mm. Own measurements, BMNH, NMNH, NNH, ZMA, UZM; wing (juv) and tarsus from Cramp (1985) and Gantlett & Harris (1988).

| WING LENGTH | | | |
|---|---|---|---|
| *albididorsalis* | | | |
| Ad ♂ | 354-366 | (359.7) | n = 10 |
| Ad ♀ | 346-360 | (353.0) | n = 16 |
| Juv ♂ | 343-355 | (349.0) | n = 5 |
| Juv ♀ | 334-348 | (341.3) | n = 4 |
| *maxima* | | | |
| Ad ♂ | 346-390 | (365.2) | n = 13 |
| Ad ♀ | 357-367 | (360.0) | n = 8 |

| TAIL FORK | | | |
|---|---|---|---|
| *albididorsalis* | | | |
| Ad summer | 65-92 | (77.7) | n = 11 |
| Ad winter | 38-75 | (53.7) | n = 20 |
| Juv/1st-winter | 35-65 | (52.9) | n = 15 |
| *maxima* | | | |
| Ad summer | 75-119 | (95.6) | n = 15 |
| Ad winter | 58-97 | (75.7) | n = 21 |
| Juv/1st-winter | 40-65 | (57.3) | n = 13 |

| BILL | | | |
|---|---|---|---|
| *albididorsalis* | | | |
| Ad | 60.9-70.0 | (64.4) | n = 24 |
| *maxima* | | | |
| Ad | 54.8-71.0 | (63.6) | n = 96 |
| Juv/1st-winter | 48.1-61.0 | (54.3) | n = 14 |

• *albididorsalis* ad ♂ 64-69 (66.3, n = 9), ad ♀ 61-65 (63, n = 11); *maxima* ad ♂ 59.4-71 (64.8, n = 34), ad ♀ 54.8-64.4 (61.9, n = 22) (own measurements).

**BILL DEPTH AT GONYS**

| | | | |
|---|---|---|---|
| *albididorsalis* | | | |
| Ad | 11.7-13.1 | (12.8) | n = 24 |
| *maxima* | | | |
| Ad | 11.9-14.4 | (13.0) | n = 40 |
| Juv/1st-winter | 11.2-12.7 | (12.3) | n = 14 |

• *maxima*: ad ♂ 12.4-14.4 (13.3, n = 34), ad ♀ 11.9-13.8 (12.7, n = 26).

**BILL DEPTH AT REAR EDGE OF NOSTRILS**

| | | | |
|---|---|---|---|
| *albididorsalis* | | | |
| Ad | 14.5-16.7 | (15.4) | n = 24 |
| *maxima* | | | |
| Ad | 14.7-17.6 | (16.0) | n = 95 |
| Juv/1st-winter | 14.1-16.7 | (15.0) | n = 16 |

• *maxima*: ad ♂ 14.9-17.6 (16.8, n = 34), ad ♀ 14.4-17.7 (15.6, n = 21).

**TARSUS**

| | | | |
|---|---|---|---|
| *albididorsalis* | | | |
| Ad ♂ | 30.5-35.0 | (33.2) | n = 15 |
| Ad ♂ | 30.0-34.0 | (32.0) | n = 15 |
| *maxima* | | | |
| Ad ♂ | 28.8-36.0 | (32.7) | n = 18 |
| Ad ♂ | 28.9-33.0 | (31.2) | n = 16 |

• Juv *maxima* 31.2 and 32.1 mm (skins, NNH).

**WEIGHT** (in grams)

| | | | |
|---|---|---|---|
| *albididorsalis* | | | |
| Ad | 350-440* | | |
| Imm | 310-410 | (353) | n = 28 |
| Juv | 320-360 | (341) | n = 13 |
| *maxima* | | | |
| Ad ♂ | 390-475 | | |
| Ad ♀ | 300-449 | | |
| Ad ♀ | 405-485 (6 specimens from Virginia, USA; NMNH) | | |

* Max. weight in October (skins, NNH). Urban *et al.* (1986) give weight between 304 and 345 g (Ghana *albididorsalis*). A bird from Mauritania weighed 440 g.

• Two juv *maxima* 270 and 290 g (skins, ZMA). Lean *maxima* in second winter 212 g (ZMA 35295). Nominate *maxima* 368-430 g (skins, NNH).

# Crested Tern

*Sterna bergii*

Photos **32-40**

### Identification in the field

The Crested Tern is an eastern counterpart of the similar-sized Royal Tern. It is slimmer than Royal. The body is elliptical and lacks obvious deep chest and clipped rear end. The slender wings are normally held angled in flight, with hand directed backwards. The Crested Tern is found along tropical coasts, which it patrols in a delicate, bounding flight almost like that of a male Montagu's Harrier *Circus pygargus* – in hard weather like a Long-tailed Skua *Stercorarius longicaudus*, making sweeps over the waves more commonly than other terns. Performs steep dives for fish from heights of several metres, but also snatches food from the water's surface.

Perched birds are large and front-heavy like Royal, with powerful greyish-yellow bill, flat crown, clearly angled nape crest and long black legs. In shape it is more reminiscent of Royal than of Lesser Crested Tern, a species with which Crested often associates.

The bill is yellow with a touch of grey or olive, and appears cold yellow (colour of a ripe grapefruit). Its shape is like that of Royal of race *albididorsalis*, but the bill has a more distinctly downcurved tip, the gonydeal angle is more obvious and the distal part of the lower mandible may be concave.

Crested Tern always has a white forehead and long untidy crest (most obvious in alert posture, with extended neck). The upperparts vary racially. Race *velox* (Red Sea to the Persian Gulf, wintering south to East Africa north of the equator) has dark grey upperparts like the British race of Lesser Black-backed Gull *Larus fuscus graellsii* – so dark that at a distance it can recall Sooty Tern (M. Ullman *in litt.*). When perched, it shows a white U shape at the tips of the secondaries (rather like adult Common Gull *L. canus*). These dark-backed birds are easily identified. East and South African races, however, have pale grey upperparts similar to or indeed paler than those of Lesser Crested Tern. They are separated from Lesser Crested by their blunter, heavier and colder yellow bill, bigger and more angular head and deeper chest. The precise colour tone of the upperparts can, however, be difficult to determine in the very strong tropical sunlight in which both species are normally seen, though Lesser Crested's orange bill (like a ripe orange) is usually immediately striking.

The primaries are paler, in fresh plumage contrasting clearly with the rest of the wing (much as on adult Kittiwake *Rissa tridactyla*). The contrast is most obvious in overcast weather, but poorer in strong sunlight. The rump and the white-edged tail are a paler grey than the back. The underparts are similar to those of Royal and Lesser Crested. Legs black.

**Adult in summer plumage** has a white band across the forehead of at most 1 cm in width. The cap is glossy black with the second-longest nuchal crest of all terns (only Elegant Tern has a longer crest). On alert birds the crest is like a horse's tail, but even when at rest it is long and ragged. The bill is yellow to greenish-yellow, greenest and darkest at the base; it may be slightly orange in tone at the start of the breeding season.

**Adult in winter plumage** has a less cleanly marked head than other crested species. It has a narrow white eye-ring, white forehead and central parts of the crown merging diffusely into white-peppered black mask. Usually the rear edge of the mask grades into a dark-spotted band on the neck sides. The upperparts are paler than in summer plumage. Pale primaries wear rapidly, and after the breeding season become less and less contrasting against the rest of the wing. Worn outer primaries are in fact very dark! Possibly parts of the plumage wear more rapidly and more dramatically on the tropical, sandblown shores with their very strong sunlight than in temperate regions. At any rate, the contrast between new and old primaries is surprisingly obvious on this species.

The bill is pale yellow to greenish-yellow, generally colder yellow than in summer plumage, and often with darker inner half.

**Juvenile** has a head similar to adult winter plumage. The upperparts are the most contrastingly patterned of the juveniles of all larger terns, with markings rather like those of juvenile Royal but with appreciably more contrast. Three dark bars are created by dark lesser and greater coverts and secondaries. These bars contrast clearly with paler central area. Greater coverts and secondaries have broad pale grey tips, which are gradually worn away. The remiges are blackish-brown with a pale wedge on inner primaries (much as on young Herring Gull *Larus argentatus*), grading evenly into grey central area of upperwing. Mantle, back and tertials are dark with pale feather edges, contrasting with grey rump and dark grey tail. Bill and legs much as in adult winter plumage.

The pale-backed races exhibit the most obvious colour contrasts. The dark *velox* is, in this plumage, too, very dark, with 'British Lesser Black-backed Gull-grey' areas, and appears strikingly dark compared with e.g. Lesser Crested Tern. Outer rectrices are very dark and contrast strongly with the otherwise grey tail, which becomes obvious when the bird spreads its tail before landing.

***PLATE 8***

**Crested Tern *Sterna bergii*, race *velox***
Size and jizz similar to Royal Tern, but bill cold yellow, never clear orange. Always shows white forehead, even in summer plumage, unlike congeners. Out of breeding plumage, mask more pale-mottled than on Royal and Lesser Crested Terns. Upperparts typically much darker than on congeners, in Western Palearctic populations appearing almost as dark as on Lesser Black-backed Gull *Larus fuscus* of ssp. *graellsi*.

1 **Juvenile.** The most well-marked juvenile *Sterna*.
2 **Juvenile moulting to first-winter.**
3 **Second-winter.** Similar to adult winter, but note darker lesser coverts and relatively much more worn outer primaries.
4 **Adult winter.** Note cold yellow bill, white-scaled mask and dark grey plumage (but see text for geographic variation).
5 **Adult summer.** Note white forehead. Yellow bill coloration often turns warmer in early breeding season, but only exceptionally shows orange tinge (see Lesser Crested Tern).

**First-summer/first-winter plumage** is similar to juvenile, but with uniformly grey back and greater coverts. With wear, the faded median coverts contrast clearly with dark bars on secondaries and coverts, especially on pale-backed races.

**Second-winter plumage** is similar to adult winter plumage, but has dark secondary bar, sometimes an incomplete dark bar across lesser coverts and dark tail sides. Retained juvenile primaries are worn and grey-brown, with worn coverts. Retains a few odd juvenile outer primaries and tail feathers up to spring of third calendar-year.

Following the next moult, the plumage is presumably as that of adult.

## Voice

A harsh *kerrerr* or *kerrak*, which is crow-like (Wallace 1973) or similar to a deep and coarse Sandwich Tern or Common Tern (Roberts 1991). Also a loud, scream-

1
2
3
4
5

ing *kree-kree* (Hollom *et al.* 1988). Other calls are said to recall Caspian Tern's.

## Moult

Varies according to timing of breeding seasons (studies of skins, photos and field studies).

Race *thalassina* (breeds in Tanzania in November: Urban *et al.* 1990).

Adults (Kenya and Tanzania) moult to adult summer plumage from March to May/June. May have acquired summer plumage in January-March, but normally not before May. Body and head are moulted to winter plumage in October-December. Primary moult similar to that of other larger terns. In August/September 5-9 inner primaries have been renewed, in November-January up to 8-9.

First-years renew mantle/back feathers, up to the inner 5 primaries and t6, and to a varying degree the greater coverts, in late winter. In June-August, 7-8 inner primaries have been exchanged. Second-years in December-January have renewed tail and coverts and have a moult limit at 5-7 inner primaries.

Race *velox* (Iran, Saudi Arabia and Somalia; breeds June-July in north, July-August in Somalia) has moulted to adult summer plumage in April-June, but can have scattered white feathers in the crown in April. Moults to winter plumage after breeding season, but a few feathers of forehead and crown are moulted during breeding. Normally in winter plumage September to March/April. Primary moult is suspended while breeding, with 4-6 inner primaries replaced, and resumed in autumn. East African birds had changed 7-9 inners in December-January.

**Juvenile** moults to first-winter plumage from December-January, starting with head, body, mantle and central tail-coverts. Primary moult presumably begins in January-February. In March-April, the inner 4-5 primaries have been renewed. During spring the tail is moulted. In the second winter (December-January), up to 6 inner primaries and most of the tail have been changed (pers. obs., Kenya).

Race *cristata* varies. Some are said to breed at six-monthly intervals (Cramp 1985), thus influencing the moult (see Sooty Tern). Adults from Thailand, China and Sulawesi are in summer plumage in February-June/July. Winter plumage is assumed from August-October, when t1-4 and inner (3) 5-6 (7) primaries are renewed.

**Juvenile**s begin the moult in November-December, when t1 and parts of the mantle/back are renewed.

Birds in first-summer to second-winter plumage have three generations of primaries (moult in innermost and two outermost), with retained juvenile secondaries; one individual out of five had retained greater coverts (July-August). Tail fresh, but t2 and 6 may be renewed. In February-April, replaces 3-8 primaries and tail feathers.

Populations from Australia and Oceania are in winter plumage in March-June, in summer plumage late September to February-May; variable, with birds from Marshall islands in summer plumage to a varying degree in October/November and April-June (related to breeding season).

Race *bergii*: adults have summer plumage in December-April (ZMO).

#### **Detailed description** (race *velox*)

Length 46-49 cm, wingspan 125-130 cm.

**Adult summer plumage:** White band of 3-8 mm on central part of forehead and 7-10 mm between base of upper mandible and crown sides. Cap black with long crest. Hindneck, mantle and underparts white. Upperparts dark grey, similar to British Lesser Black-backed Gull *graellsii*, sometimes faintly tinged brown (most obvious with wear). Tertials, secondaries and inner primaries have white edges and tips. Rump and tail slightly paler grey. Tail feathers grey with darker outer webs and narrow pale edges; t6 has pale tip of about 5 mm, which is rapidly worn off. Secondaries blackish-grey. Inner 4-5 primaries silver-grey (in fresh plumage) with white inner webs; outer primaries have dark grey outer webs. Underwing white, with grey tips about 6 mm wide on 4-6 outermost primaries and grey-toned lesser coverts and secondaries. With wear, secondaries, tertials and outer tail feathers acquire a pale brownish-grey tint, inner primaries become dark grey and outermost primaries grey-brown to blackish. Central primaries can become dark-tipped also on upperside.

Bill chrome-yellow to greenish-yellow, sometimes with greener base or, during breeding season, with faint tinge of orange. Upper mandible has slight curve at tip. Gonydeal angle prominent, generally most obvious on males; females may lack gonydeal angle. Tip of lower mandible may be concave. Legs black with completely or partially yellow soles.

**Adult winter plumage:** Forehead white, grading diffusely into black-spotted ('white-peppered') crown. Cap from eye to nape black with white feather tips. Lower rear edge of cap angled; may grade into incomplete dark neck band. Cap varies, and some have broader white feather tips forming coarsely spotted pattern. A few are very pale-headed (like winter-plumaged Royal Tern) and have only narrow black mask behind eye or narrow dark streaks in crown and nape. Has narrow white eye-ring, but this can be lacking in front of eye as rear part of lores is black and forms a broad black spot in front of eye.

Appearance of upperparts depends on wear and moult: mixture of worn grey-brown and fresh dark grey feathers can produce an untidy pattern. Birds which are moulting greater coverts reveal white bases to remiges, like moulting dark-backed large gulls such as Great Black-backed *Larus marinus*. Fresh innermost primaries silvery-grey, contrasting with remaining worn dark ones. Worn central primaries may have dark tips above. Wear obvious after breeding season.

Bill pale yellow to greenish-yellow, sometimes with dark olive-grey or grey-brown tinge at base.

**Juvenile:** The most contrastingly marked juvenile *Sterna*. Varies individually (and racially: pale-backed races show most contrast; see Geographical Variation).

Head much as winter-plumaged adult. Forehead, lores and sides of head white with dense black spots. Throat white. Mask (crown, ear-coverts and nape black) with pale feather edges, broadest in fore region. Cap angled at lower edge and grading variably into grey-spotted neck sides and throat sides, which can form incomplete neck band. Narrow white eye-ring.

**CRESTED TERN** QUICK KEY TO IDENTIFICATION

1. **Elegant, long and slim sea tern with strongly angled wings and long cold yellow bill.**
2. **Perched birds are heavy, with long greenish-yellow bill, white forehead and shaggy crest.**
3. **Adult of race *velox* has the darkest grey upperparts of all *Sterna* terns, similar to British Lesser Black-backed Gull (of race *graellsii*). African races south of equator have pale upperparts similar to Lesser Crested Tern.**
4. **In late winter and spring, silvery-grey primaries are distinctly paler than rest of upperparts.**
5. **The yellow bill is cold in colour, with a green tint, and often has darker grey basal part.**
6. **Juveniles and first-winters show very rich contrasts, with almost black bars across lesser and greater coverts and secondaries and pale wedge on inner primaries.**
7. **Outside breeding season, has white-spotted crown and often dark incomplete band on throat sides and neck sides. Facial mask therefore larger and more 'untidy' than on other crested terns. Only a narrow white eye-ring.**

Mantle, back, scapulars and tertials blackish-brown to blackish-grey with broad white to pale grey edges. Rump and uppertail-coverts paler with blackish-grey spots, broadest on rump.

Primaries grey-black with white edge to inner webs, greyer towards base to about 6 mm from tip; inner 4-6 primaries have narrow white edges and tips. Secondaries, primary coverts and greater wing-coverts dull black with white tips. Median and longest lesser coverts grey, medians sometimes with diffuse darker centres; remaining lesser coverts blackish-brown. Underwing and leading edge of upperwing white. Tail dark grey; fresh tail feathers have narrow white edges and tips, broadest on t1-2.

Bill and legs as adult winter plumage, but legs sometimes greyish-yellow with black spots, especially on front of tarsus and on upperside of toes. Bill can have grey inner part.

**First-winter plumage:** Head as adult winter plumage, but crown sometimes black with narrow white feather centres and contrasting less with black mask. Grey spots or short streaks on throat sides and neck sides form variable neck band. Mantle and back mid-grey. Wing similar to juvenile, but some have new uniform grey greater coverts. Bar on lesser coverts greyish-black to brownish-grey. The majority of remiges and tertials are juvenile up to midwinter, gradually becoming brownish-black through wear. In April, 3-7 outer primaries and some outer tail feathers are juvenile.

During summer this plumage is replaced by second-winter plumage, which is as adult apart from retained juvenile outer primaries and primary coverts together with secondaries. Tail generally darker, with variable dark terminal band. Up to 5 outer primaries and their coverts can be juvenile up to December.

1
2
3
4
5
6
7
8

**PLATE 9**

**Crested Tern *Sterna bergii*, race *velox* (1-6) and race *thalassina* (7-8).**

*Velox* (Only breeding subspecies in Western Palearctic) is the largest and darkest race. Upperparts typically are darkest among larger terns, often close to Lesser Black-backed Gull of subspecies *fuscus*.

1 **Juvenile.** Wing pattern strong, recalling certain juvenile gulls. Note three dark bars in inner wing.
2 **Juvenile.**
3 **First-winter.**
4 **First-summer.**
5 **Adult winter.**
6 **Adult summer.**

*Thalassina* (tropical East Africa) is the palest subspecies, approaching Sandwich Tern or Lesser Crested Tern in upperpart coloration. Other subspecies are intermediate between *velox* and *thalassina* (see text).

7 **Adult summer.** Compare upperpart coloration with that of *velox* and Lesser Crested Tern. Best separated from latter by cold yellow bill colour: in summer plumage on white forehead, in other plumages on white-mottled, unevenly marked hood. See text.
8 **First-winter.** Distinguished from older birds by darker lesser coverts and secondaries and more worn outer primaries.

**Second-summer plumage:** Resembles adult, but perhaps with some white feather tips in crown.

## Geographical variation

Involves mainly the colour of upperparts. Race *velox* (Red Sea, Persian Gulf and northern part of Indian Ocean, wintering along East African coasts, mainly north of equator: Britton 1980; Lewis & Pomeroy 1989) is biggest and darkest and has the longest bill, which is powerful as that of Royal Tern (*albididorsalis*). Upperparts dark grey, much as British Lesser Black-backed Gull. See Measurements.

Race *thalassina* (western parts of Indian Ocean from Tanzania to Madagascar, in East Africa commonest south of equator: Lewis & Pomeroy 1989) is smallest and palest, but becomes gradually larger and darker towards southwest Africa. Upperparts paler grey than *velox*, varying from pale grey as Sandwich Tern (East Africa) to darker grey (as or darker than Common Gull) farther south. Forehead band of adult summer (4) 7-11 mm. Juvenile has broader pale feather edges on mantle/back than *velox*, and can have white rump.

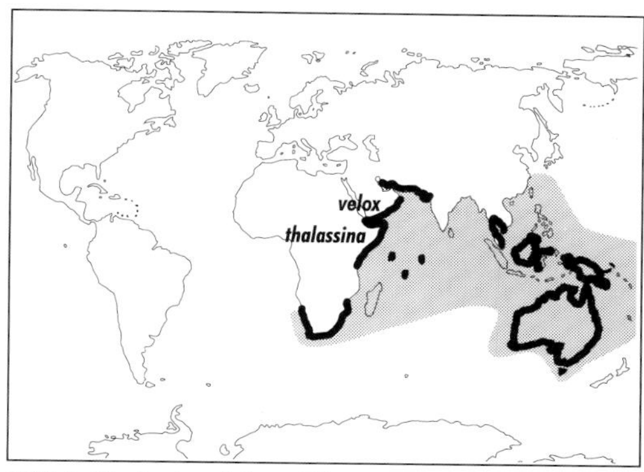


***MAP 4*** Distribution of Crested Tern *Sterna bergii*.

Race *bergii* (South Africa) is bigger than *thalassina*. Upperparts vary, but are generally dark grey as Common Gull. Tail and rump uniform with back. White band across forehead narrower: 2.5-6 (8) mm. Gonydeal angle generally more prominent than in *thalassina*.

Race *cristata* (Southeast Asia, China and Australia) resembles *bergii*. Upperparts vary from as dark as *velox* (Southeast Asia and north Australia) to as pale as Common Tern (in west and south Australia); in Southeast Asia, between *velox* and *thalassina* in colour. Tail and rump concolorous with back. White forehead band in adult summer plumage 5-9 mm (5-7 mm in Australia). Bill is lemon-yellow in breeding season, otherwise greenish-yellow. Australian populations have relatively short bill, and greyish-white uppertail-coverts and tail.

### Measurements

In mm. Own measurements, BMNH, NMNH, NNH, ZMA, UZM, NRK, ZML, ZMO.

**WING LENGTH**

| | | | |
|---|---|---|---|
| *velox* | | | |
| Ad | 354-381 | (366.0) | n = 30 |
| Juv/1st-winter | 332-358 | (342.6) | n = 20 |
| *cristata* | | | |
| Ad | 325-365 | (343.7) | n = 41 |
| Juv/1st-winter | 325-355 | (336.3) | n = 10 |
| *bergii* | | | |
| Ad | 344-375 | (357.5) | n = 18 |
| *thalassina* | | | |
| Ad | 322-356 | (337.0) | n = 25 |

• Average for *velox* ad ♂ 362.3, ad ♀ 369.8; for *cristata* ad ♂ 344.0, ad ♀ 342.4.

**TAIL FORK**

| | | | |
|---|---|---|---|
| *velox* | | | |
| Ad | 72-112 | (87.6) | n = 36 |
| Juv/1st-winter | 35-55 | (46.3) | n = 7 |
| *cristata* | | | |
| Ad | 55-104 | (85.0) | n = 66 |
| Juv/1st-winter | 38-66 | (43.6) | n = 10 |
| *bergii* | | | |
| Ad | 79-106 | (89.8) | n = 12 |
| *thalassina* | | | |
| Ad | 65-100 | (79.3) | n = 25 |

• Average for *velox* ad ♂ 82.3, ad ♀ 89.5; for *thalassina* ad ♂ 80.6, ad ♀ 78.8. Juv *bergii* 50-64, four juv *thalassina* 44-54.1 (juvs BMNH, UZM, NMNH).

**BILL**

| | | | |
|---|---|---|---|
| *velox* | | | |
| Ad | 57.8-68.8 | (64.6) | n = 37 |
| Juv/1st-winter | 53.8-62.5 | (58.9) | n = 7 |
| *cristata* | | | |
| Ad | 54.0-67.4 | (60.7) | n = 68 |
| Juv/1st-winter | 49.7-62.5 | (57.7) | n = 26 |
| *bergii* | | | |
| Ad | 57.0-67.7 | (62.3) | n = 45 |
| *thalassina* | | | |
| Ad | 53.5-64.0 | (56.7) | n = 29 |

• For *velox*, ad ♂ 60.0-68.8 (66.3), ad ♀ 57.8-68.1 (61.6); average for *thalassina* ad ♂ 56.5, ad ♀ 57.7.

**BILL DEPTH AT GONYS**

| | | | |
|---|---|---|---|
| *velox* | | | |
| Ad | 10.7-13.9 | (11.8) | n = 29 |
| *cristata* | | | |
| Ad | (9.5-) 10.0-13.0 | (11.3) | n = 50 |
| *bergii* | | | |
| Ad | 10.6-12.5 | (11.5) | n = 45 |
| *thalassina* | | | |
| Ad | 10.9-12.4 | (11.7) | n = 22 |

**BILL DEPTH AT REAR EDGE OF NOSTRILS**

| | | | |
|---|---|---|---|
| *velox* | | | |
| Ad | 13.2-16.2 | (14.7) | n = 29 |
| *cristata* | | | |
| Ad | 12.2-16.0 | (14.2) | n = 55 |
| *bergii* | | | |
| Ad | 13.9-16.5 | (14.8) | n = 43 |
| *thalassina* | | | |
| Ad | 12.1-15.7 | (14.3) | n = 22 |

**TARSUS**

| | | | |
|---|---|---|---|
| *velox* | | | |
| Ad + 1st/2nd-winter | 29.7-36.1 | (32.4) | n = 41 |
| *cristata* | | | |
| Ad + 1st/2nd-winter | 22.6-32.0 | (28.4) | n = 74 |
| *bergii* | | | |
| Ad + 1st/2nd-winter | 28.0-32.2 | (29.6) | n = 41 |
| *thalassina* | | | |
| Ad + 1st/2nd-winter | 27.2-30.8 | (28.5) | n = 20 |

**WEIGHT** (in grams)

| | | |
|---|---|---|
| *velox* | | |
| Ad | 340-397 | |
| *thalassina* | | |
| | 325-350 | |
| *cristata* | | |
| | (274) 325-383 | (480)* |

* Both extremes from skins, BMNH.

# Lesser Crested Tern

*Sterna bengalensis*

Photos **41-48**

### Identification in the field

The Lesser Crested Tern is the smallest crested, 'yellow-billed' tern with the brightest orange bill. In size and proportions it recalls Sandwich Tern – it looks like an orange-billed Sandwich Tern with uniform grey upperparts, the latter also distinguishing this species from Royal and Elegant Terns, which have white rump and tail. The bill is bright orange (like a ripe orange), similar to that of Sandwich in shape and length but generally with broader base (most obvious on the shortest-billed individuals); it is distinctly more slender than Royal's and normally shorter than that of Elegant. Note, however, that long-billed birds have a bill length as latter, but then with relatively more obvious gonydeal angle. The species is similar in shape to Sandwich Tern, but body and tail appear longer and the wings longer and narrower (and more centrally placed).

Compared with Crested Tern and Royal Tern, it is more delicately built, with smaller head and shorter crest. The head shape varies according to level of activity. At rest it can appear round-headed with the highest point immediately above the eye (Hurford 1989; Clement & Batten 1989), while birds in territorial conflict become extremely flat-headed with bristling crest. The head and bill then form a long and narrow fore area. The legs are shorter than Crested Tern's, as those of Sandwich in length. (The claim that perched birds are 50% taller than Sandwich (Baker 1984) is not supported by measurements.) At rest, the wingtips project clearly beyond the tail. The underwing is white, with dark rear edge to outer wing formed by tips of 5-7 outer primaries; the trailing edge is broader, longer and darker than on Sandwich Tern.

Lesser Crested Tern is, like Crested, very much a marine bird. The flight recalls that of Sandwich Tern, but is often slower – which, in combination with the orange bill, which is often held downwards, can evoke thoughts of Common Tern. It forages like Sandwich Tern, with steep plunges from some height, but also in the manner of Common Tern, with lunges towards the surface of the water.

Mixed flocks of terns are a common feature along tropical coasts, where several similar species occur. In the western part of the region (e.g. in West Africa), separation from Royal Tern is often difficult. Lesser Crested is clearly smaller, with slimmer bill and uniform grey upperparts. The overall impression is of an 'orange-billed Sandwich Tern', whereas Royal Tern is a 'Caspian in miniature' with white rump and tail. The primaries are moulted later than those of Royal; adults moult the inner primaries in autumn, when Royal is moulting the outers.

In the east, mixed flocks of Crested and Lesser Crested Terns are common. Crested has a more powerful, cold yellow bill and more angular head, altogether having a hefty and angular front-heavy appearance. Crested Tern's upperparts, however, are noticeably darker only on northern and eastern races (within the region of the Red Sea to the northern part of the Indian Ocean), more southerly populations (East and South Africa south of equator, and Australia) having upperpart colour similar to that of Lesser Crested Tern. Elegant Tern also represents a problem, though it has white rump to tail and generally longer bill and crest. Cayenne Terns (race *eurygnatha* of Sandwich) have a yellower bill, often with a tinge of grey (which Lesser Crested never shows). See below for differences in the various plumages.

**Adult** has an orange bill with diffuse paler yellow tip, which against the light shows less translucency than that of Royal. The upperparts are pale grey, populations from the Mediterranean Sea and North Africa being a shade darker than Sandwich Tern, but otherwise similar to latter. Rump and tail are pale grey, as back, but the rump may be slightly paler. Sharp tropical sunlight often makes the upperparts paler; lack of contrast between back and rump/tail is then more important than actual colour.

In fresh plumage (spring), the silvery-grey primaries are somewhat paler than the rest of the upperparts (though not so obviously as on Crested Tern of race *velox* in fresh plumage). During the summer and into winter, any unmoulted primaries gradually darken, becoming first concolorous with and later darker than the rest of the wing; the pale shafts then appear as pale streaks on the 4-5 outer primaries. The legs are black.

**Adult in summer plumage** has a black cap (April-July/August), but white feathers appear in the front part of the cap during the breeding season (as on Sandwich Tern). The cap is similar to that of Sandwich, but the crest is generally longer and more bristly and the white wedge between gape and cap generally broader. These characters, however, are almost impossible to use without direct comparison. At rest, the crest is slightly drooping, but is not so obviously long and dishevelled as that of Crested Tern.

The bill is orange, rather similar in colour to that of Royal Tern of western race *albididorsalis*.

**Adult winter plumage** has white head with black mask similar to Royal's. Compared with Royal, the mask is generally broader, and more solid in front of the eye. The white eye-ring is therefore distinct only behind the eye, and narrow (usually barely visible) in front of the eye, which only rarely appears isolated by white as on Royal. The black mask is complete on the nape, with a sharp border against the white crown and some dark streaking where the two meet. Crested and Sandwich Terns have a distinctly white-spotted dark nape, Crested also a broader white eye-ring and often a suggestion of a dark neck band. During the moult the forehead becomes dark-spotted, so that the mask becomes broader and more diffusely demarcated.

The bill is uniformly yellow to yellowish-orange, similar in colour to that of Royal. It is always warm yellow (red-tinted), an important difference from Crested Tern's more powerful, cold yellow bill, which furthermore usually has an element of grey in it.

**Juvenile** recalls juvenile Royal Tern, but is smaller. Three dark wingbars (lesser and greater coverts plus secondaries) are paler than those of Crested Tern. Upperpart feathers and tertials have dark centres and pale edges. Rump and uppertail-coverts are paler than on adult. The tail is slightly paler grey than the back and has a diffuse dark terminal band, broadest on the outer rectrices. The primaries are dark. The bill is warm yellow.

---

***PLATE 10***

**Lesser Crested Tern *Sterna bengalensis***
Similar in size to Sandwich Tern, but with orange bill and slightly darker, uniform grey upperparts. Bill uniform orange (as a ripe orange), similar in coloration to bill of Royal Tern.

1 **Juvenile.**
2 **First-winter (spring).** Separated from adult winter by darker bar over lesser coverts and retained winter head in summer.
3 **Adult winter.**
4 **Adult summer.**

1
2
3
4

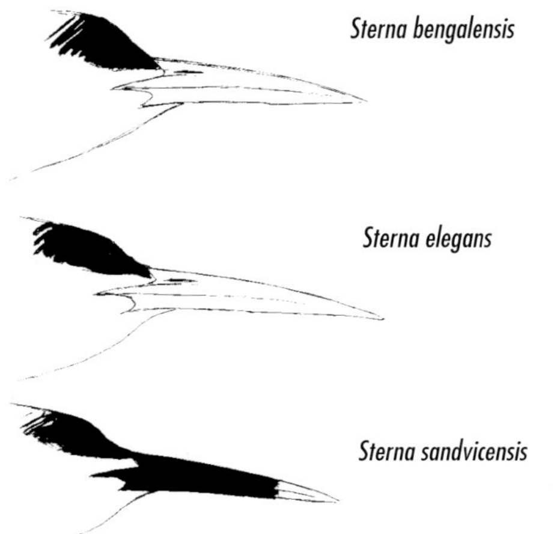


***FIGURE 4*** Differences in bill shape between Lesser Crested Tern, Elegant Tern and Sandwich Tern. Note long, drooping bill of Elegant Tern. Short-billed individuals of Elegant are more problematic. Note that Lesser Crested Tern shows a better-marked gonydeal angle (situated halfway or more towards the tip of the lower mandible). Elegant Tern shows gonydeal angle about halfway towards bill tip which, although well defined, is less visible in the field.

Sandwich Tern size and flight action are important for separation from Royal Tern. Young Crested are more heavily dark-patterned, with cold yellow bill and even more obvious wing markings; almost black and white with extra dark bar on median coverts.

**First-winter plumage** is similar to juvenile, but in the middle of winter acquires a grey back and some grey median and greater coverts. These new feather areas are clearly paler than similar ones on adults. More important for ageing are the dark-centred juvenile tertials, though these are exchanged in late winter for paler grey ones.

The wing is otherwise juvenile, but with more distinct pale primary wedge formed by new pale inner primaries. The central part of the tail and rump is pale grey. The bill is not so yellow-orange as the adult's but slightly duller in colour. Tarsus and feet may be yellow and contrast with dark 'knees' and 'thighs'.

During winter the central parts of the wing fade to whitish. At the same time the cap becomes dull and brownish.

**First-summer plumage** varies. Individuals which retain dark juvenile lesser coverts and secondary bar are easily aged; more advanced birds are similar to adult winter, but have dark primary coverts (pale grey on adults) which 'lengthen' the dark leading edge of the outer wing. Contrast between new inner primaries and faded dark outers is often very obvious, especially in spring when the majority of adults have fresh, pale primaries. The head is as adult winter plumage, but the cap tinged brown. The outer tail feathers often show elements of dark coloration. The bill is greyish-yellow to yellow-orange. The tarsus may still have pale elements.

**Second-winter plumage** resembles adult, but has dark secondary bar and some dark colour on the outer 2-3 tail feathers. Some also retain vestiges of a dark bar across the lesser coverts. The tertials are generally darker grey with more distinct pale edges than on adult. Any unmoulted outer primaries and their coverts are dark and worn. In midwinter, separated from first-winter plumage by the fact that only the outer primaries are darker, as first-winters on the whole have juvenile remiges.

## Voice

Resembles that of Sandwich Tern, but not quite so sharp and a trifle deeper (Brichetti & Foschi 1987; Thompson *et al.* 1985; Roberts 1991). Not so obviously disyllabic as Sandwich Tern's (Hollom *et al.* 1989). A high thin *kreek* has also been described (Roberts 1991), perhaps the begging call of the juvenile.

## Moult (West Palearctic populations)

**Adult** acquires **winter plumage** in a complete moult, which starts with inner or central primaries, t1 and some head feathers and scapulars in late July-August. White feathers appear around bill base, forehead and crown from end of May or during the breeding season (as with Sandwich Tern), with head winter-plumaged end of July at earliest. Moult of the head, most of the body and the tail is completed in October-November. Primary moult commences in late summer with any retained outer primaries. In November 2-3 inner primaries have been renewed (Gambia, Hans Larsson verbally), in December-January 5-7 inner primaries have been changed; by late January at the earliest all primaries are renewed, but occasional individuals have the outer primary growing in April. Primary moult is generally later than that of Royal Tern.

**Adult** acquires **winter plumage** in a partial moult, which includes head and underparts, parts of upperparts and scapulars and t5-6. The inner primaries are moulted from late November to late January. Head and body are moulted late February to early April, with forehead feathers moulted last. The primary moult is arrested when head and body moult is completed, with inner 3-5 (6-7) primaries replaced, but sometimes all primaries are exchanged before breeding.

**Juvenile** has a complete moult to **first-winter plumage** which begins in November-January with head, body, t1 and median and greater coverts. Moult of body feathers is normally completed in March-April, tail moult in July-August (but can be delayed until winter; see below). Primary moult begins in January-February (March); in the first winter 4-5 (8) inner primaries are renewed. A new moult series may begin during spring with inner primaries (see below). Two moult series may be found in the primaries during the first summer, when the inner/central and outer primaries are moulted.

Moult to **second-winter plumage** is complete. It commences with inner primaries in May-July before the first moult cycle is finished. In midwinter, 1-2 (4) outer primaries are usually left from the previous moult cycle, and these are replaced in January-April (pers. obs. Kenya, December-January; skins). Moult of head and body is completed in October, the tail normally later; t5-6 are usually very worn in December-January. Secondaries are normally moulted during autumn and winter, the central ones last.

In the second winter up to spring (third calendar-year) the upperparts are as on adults, but outer tail feathers often very worn; 4-5 inner primaries normally renewed in June-August.

Subsequent moults presumably as for adults; some have white-tipped feathers in the cap and dark tail feathers (t4-5) in second-summer plumage, when outer primaries are normally worn in April-May (can be retained until autumn, rarely until following spring).

**LESSER CRESTED TERN** QUICK KEY TO IDENTIFICATION

1. **Orange-billed tern similar in size and shape to Sandwich Tern.**
2. **Rump and tail grey, uniform with back.**
3. **Bill brighter and more uniformly orange than Elegant Tern's, never cold yellow as on Crested Tern.**
4. **Normally flies with bill horizontal, unlike Sandwich Tern.**
5. **Crest shaggy and angled.**
6. **Juveniles have yellow bill and dark bars on lesser and greater coverts.**
7. **In winter plumage resembles Royal Tern, but with narrower white eye-ring (broadest behind eye) and broader black mask.**
8. **In second-winter plumage resembles adult, but with dark secondary bar, and dark outer (2-4) primaries and tail sides.**

## Detailed description

Length 35-37 cm, wingspan 92-105 cm.

**Adult summer plumage:** Cap black, crest shaggy and somewhat drooping. Nape, lower part of lores, mantle and underparts white, belly sometimes greyish-white. White wedge 3-5 mm broad between lower edge of cap and gape. Upperparts pale grey, as on Sandwich Tern or Crested Tern (race *thalassina*), sometimes slightly darker and tinged blue-grey. Rump and tail uniform with back (rump palest). Tail feathers pale grey, sometimes

**PLATE 11**

**Lesser Crested Tern *Sterna bengalensis***

1 **Juvenile.**

2 **Juvenile.**

3 **First-winter.** Distinguished from adults by darker lesser-covert and secondary bars, and dark primary coverts.

4 **First-summer / second-winter.** Distinguished from adult by presence of darker secondaries and primary coverts, relatively more worn outer primaries and dark tail spots. As in congeners, first-summers retain winter head.

5 **Adult winter.** Note rather plain upperparts with concolorous mantle, rump and tail.

6 **Adult summer (before breeding season).** Develops white forehead from the middle of breeding season (as Sandwich Tern). Outer primaries become gradually darker following breeding season.

with whitish inner webs; rarely, whitish. T6 has darker grey outer web and a couple of millimetres of paler tip. In spring, t4-5 are worn and darker grey-brown than rest of tail. Tertials sometimes have darker centres than remaining upperpart feathers.

Primaries pale grey, contrasting only poorly with darker upperparts. Outer webs silver-grey with dark grey streak of about 5 mm along shafts. Remiges grey with narrow (1-2 mm) white tips (similar to Sandwich Tern of race *acuflavida*), tips broadest on inner primaries. During spring, the inner 5-6 primaries are freshest, and somewhat paler than the outers. Outer 5-6 primaries have broad but diffuse dark tips, most obvious on underside. Inner primaries and all secondaries when backlit appear less translucent than on Sandwich Tern.

Bill orange to orange-yellow (especially Mediterranean race *emigrata*). It is dagger-shaped with slightly curved upper mandible, and with poorly marked gonydeal angle (can be lacking) 45-50% out from base of lower mandible. Bill tip sometimes slightly paler yellow. Legs black.

**Adult winter plumage:** Much as adult summer plumage, but forehead, lores and crown white; crown has variable dark spotting and streaking.

Black 'loral triangle' in front of eye merges into black mask through ear-coverts to nape. White eye-ring is broadest behind eye, usually lacking in front of eye. Upperparts sometimes darker than in summer plumage. Wing contrast depends on wear: contrast between new inner and dark worn outer primaries is most obvious in winter. Bill yellow to yellowish-orange, generally yellower than in summer plumage.

**Juvenile:** Head much as adult winter plumage, but crown more clearly dark-spotted. Recently fledged young have a tinge of yellow-brown in forehead, lores and upperparts. Upperparts as on Royal Tern. Lesser and greater coverts together with secondaries are dark grey with paler tips (form dark bars across wing). Back, scapulars, inner wing-coverts and tertials have variable grey-brown to brown centres and pale edges. Tail feathers dark grey, generally darkest on outer part, with white bases and edges. Lacks pale tips to t4-6 (see Elegant Tern). Central tail feathers darkest. T6 has pale grey outer web. The tail becomes browner with wear. Remiges dark grey, secondaries and inner primaries with broad white tips and inner webs.

Bill greyish-yellow, olive-yellow, warm yellow or orange-yellow. Feet yellow, tarsus black with yellow spots.

**First-winter plumage:** Much as juvenile, apart from uniform grey back from November/December. Juvenile primaries and secondaries, lesser and greater coverts, outer part of tail and sometimes tertials are retained on the whole until January-February (or later), and become brownish with wear. Greater coverts may be uniform grey. New inner primaries form pale grey wedge. Tail darker grey than back and rump. Bill and legs as those of juvenile.

**First-summer plumage** as adult winter plumage, but cap is brown-toned and worn. Retains dark secondary bar, 4-5 outer primaries and their coverts and also outer tail feathers from juvenile plumage; juvenile feathers dark and worn. Tertials generally darker grey with more prominent pale edges than on adults; may retain a few odd juvenile tertials.

Legs dark, but with pale spots on tarsus until autumn of second calendar-year.

**Second-winter plumage:** As adult winter plumage, but with dark secondary bar (most obvious on central feathers) and sometimes a few dark lesser coverts. In December-January, 2-4 (5) outer primaries and their coverts are grey-brown from wear, and outer 1-2 tail feathers normally heavily worn. Outer tail feathers, tertials and primary coverts generally darker grey than those of adult. Legs black, sometimes with paler soles.

**Second-summer plumage:** As adult summer plumage, but with white feather bases in forehead, lores and forecrown, most obvious in worn plumage. Any worn outer primaries very dark. A bird in Pakistan in April with such dark wingtips that it recalled Kittiwake *Rissa tridactyla* was probably an unmoulted adult or second-summer individual (M. Ullman *in litt.*).

Certain ageing in the field in this plumage is not recommended, as adults moult to winter plumage from the middle of the breeding season.

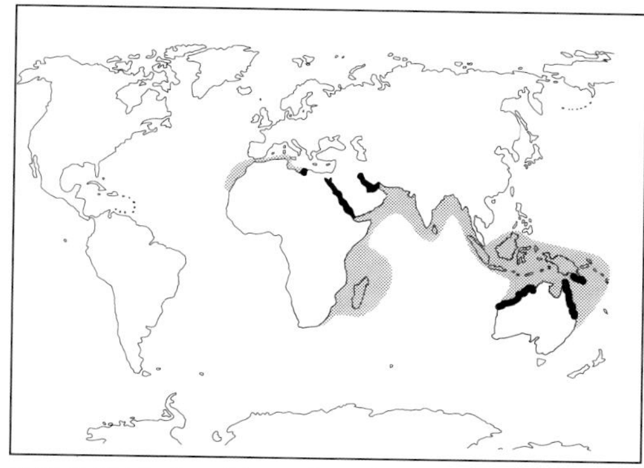

***MAP 5*** Distribution of Lesser Crested Tern *Sterna bengalensis.*

## Geographical variation

Minimal and unclear. The races *emigrata* (Mediterranean Sea) and *torresii* (Indonesia to Australia) are slightly paler than *bengalensis* (Indian Ocean between East Africa and India), but intergrades frequent and racial status unclear; populations from the Red Sea and the Persian Gulf to Pakistan are intermediates between *bengalensis* and *torresii*. Race *bengalensis* averages somewhat smaller than Sandwich Tern (Gantlett 1988). Eastern *torresii* (Java) have upperparts similar to those in West Palearctic (skins, NNH), but become progressively darker towards Australia (like Black-headed Gull *Larus ridibundus* or Common Gull *L. canus*); some have darker upperparts even than Australian Crested Terns (contra Slater *et al.* 1986, Pizzey *et al.* 1980). Wings average shorter than on other races (see Measurements).

## Hybrids

Mixed pairs of Lesser Crested and Sandwich Terns have been recorded in colonies of Sandwich Terns in the Mediterranean (Brichetti & Foschi 1987) and also in Britain. Fledged juveniles have been described by Steele & McGuihan (1989) and Verroken (1990). The description below is largely from Steele & McGuihan (1989).

Size as Sandwich Tern or a little bigger and heavier. Head as Sandwich, but with darker forehead, pale brown area from bill base to above eye, dark lores and narrow pale eye-ring. Upperparts pale grey, with narrow dark streaks or spots on scapulars. Rump pale greyish-white. Outer primaries dark brown-grey with very narrow pale edges, inner primaries paler as on young Herring Gull *L. argentatus*. Secondaries dark grey with narrow white trailing edge, tertials dark blackish-grey with white edges. Greater primary coverts dark brown-grey, possibly with narrow paler edges. Greater coverts grey with dark centres. Diffuse grey bar across lesser coverts; inner lesser coverts whitish-grey, as back. Underparts white (pink tinge has been noted: Verroken 1990).

Underwing white with dark tips on inner webs of outer primaries. Tail white with dark tips on outer feathers (as juvenile Sandwich Tern); whitish tip to tail feathers and white outer web to outermost rectrices form a white border around the tail.

On Steele & McGuihan's bird, the brown coloration and tail markings differed from those of the two parent species involved.

Legs black, generally slightly longer than on Sandwich Tern. Bill dirty yellow, a shade paler towards tip and with faint greyish tone in centre of upper mandible (Steele & McGuihan 1989) or orange with yellow tip (Verroken 1990).

### Measurements

In mm. Own measurements, BMNH, NNM, UZM, NRK, ZMO, NMNH. Race *bengalensis* (Red Sea, Persian Gulf and East Africa).

**WING LENGTH**

| | | |
|---|---|---|
| Ad | 280-324 (299.4) | n = 75 |
| Juv/1st-winter | 280-300 (291.0) | n = 35 |
| 2nd-winter/summer | 285-304 (297.2) | n = 36 |

• Eight adult *emigrata* (Mediterranean, Morocco) 294-328 (314.2); adult *torresii* from Sumatra, Java and Bali 269-308 (295.0, n = 22).

**TAIL FORK**

| | | | |
|---|---|---|---|
| Ad ♂ | 60-83 | (69.9) | n = 27 |
| Ad ♀ | 55-78 | (61.9) | n = 27 |
| Juv/1st-winter | 30-64 | (45.8) | n = 53 |
| 2nd-winter/summer | 48-78 | (63.6) | n = 35 |

• Ad *torresii* from Sumatra, Java and Bali (March-April) 45-87 (57.2, n = 20); when worn, 30-75.

**BILL**

| | | | |
|---|---|---|---|
| Ad | 47.2-62.0 | (53.4) | n = 85 |
| Juv/1st-winter | 43.9-52.3 | (49.1) | n = 42 |
| 2nd-winter/summer | 47.9-56.4 | (54.1) | n = 22 |

• Six adult *emigrata* (Mediterranean, Morocco) 48.0-60.2 (55.4). Average ad ♂ 54.3, ad ♀ 52.7.

**BILL DEPTH AT GONYS**

| | | | |
|---|---|---|---|
| Ad ♂ | 8.3-10.9 | (9.5) | n = 50 |
| Ad ♀ | 8.0-9.8 | (8.8) | n = 27 |
| Juv/1st-winter | 8.1-10.0 | (8.9) | n = 64 |

• Nine adult *emigrata* (Mediterranean, Morocco) 8.2-10.8 (9.6).

**BILL DEPTH AT REAR EDGE OF NOSTRILS**

| | | | |
|---|---|---|---|
| Ad | 10.1-13.3 | (11.7) | n = 93 |
| Juv/1st-winter | 9.8-11.8 | (10.8) | n = 67 |

• Eight adult *emigrata* (Mediterranean) 10.0-13.0 (11.5). Average *bengalensis* ad ♂ 11.7, ad ♀ 11.4. Cramp (1985) gives adult *torresii* as 11.2-12.9 and adult *bengalensis* as 9.9-12.0.

**TARSUS**

| | | | |
|---|---|---|---|
| Ad | 23.0-29.0 | (25.3) | n = 75 |
| Juv/1st-winter | 23.3-28.6 | (25.6) | n = 64 |

• Tarsus length identical on ♂♂ and ♀♀. Nine adult *emigrata* (Mediterranean) 25.2-30.2 (27.5).

**WEIGHT** (in grams)

160-235 (East Africa)

# Sandwich Tern

*Sterna sandvicensis*

Photos **49-59**

### Identification in the field

Sandwich Tern is the northernmost breeder of the 'crested' terns and the only one which is black-billed. It is pale and long-winged with flat crown, angular nape and narrow bill. The underparts are white, the upperparts pale grey with white rump and tail.

Sandwich Tern has a powerful rather than a delicate flight, with fairly quick and deep wingbeats. In flight it is slim ('starved'), with head and narrow bill the dominating features. The oval-shaped body is deepest across the breast, but the rear end cropped. The lean and emaciated impression is reinforced by the long and narrow angled wings, especially obvious against the light, when secondaries and inner primaries are clearly translucent. The underwing is white, with grey tips to the outermost 4-5 primaries (shorter and fainter than on Crested and Lesser Crested Terns). The tail is up to 1.5 times the wing breadth, but the tail projection is difficult to see from sideways on (or in sharp sunlight), and the tail streamers are often worn away in summer.

The long slender bill is clearly narrower than the head at its base, and looks like a black peg inserted into the forehead, especially when seen from in front or from below. It is straight and characterless in shape, without any obvious gonydeal angle.

The species generally forages at deeper waters than Common and Arctic Terns, patrolling the coastline at some height with bill directed downwards. Suddenly it makes dramatic, often vertical dives from up to 5-7 m, and may disappear for several seconds beneath the surface. At shallower water it performs shorter dives from more acute angles. Like Crested and Lesser Crested Terns, Sandwich is well adapted for foraging in strong winds, and is not troubled by blustery weather.

When perched, it has an angular head with flat crown and 90° angle at nape, formed by a short broad crest. Only alert birds with upstretched neck show a slightly drooping crest. Narrow bill, flat crown and broad, angled crest give the species a 'tough' facial expression all of its own, rather like that of the tropical crested terns. For differences from Gull-billed Tern, see latter.

**Adult in summer plumage** has a glossy black cap. The bill is black with distinct yellow tip. The upperparts are silver-grey with white tail and rump. The inner primaries contrast with the 3-6 outers, which in spring are only slightly darker, most obvious as a narrow, dark grey wedge on the central primaries. During summer the hand becomes progressively darker, and in July-September the outer part of the hand is normally conspicuously dark. Some, however, have only a faint dark (Common Tern-like) wedge, while the most heavily worn individuals have up to 6 outer primaries dark with pale shafts and tips. The white secondaries are also worn in summer.

Adults gradually acquire winter plumage soon after the breeding season. Both this and the different appearance of the primaries mean that in late summer the species differs clearly from spring birds.

Black cap and bill, white underparts and pale upperparts give adults an appearance approaching that of Roseate Tern. The latter, however, is smaller, lacks a dark line on the trailing edge of the primaries, in summer has a dark primary wedge closer to the wingtip (around second-outermost primary) and shorter wings/longer tail. In summer, any red at the bill base easily distinguishes Roseate Terns from Sandwich. Perched Roseate lacks a nape crest and has red legs.

**Adult winter plumage** is acquired early. Even in early June the first white feathers can appear in the forehead, with the earliest birds having a winter head in late June. Birds with white forehead become increasingly common during July, and totally predominate in August (see Moult). In winter plumage the head is white with narrow black U-shaped mask behind eye; initially this mask is concealed by white feather edges, and up to mid September can be reduced to a black streak barely broader than the eye. Occasional individuals are almost white-headed. The eye stands out as a large isolated black spot, accentuated by a black U-shaped loral patch and broad white eye-ring. The upperparts are much as in summer plumage. Old primaries become blackish. When the moult in late autumn has reached 2-3 outer primaries, the wing markings briefly become similar to those of Little Tern. Birds which acquire new, silver-grey primaries early (at same time as the mask is mottled white) appear very pale. Theoretically they can be confused with Forster's Tern in fresh winter plumage. Head shape and size are of course useful, but also the shape of the black mask and the white eye-ring: on Sandwich the mask is uniform in width and continues through the nape as a complete black band; Forster's has a black oval-shaped mask restricted to the area around and behind the eye, lacks a white eye-ring, but has a white nape.

**Juvenile** is smaller, more compact and more round-winged than adult. The shorter bill is black, with at most a few millimetres of yellowish-grey at the tip (darker and more diffuse than on adult; at a distance barely visible). The shorter bill is relatively thicker than the adult's; it can recall that of Gull-billed Tern, but is narrower and characterless, lacking Gull-billed's distinctly curved tip and prominent gonydeal angle.

The head appears more rounded than the adult's, as the crest is shorter. The cap is black with pale spots on forehead and crown, on newly fledged birds dark, but later in summer (from mid July) the forehead becomes white. Fresh birds are tinged yellow-brown on mantle, back and coverts. The upperpart feathers have

---

***PLATE 12***

**Sandwich Tern *Sterna sandvicensis*.**
The most widespread of the crested terns in our region. Size similar to that of Black-headed Gull *Larus ridibundus*. A slender, long-billed sea tern with narrow wings and moderately elongated outer tail feathers. Narrow, black bill separates the species from congeners. Birds older than 1 year show clearly contrasting yellow bill tip. Upperparts pale grey with white rump and tail, similar in coloration to Royal Tern. Noisy.

1 **Adult summer (March-May).** Complete black cap and pale outer primaries. Pale edges and tips to fresh primaries (see text) fit Western Palearctic race *sandvicensis*; Nearctic *acuflavida* shows more narrow and even tips on fresh primaries.

2 **Adult summer (June-July).** During breeding season, outer primaries gradually darken (and white hood is developed).

3 **Adult summer moulting to winter.** From beginning of June, white forehead and winter head develop). In late summer, typically appears white-fronted with darker wedge on outer primaries (seen here as contrast between inner and outer primaries).

4 **Adult summer Cayenne Tern (sub)species *eurygnatha*.** As Sandwich tern *acuflavida*, but bill yellow, varying from orange to straw-yellow, often with darker central areas. Crest often appears longer than on typical Sandwich Tern.

5 **Adult summer Cayenne Tern of the darkest-billed type.** Similar to Sandwich Tern *acuflavida*, but generally with broader yellow tip to bill. The darkest extreme in Cayenne Tern.

1
2
3
5

dark V-shaped markings (strongest on back, scapulars and tertials, which can be barred pale and dark). Lesser coverts are normally uniform in colour with rest of coverts, and do not therefore form a clear dark leading edge to the arm; on the other hand, the greater coverts may appear paler than the rest of the wing. Overall, however, the upperwing is rather lacking in contrasts – what one sees from a distance is the dark tail sides, not features such as dark bars on coverts and remiges as with other similar species. On perched birds, the dark-patterned tertials are the most obvious feature at longer ranges. The tail does vary, it is true, but dark corners are always obvious (almost recalling Black-eared Wheatear *Oenanthe hispanica*!) and visible at longer ranges than other characters.

Juveniles moult early to first-winter plumage, and even in late July the upperparts are normally a mixture of juvenile and new, grey feathers. In early August, the first ones to have moulted have uniform grey back and adult-like head (the majority are thus from mid August). Some juvenile upperpart feathers may be retained into the early winter.

**First-winter plumage** is much as adult winter plumage, but has dark tail corners, narrow dark bars on lesser coverts and secondaries (contrasting with new, pale grey central part of wing) and dark primary coverts. The inner greater coverts have dark tips and edges (Vinicombe 1988). Birds in first-winter plumage possibly have less black on the nape than adults.

**First-summer plumage** is similar to adult winter plumage, but normally has a darker crown, dark tail sides and a few darker grey upperpart feathers, coverts and tertials. The outer 1-3 (4) primaries are in moult (see adult). Dark juvenile primaries contrast well with the rest of the wing. Narrow dark bar may be present across lesser coverts.

Subsequent plumages are poorly known. **Second-winter plumage** is adult-like, but some dark-tipped outer tail feathers and darker greater primary coverts may be retained.

**Second-summer plumage** adult-like, but with white feather fringes in cap and dark, very worn outer tail feathers. Tertials and secondaries possibly darker grey than on adults.

## Voice

Adults have a characteristic coarse and far-carrying *kreeit* or *kjerr-it*, often disyllabic. Penetrating and frequently used, this is a characteristic call when flocks assemble. It has been reported as sounding 'like amalgam being pressed into a tooth' (Bruun *et al.* 1987). Juveniles have a squeaky, non-guttural *pee-up*, quite unlike adult's more powerful call; heard mostly from juveniles accompanying adults.

**Detailed description** *Sterna sandvicensis sandvicensis* (West Palearctic)

Length 36-41 cm, wingspan 95-105 cm.

**Adult summer plumage:** Cap black with elongated nape feathers. White wedge between gape and cap 3-4 mm broad. During early stages of moult to winter plumage, the forehead becomes white and the forecrown partly white-flecked. In mid to late June, 25% of west European breeders have a white-flecked crown, a few having a winter head (Robinson 1940; pers. obs.). Lower nape and mantle white. Upperparts pale grey, scapulars and tertials with variable white tips. Rump to tail white; t5-6 sometimes grey-tinted, rarely grey with 7-8 mm of white at tips. Rump rarely pale grey, as back.

Underparts white, sometimes with pink tinge to throat, breast and belly (most pronounced early in breeding season).

5-6 inner primaries pale silver-grey. 4-5 (6) outer primaries have dark grey outer webs and streaks along inner webs contrasting with white shafts. Fresh primaries have pale edges 2-3 mm broad on inner webs, 1-2 mm broad on outer webs, and 3-5 mm of pale colour at tips, which, however, is soon worn away. In early summer, 4-6 outer primaries are grey with a silvery tinge, which gradually disappears with wear during the summer. They become progressively darker in summer, and on the majority form a dark outer area on the hand contrasting with paler inner primaries. The outer webs of the fresh inner primaries have white edges 2-3 mm wide, though these are rapidly worn away. Secondaries and upperwing-coverts pale grey with white tips and inner webs. Underwing white with narrow blackish-grey tips to 4-5 outer primaries (can be faded or worn off in late summer and autumn).

Bill black with yellow tip of 8-14 mm (males 8-14 mm, females 8-12 mm). The bill is narrow, lacking prominent gonydeal angle. Legs black, soles sometimes yellow. Scattered yellow spots may be present on tarsus and 'knee' (presumably a subadult character).

**Adult winter plumage:** Forehead, lores and crown white. The crown has variable black spots, broadest towards nape. Black U-shaped patch in front of eye frames front edge of latter. Narrow white eye-ring is broadest at rear. Black U-shaped band from behind eye and through the nape, in fresh plumage (up to mid September) partially concealed by white feather fringes: may then be reduced to a narrow streak, of same width as eye.

Otherwise as adult summer plumage, but worn outer primaries and inner secondaries are greyish-black, later grey-brown; replaced in September-December. Birds with 1-3 old outer primaries acquire a narrow dark leading edge. In January-May all remiges are normally silver-grey and fresh, but during spring the central primaries may have grey outer webs.

**Juvenile:** Cap black with broad sandy-brown tips to fresh feathers, paler and more faded with wear, especially on forehead and lores. Dark loral patch. Nape and mantle white, sometimes spotted dark. Underparts white.

Fresh feathers on upperparts have yellow-brown edges, which soon disappear with wear. Back and scapulars pale grey with blackish-brown subterminal bars or U-shaped markings. Palest birds have only narrow and broken dark vermiculations, but the majority have these markings darker and broader. On the darkest birds, dark markings dominate over pale coloration and form a strong dark-and-pale patterning. Tertials black with white spots, subterminal bars and edges. Rump and uppertail-coverts white with variable dark brown outer part and subterminal spots.

Tail feathers pale grey with dark outer area and narrow pale bars near the tip. Some have only outer two pairs of rectrices dark-tipped; others have dark tips to all tail feathers, broadest on the outermost (sometimes over 50% dark), which have markings as on tertials. T1-2 have the weakest dark spots, restricted to near the tip.

Primaries dark grey (lack adult's silver coloration). Primary coverts and lesser upperwing-coverts dark grey to grey-brown with paler edges, sometimes darker centrally. Median and greater coverts together with primary coverts mid-grey with diffuse pale grey edges of up to 3 mm in width (broadest on greaters), and white subterminal spots or bars near tip. Median coverts and longest lesser coverts vary: on the palest birds pale grey and contrasting with dark alula, but more usually greyish-black as back and scapulars; on the darkest birds predominantly dark.

Bill shorter than adult's. Black or with 1-3 (6) mm of tip horn-coloured. Bill edges blue-grey, pink or yellow on newly fledged individuals (Cramp 1985; Mitchell 1989). Juvenile with yellow bill (yellower than yellow tip of adult's) has been described (Mitchell 1989). Legs dark, a few per cent having pale spots on 'knees' and feet.

**First-winter/first-summer plumage:** Much as adult winter plumage, but with juvenile outer, dark-tipped tail feathers. T1-2 are moulted in December-January, but the outers are in most cases retained until May-June, when they are heavily worn and contrast noticeably with rest of tail. In summer and early autumn the outer 4-5 primaries are darker than on adult, contrasting with new inner primaries. Dark grey, pale-edged juvenile primary coverts are moulted at same time as their associated primaries. Faint darker bars may be present on lesser coverts and secondaries.

Bill black with 5-14 mm of yellow at tip; sometimes all black.

**Second-winter plumage:** Directly replaces first-winter plumage in first summer. Resembles adult winter plumage, but unmoulted primaries and primary coverts darker. Tertials generally darker grey than on adults, with broader pale edges. Some tail feathers may show elements of dark colour.

The primaries begin a second moult series in June-July. Second-calendar-year birds for the most part have two active moult cycles in June-September.

**Second-summer plumage:** Much as adult summer plumage apart from following. White spots may be present in lores and crown; forehead may be white (Baker 1993). Some dark-tipped greater primary coverts may possibly be present (seen on a Danish individual in late May in association with two outermost brownish, worn primaries); inner primaries and all secondaries whitish-grey. In midsummer, 10-25% of inner primaries have been moulted. Some have dark-tipped outer tail feathers (skins from Africa, NRM). A new moult series in primaries commences in June-September.

## Moult

**Adult** has complete moult to **winter plumage**. The moult starts with scattered

1
2
3
4
5

**PLATE 14**

Development of head from summer to winter plumage in Sandwich Tern *Sterna sandvicensis.* During breeding season, white feathers start to appear in forehead and central part of lores. By middle of summer (end of June to early July) forehead and crown whiten, and by late July most show complete or almost complete winter head (compare Gull-billed Tern).

**PLATE 13**

**Sandwich Tern *Sterna sandvicensis***

1 **Juvenile.** Recently fledged individual (June/early July). Note dark-spotted forehead and pale bill centre. Upperparts appear scaled - in fresh plumage with a pale buff tinge (see plate 12). This plumage is soon replaced by first-winter (2).

2 **Juvenile moulting to first-winter.** In late summer similar to adult winter, but upperparts a mixture of juvenile and uniform grey first-winter feathers. Note juvenile tertials. Bill uniform or with restricted yellow tip compared with adult.

3 **First-winter (spring).** Note darker lesser coverts and tertial centres, as well as restricted yellow bill tip compared with adults. May have wholly black bill into first summer.

4 **Adult winter (December-January).** Black mask similar to e.g. Lesser Crested and Royal Terns (fresh winter mask may appear much smaller owing to pale feather tips). Following end of primary moult (around January) appears very pale-winged.

5 **Adult summer.**

feathers in central crown, upper lores and crown sides in (early) mid June, normally late in breeding season. Winter head is acquired in late June at the earliest (presumably non-breeders or failed breeders), areas around bill base being the last to be moulted. In early July the majority have scattered white feathers in the forehead, and 35-50% have pure white forehead. In mid to late July most have white forehead and dark-spotted crown, and 25-50% have a winter head. The proportion with full winter head increases from about 35-50% in late July to 90-100% in late August (pers. obs., south Scandinavia). A few retain a summer head up to early September.

Tail moult begins in late July, and is normally completed by early October. Moult sequence is normally t2-t1, t3-t6 (Cramp 1985), but t6 may be moulted before t3-5. During autumn the outer tail feathers are very worn; t6 may, however, be renewed before t4-5. T4-5, body, coverts and tertials are moulted in late August-September. Some greater coverts are occasionally moulted from mid July. The moult is normally completed by late October.

Primary moult commences after the breeding season (late July to late August); the majority have renewed the innermost 5-6 primaries by late September, but the moult is restricted near north European breeding sites. More usually the primaries are in active moult at stop-over sites during migration (in Europe, e.g. the

**SANDWICH TERN** QUICK KEY TO IDENTIFICATION

1 **Pale and slim tern with narrow black, yellow-tipped bill.**
2 **Flat crown and angled nape combined with black bill diagnostic.**
3 **During summer and autumn, dark markings in outer wing (from black wedge in central primaries to darker outer part of hand) characteristic.**
4 **The slender bill appears 'stuck on', like a black peg or stick.**
5 **From as early as July the forehead is normally white and the winter cap is formed.**
6 **Juveniles have distinctly dark-tipped tail.**
7 **Juveniles have dark-spotted upperparts, but rarely show obvious wing-covert bars.**
8 **Call of adults an upward-inflected, hoarse 'kree-it', used frequently. Juveniles' call more 'throatless' and non-characteristic; often heard from begging juveniles accompanying adults.**
9 **Cayenne Tern is rather like typical Sandwich, but has dull yellow to dull orange bill, often with greyish elements and redder base.**

Wadden Sea and in the Netherlands, where active moult is common in August-September). Many birds scrutinised in the Netherlands had exchanged 6-7 (8) inner primaries by mid to late September (own studies). Ginn & Melville (1982) state that a third moult series may begin in late summer and autumn, when primaries 4-5 have been renewed twice. Birds from south Europe in October-November had renewed the inner 5-8 primaries. The moult may be completed by late October (Cramp 1985), but in December-January the majority have primaries 8-10 still growing out (pers. obs., Morocco).

**Adult** has a partial moult to **summer plumage**. The moult includes head, 4-5 inner primaries, body and tail. The head is moulted mid February to late March. Normally has a summer cap on arrival in breeding quarters, but odd white feathers may be present in the front part of the cap in April. Of 3,000 individuals scrutinised in Denmark in late May, one had scattered white feathers in the forehead and crown. Body and tail are probably moulted in February-March.

New primary moult may commence in November-December after arrival in the winter quarters, and be arrested in late winter (late January-March) with about 4-6 innermost renewed. Up to three moult series in the primaries may be in progress simultaneously (Ginn & Melville 1982). Two to three active moult series have been found on skins (e.g. innermost primary moulted when 5-6 have grown out). Outer primary may be growing in March-early June (race *acuflavida*). Body and tail are renewed in February-March, but tail moult varies, and often the outer rectrices are very worn in spring and summer. Some moult these in spring, while the rest of the tail is not renewed.

**Juvenile** has a complete moult to **first-winter plumage**. Some begin the moult in late July, and have uniform grey back and white forehead/lores in early August. The majority moult in late August to late September, and acquire a grey back and adult-like head gradually during the autumn.

In late September-October, head, body, most of the upperwing-coverts, t1 and a few tertials have been renewed. In January-February the plumage is fully moulted apart from most primaries (see below), primary coverts and usually t5-6. T6 may, however, be moulted before t4-5. Primary moult commences in December-February and is arrested in May-June; 3-7 (9) inner primaries are renewed in April-May.

In June-July a new moult series begins in the primaries; rarely, this is started as early as May (Baker 1993; pers. obs.). 3-4 inner primaries are replaced in autumn; three generations of primaries may be present in late spring and summer. In first summer moults directly into second-winter plumage. Subsequent moults are similar to those of adults, but commence in June; in midsummer 10-25% of inner primaries have been replaced, and in September-October 5-6 inner primaries have been renewed.

## Geographical variation

Nominate *sandvicensis* (northwest Europe to the Black Sea and the Caspian Sea) described above. The race *acufla-*

vida (North America and the Caribbean to Cuba, Bonaire and the Virgin Islands) is smaller, with shorter bill and perhaps paler upperparts. Yellow bill tip generally broader, in southern USA 8-18 mm, usually broader and more diffuse in the Caribbean. The 3-4 outermost primaries have 1-1.5 mm of narrow pale edges and tips (*sandvicensis* has 2-4 mm of pale on inner web, 3-5 mm of pale at tip and 1-2 mm pale on outer webs). The difference is of use only on birds with fresh primaries. See also Measurements.

**Juvenile** *acuflavida* has darker (solid) feather centres on mantle, scapulars and tertials, giving chequered upperside pattern; edges of these feathers whitish. Tertial pattern similar to that of Lesser Black-backed Gull *Larus fuscus*. Fresh birds may have the back almost covered by pale feather edges. The secondaries generally have a more distinct dark bar than on *sandvicensis*.

Moult as in *sandvicensis*; in February, 2-3 outer primaries may still be unmoulted (compare *sandvicensis*).

Race *acuflavida* has been found in the Netherlands and in England in November-December (ringed birds: Scharringa 1979; Ouweneel 1989). In the Netherlands, Sandwich Terns regularly occur in November-December which possibly originate from American populations (Ouweneel 1989).

Cayenne Tern *S.* (*s.*) *eurygnatha* (south Caribbean from north of Venezuela through South America) is similar to Sandwich Tern, but has a yellow to orange bill, in Caribbean populations often with greyer central and basal part. The bill can be red or dull orange, but is never so bright orange or fiery red as on Lesser Crested or Elegant Terns. Nuchal crest generally longer and more shaggy than on Sandwich Tern, and upperparts generally darker grey. In Caribbean generally smaller than Sandwich (see Measurements), but becomes gradually bigger and longer-billed in south. In Brazil/Argentina, some have a bill as long as that of Elegant Tern.

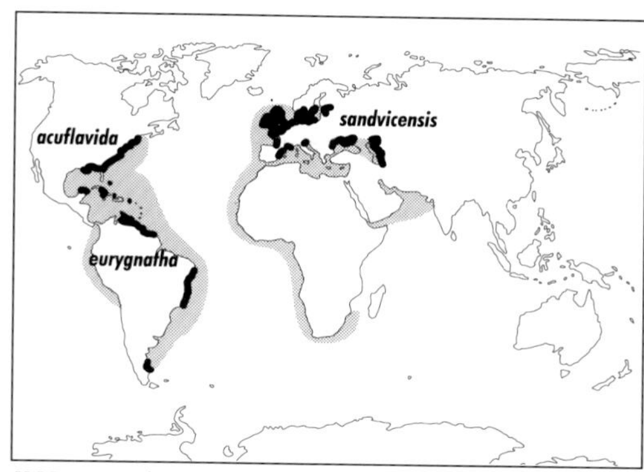


***MAP 6*** Distribution of Sandwich Tern *Sterna sandvicensis*.

Bill on populations from north Venezuela, Netherlands Antilles and to a lesser extent on Trinidad and Tobago variable. It can recall that of Sandwich Tern, but is paler grey-toned with broader and more diffusely demarcated pale tip (minimum 16 mm) (5-25% in Bonaire, Curacao, Aruba: Voous 1983). The majority have a straw-yellow bill (38-84% in Caribbean populations: ffrench 1973), often with grey tinge (especially on inner and central area), the remainder being intermediates.

Populations from South America (Brazil southwards) are bigger and longer-billed. In Argentina, in summer plumage in December (skins, ZMA). Yellow bill gradually predominates southwards, where birds with orange bill occur. As far south as Argentina, occasional individuals show a black bill base or elements of black (Kjellén 1992).

Upperparts otherwise as *sandvicensis* and *acuflavida*, but sometimes darker grey. Inner secondaries generally have darker centres, which can form faint dark secondary bar. Winter plumage much as for Sandwich Tern. Mask then becomes black, isolated from eye by white eye-ring (unlike Elegant Tern).

1
2
3
4
5
6
7
8
9
10

**PLATE 15**

**Sandwich Tern *Sterna sandvicensis***

1 **Juvenile.** (July-early August). Note scaly upperparts and coverts (soon replaced by uniform grey first-winter feathers). Broad dark tip to tail is the most striking feature in autumn. As other juvenile terns, appears more compact, short-billed and tailed, and blunter-winged than adults.

2 **First-winter (autumn).** See caption for juvenile.

3 **First-winter.** In flight, Sandwich Tern shows shorter and less prominent dark bar on tips of primaries than other similar (crested) species.

4 **First-summer (spring).** Similar to adult winter, but with dark secondary (and sometimes lesser-covert) bar, dark-tipped tail and much more worn outer primaries. As in congeners, retains winter head in first-summer.

5 **First-summer (late summer/autumn).** similar to adult winter, but note retained juvenile dark primary coverts (and 1-2 outer primaries heavily worn). May show some dark in tail.

6 **First-summer.** See caption 5.

7 **Adult winter.**

8 **Adult summer (spring).** Note full black cap and rather plain, fresh primaries.

9 **Adult summer (June-early July).** White feathers start to appear on forehead during breeding. Outer primaries gradually abraded during summer, typically appearing as dark wedge on outer wing in late summer until winter moult (November-December).

10 **Adult summer.**

**Juvenile** similar to that of *acuflavida*, but with greyish-yellow bill, often with some black. Tertials have more solid dark centres and pale edges (rather like young Lesser Black-backed Gull). Upperparts have broader, blackish-brown subterminal spots and yellowish-brown edges. Both tertials and mantle/back feathers thus appear as even more solid dark spots than on *sandvicensis*. Primaries have, as *acuflavida*, narrow pale edges 1-1.5 mm broad.

### Measurements

In mm. Race *sandvicensis*: own measurements, Scandinavia, Britain (BMNH, NNM, ZMA, UZM, MN, ZRM, ZML, ZMU, ZMO). Adult wing length from Cramp (1985) (Netherlands, April-October) and Glutz (1984) (west Europe); measurements of juveniles from July-September. Race *acuflavida*: North America, April-October (BMNH, NMNH, NNH, ZMA). Race *eurygnatha*: Netherlands Antilles, May-August, Argentina, December-February (ZMA, NNH).

WING LENGTH

| | | | |
|---|---|---|---|
| *sandvicensis* | | | |
| Ad ♂ | 290-325 | (308) | n = 33 |
| Ad ♀ | 283-320 | (304) | n = 16 |
| Juv ♂ | 290-308 | (302) | n = 13 |
| Juv ♀ | 287-307 | (296) | n = 22 |
| *acuflavida* | | | |
| Ad ♂ | 275-305 | (294.7) | n = 42 |
| Ad ♀ | 283-302 | (295.9) | n = 21 |
| Juv | 248-296 | (274.7) | n = 6 |
| *eurygnatha* (Netherlands Antilles) | | | |
| Ad ♂ | 284-310 | (295.1) | n = 15 |
| Ad ♀ | 282-296 | (289.5) | n = 12 |
| *eurygnatha* (Argentina, Brazil) | | | |
| Ad ♂ | 299-327 | (315.6) | n = 9 |
| Ad ♀ | 300-324 | (314.0) | n = 5 |

Two juv *eurygnatha* 251 and 258(ZMA).

• Van Halewijn (1990) gives for *acuflavida*: from North America, ad ♂ 274-307 (293, n = 11), ad ♀ 277-302 (290, n = 10); from West Indies, ad ♂ 276-300 (288, n = 8), ad ♀ 265-294 (283, n = 11).

• Wing length of *eurygnatha*: Aruba, Guyana, ad ♂ 283-301 (291.5, n = 20), ad ♀ 270-295 (287, n = 11); Brazil, ad ♂ 285-297 (293, n = 6), ad ♀ 283-303 (291, n = 6); Argentina, ad ♂ 294-322 (311, n = 20), ad ♀ 294-320.5 (310, n = 9).

TAIL FORK

| | | | |
|---|---|---|---|
| *sandvicensis* | | | |
| Ad ♂ | 48-90 | (67.3) | n = 86 |
| Ad ♀ | 46-83 | (69.4) | n = 62 |
| Juv | 29-48 | (40.8) | n = 55 |
| *acuflavida* | | | |
| Ad ♂ | 40-74 | (51.0) | n = 40 |
| Ad ♀ | 45-60 | (49.2) | n = 22 |
| Juv | 27-50 | (36.6) | n = 8 |

*eurygnatha* (Netherlands Antilles)

| | | | |
|---|---|---|---|
| Ad ♂ | 50-70 | (60.3) | n = 15 |
| Ad ♀ | 44-63 | (55.3) | n = 8 |

*eurygnatha* (Argentina)

| | | | |
|---|---|---|---|
| Ad ♂ | 50-70 | (56.1) | n = 10 |
| Ad ♀ | 58-77 | (64.5) | n = 4 |

• Tail of measured *acuflavida* more worn than in *sandvicensis*.

#### BILL

*sandvicensis*

| | | | |
|---|---|---|---|
| Ad ♂ | 51.0-64.2 | (55.5) | n = 88 |
| Ad ♀ | 48.1-57.2 | (53.1) | n = 67 |
| Juv* | 32.1-47.1 | (40.5) | n = 56 |
| 2nd cal-yr** | 49.5-56.1 | (52.9) | n = 10 |

* Jul-Nov
**(Jan-May)

*acuflavida*

| | | | |
|---|---|---|---|
| Ad ♂ | 48.5-56.4 | (52.4) | n = 48 |
| Ad ♀ | 46.5-54.6 | (51.0) | n = 22 |
| Juv | 37.0-50.3 | (42.1) | n = 7 |

*eurygnatha* (Netherlands Antilles)

| | | | |
|---|---|---|---|
| Ad ♂ | 52.1-60.5 | (55.3) | n = 15 |
| Ad ♀ | 48.0-56.0 | (52.9) | n = 8 |

*eurygnatha* (Argentina)

| | | | |
|---|---|---|---|
| Ad ♂ | 56.5-61.9 | (59.6) | n = 9 |
| Ad ♀ | 53.5-59.8 | (57.4) | n = 5 |

• Van Halewijn (1990) gives for *acuflavida*, USA: ad ♂ 50-57 (54.8, n = 13), ad ♀ 47-56 (52.3, n = 10). Race *acuflavida*, West Indies: ad ♂ 49-57 (52.6, n = 14), ad ♀ 43-53.3 (49.9, n = 6). Race *eurygnatha*: Aruba, Guyana, ad ♂ 52.2-60.4 (56.0, n = 22), ad ♀ 47.8-56.2 (52.5, n = 11); Brazil, ad ♂ 53.4-57.0 (54.2, n = 6), ad ♀ 47-55 (52.6, n = 9); Argentina, ad ♂ 55-62 (59.2, n = 20), ad ♀ 53.0-60.9 (56.7, n = 9). One ad ♂ *eurygnatha* from Brazil had bill 52.7 (NNH).

* Juveniles acquire adult bill length after about one year. Young that have just fledged have bill length of 25-35 mm (own measurements). Two juv *eurygnatha* 37.4 and 40.8 (ZMA).

#### BILL DEPTH AT GONYDEAL ANGLE

*sandvicensis*

| | | | |
|---|---|---|---|
| Ad ♂ | 7.9-11.0 | (9.2) | n = 88 |
| Ad ♀ | 7.8-9.1 | (8.3) | n = 67 |
| Juv | 6.6-9.0 | (7.5) | n = 48 |

*acuflavida*

| | | | |
|---|---|---|---|
| Ad ♂ | 8.5-10.0 | (9.4) | n = 48 |
| Ad ♀ | 8.2-9.4 | (9.1) | n = 22 |
| Juv | 8.2-9.8 | (9.1) | n = 7 |

*eurygnatha* (Netherlands Antilles)

| | | | |
|---|---|---|---|
| Ad ♂ | 9.2-10.1 | (9.8) | n = 15 |
| Ad ♀ | 8.8-9.9 | (9.4) | n = 8 |

*eurygnatha* (Argentina)

| | | | |
|---|---|---|---|
| Ad ♂ | 10.0-11.1 | (10.6) | n = 9 |
| Ad ♀ | 8.8-10.4 | (10.0) | n = 5 |

• Two juv *eurygnatha* (Netherlands Antilles) 8.3 and 8.5 (ZMA).
• One ad ♂ *eurygnatha* from Brazil 9.5 (NNH).

#### BILL DEPTH AT REAR EDGE OF NOSTRILS

*sandvicensis*

| | | | |
|---|---|---|---|
| Ad ♂ | 10.3-12.1 | (11.2) | n = 88 |
| Ad ♀ | 9.7-12.2 | (10.7) | n = 67 |
| Juv | 7.5-10.9 | (9.2) | n = 48 |

*acuflavida*

| | | | |
|---|---|---|---|
| Ad ♂ | 9.3-12.4 | (11.2) | n = 48 |
| Ad ♀ | 9.7-11.6 | (10.7) | n = 23 |
| Juv | 9.2-10.8 | (10.0) | n = 7 |

*eurygnatha* (Netherlands Antilles)

| | | | |
|---|---|---|---|
| Ad ♂ | 10.3-12.1 | (11.6) | n = 15 |
| Ad ♀ | 10.3-11.8 | (10.9) | n = 8 |

*eurygnatha* (Argentina)

| | | | |
|---|---|---|---|
| Ad ♂ | 11.3-12.7 | (12.1) | n = 9 |
| Ad ♀ | 11.2-11.8 | (11.5) | n = 5 |

• Two juv *eurygnatha* (Netherlands Antilles) 8.4 and 10.1 (ZMA).
• Average for juv ♂ 10.0, juv ♀ 9.3.
• One ad ♂ *eurygnatha* from Brazil 11.9 (NNH).

#### TARSUS

*sandvicensis*

| | | | |
|---|---|---|---|
| Ad ♂ | 23.3-30.0 | (27.2) | n = 88 |
| Ad ♀ | 23.3-29.0 | (25.8) | n = 67 |
| Juv | 20.0-29.0 | (24.4) | n = 48 |

*acuflavida*

| | | | |
|---|---|---|---|
| Ad ♂ | 23.1-28.8 | (26.1) | n = 48 |
| Ad ♀ | 24.6-28.3 | (25.8) | n = 23 |
| Juv | 23.0-27.4 | (25.3) | n = 7 |

*eurygnatha* (Netherlands Antilles)

| | | | |
|---|---|---|---|
| Ad ♂ | 23.8-27.0 | (25.4) | n = 15 |
| Ad ♀ | 21.8-26.1 | (25.0) | n = 8 |

*eurygnatha* (Argentina)

| | | | |
|---|---|---|---|
| Ad ♂ | 25.0-28.9 | (27.2) | n = 9 |
| Ad ♀ | 26.2-27.0 | (26.5) | n = 5 |

• Two juv *eurygnatha* (Netherlands Antilles) 22.8 and 24.7 (ZMA).
• One ad ♂ *eurygnatha* from Brazil 23.8 (NNH).

#### WEIGHT (in grams)

205-283 (240) 102*

• According to Glutz (1984), Langewerder, eastern Germany. ♂♂ average the heavier. Two ♀♀ Britain, late September to early October, weighed 284 and 291 (Cramp 1985). Juvs (Netherlands, August) 200-245, up to 250 in September (Cramp 1985).

# Elegant Tern

*Sterna elegans*

Photos **60-66**

## Identification in the field

The Elegant Tern breeds along the Pacific coast between southern California and Central America. It has been recorded in Europe only a few times (Alström *et al.* 1992; Boesman 1992), including co-breeding with Sandwich Tern in France in 1974-85. Hybrid young have hatched, and may possibly be responsible for records of Elegant Tern from Belgium and Ireland (P.J. Dubois *in litt.*; A.B. van den Berg *in litt.*). See also Sandwich Tern of Cayenne race *S.* (*sandvicensis*) *eurygnatha*.

Elegant Tern is reminiscent of Lesser Crested Tern, but has a longer bill and crest, and the pale grey upperparts contrast with white rump and tail – the most important character compared with Lesser Crested. Within the normal range, Royal Tern is the only similar species. It is bigger, more powerful and longer-legged, with broader bill. In flight, Elegant Tern is extremely slim and elegant. It flies with thrusting and well-accomplished wingbeats, clearly lighter than Royal Tern.

The slender bill droops slightly at the tip. On the longest-billed individuals the bill is obviously longer than the head, which in combination with drooping upper mandible gives the species something of a skimmer-like appearance. Short-billed birds, however, differ minimally from Lesser Crested Tern. The bill is yellowish-orange to red, often with paler yellow tip and darker tomato-red inner part. Against the light the bill tip is clearly translucent and the colour contrast of the bill becomes generally more obvious than on Royal and Lesser Crested. The lower mandible is straight, but the gonydeal angle is often well suggested, though not so much as on most Lesser Crested Terns. That the gonydeal angle is normally lacking, which has often been stressed, is not, however, correct, though on the long bill it does not normally stand out very prominently. The ratio of bill length to bill depth is given as 1:5-5.5 (on Lesser Crested 1:4-4.5) (Boesman 1992).

The Elegant Tern has the longest crest of all terns: drooping tufts of feathers like the hair of long-haired punks! Alert birds with neck extended appear high-crowned with the crest like a dangling horse's tail.

The upperparts are paler grey than on Lesser Crested Tern, but perhaps a mere shade darker and more brownish than on Sandwich Tern. They are, however, so light in colour that the primaries never appear obviously paler as on Lesser Crested. Rump and tail are white with a weak pale grey tinge, and normally contrast well with the grey back (J. R. Hough *in litt.*). The underparts are white. Only 4-5 outer primaries have dark tips, possibly slightly paler than on Lesser Crested.

As with other terns, the primaries are palest in late winter and spring, and darken with wear during the summer. In late summer and autumn, the outer unmoulted primaries are therefore dark and contrast with new inner ones. The legs are black, sometimes red-brown.

**Adult summer plumage** has a black cap with long nuchal crest. The underparts may have a pink tinge, which in such cases is diagnostic in comparison with other red-billed crested terns (Gantlett & Harris 1988). Some have darker central primaries contrasting with paler surrounding ones.

**Adult winter plumage** has a white fore-

1
2
3
4
5

**PLATE 16**

**Elegant Tern *Sterna elegans***

As Lesser Crested Tern, but with on average longer and more drooping bill. Birds with the longer bill (♂) appear most slender. Bill orange, mostly with lighter, yellow tip and darker, blood-red to tomato-red base to bill (most obvious with ♂).

1 **Juvenile.** Fresh plumage.
2 **First-winter.** End of autumn.
3 **Adult winter.** End of autumn and winter.
4 **Adult summer.**
5 **Adult summer.** Long drooping crest (longest of all crested terns).

head merging diffusely with black mask from the eye to the nape (appears bald with black pony-tail, rather like an ageing hippie!). The mask is broader and more triangular than on Royal, Crested and Lesser Crested Terns. Black loral triangle in front of eye passes directly into the mask, so the eye is not isolated by white: only at close range is a narrow white eye-ring visible (see Royal and Lesser Crested Terns).

**Juvenile** resembles juvenile Lesser Crested, but the upperparts are more variegated, with strongly brown-tinted back, scapulars and wing-coverts. The bill is a greyish-yellow orange in colour, shorter than adult's, and often has blackish elements, especially at edges of upper mandible (J. Alderfer *in litt.*).

Like other terns, birds in **first-winter plumage** have remnants of juvenile wing-coverts, dark secondary bar and unmoulted, juvenile outer primaries. The bar on the lesser coverts is possibly moulted out more quickly than on Lesser Crested Tern: combination of mainly juvenile remiges and pure grey upperparts is common.

In **first-summer plumage** retains the winter-plumage head, juvenile secondaries and outer primaries and dark-tipped outer tail feathers, which are by then heavily worn. Outer 2 (3) tail feathers differ from those of Lesser Crested in having

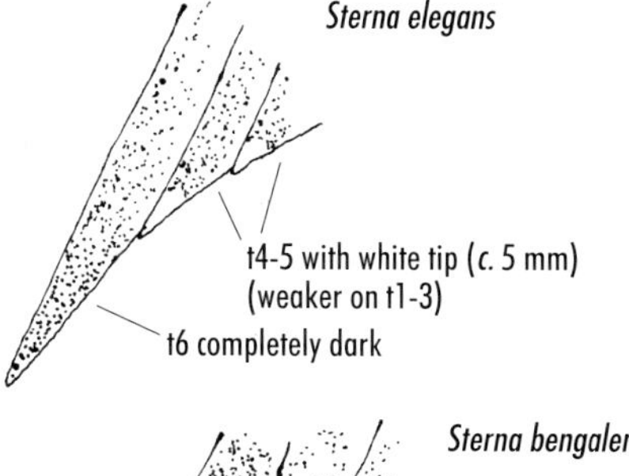


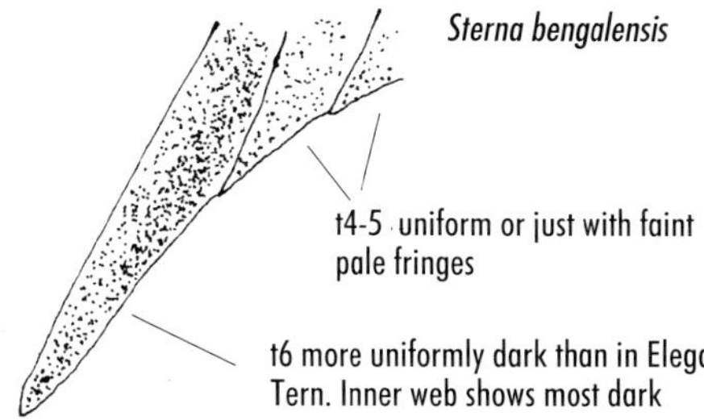


***FIGURE 5*** Elegant Tern *Sterna elegans* and Lesser Crested Tern *Sterna bengalensis.* Tail pattern of (juvenile) first-summer birds.

narrow white tips. New tail feathers are darker grey than on adults.

**Second-winter plumage** resembles adult winter plumage, but has unmoulted juvenile outer primaries until around January, remnants of dark secondary bar and darker grey tail than adults.

## Voice

Recalls that of Sandwich Tern, but is deeper and rather like that of Lesser Crested (Alström *et al.* 1992).

### Detailed description

Length 39-43 cm, wingspan 76-81 cm.

**Adult summer plumage:** Cap black with long, shaggy and drooping crest. Upperparts pale blue-grey (similar to Sandwich Tern). Rump and tail white; t(3-4)5-6 may have 4-6 cm of grey on outer part and narrow whitish-grey tips of up to 1 cm in breadth. Secondaries pale grey with white trailing edge. Primaries pale grey with dark grey outer

***MAP 7*** Distribution of Elegant Tern *Sterna elegans.*

webs to 1-2 outer primaries and dark tips to 4-5 outers. With wear (late summer and autumn), primaries become darker.

Underparts white, sometimes with pink tinge to body early in breeding season. Occasionally shows pale grey tinge to belly (rarely perceptible in the field). Bill yellow-orange to reddish-orange, often with paler, greyish tip and darker tomato-red base (strongest at start of breeding season). Males have most contrastingly marked bill, females more uniform orange, though with yellow tip (C. Wilds pers. comm.). On the longest-billed individuals, the bill is distinctly downcurved at the tip. Lower mandible straight with poorly marked gonydeal angle (may be lacking). Legs black to dark reddish-brown, rarely bright red.

**Adult winter plumage:** Forehead and lores white, crown to nape black; transition between forehead and crown black-spotted in front of eye. Black patch in front of eye broad and rounded, passes directly into broad dark triangular facial mask. White eye-ring weak, in form of two white arcs above and below eye, visible only at close range. Bill sandy-red with paler yellow tip.

**Juvenile:** Head much as adult winter plumage. Back, rump and scapulars grey with dark bases and subterminal markings. Lesser and greater upperwing-coverts and primary coverts dark grey-brown, median coverts pale grey. Remiges dark grey with pale tips to secondaries and inner primaries. Tail feathers dark grey with white edges and diffusely darker tips to t(4)5-6; t4-5 have whitish-grey tips about 5 mm broad. Bill yellow to orange-yellow, often with blackish elements, especially on edges of upper mandible. Legs black, often with variable elements of yellow, tarsus occasionally greyish-yellow.

**First-winter/first-summer plumage:** Much as juvenile, but with grey back and often uniform grey coverts. Tail feathers darker grey: t(4)5-6 have white tips (5-6 mm). During first summer, inner 1-5 primaries are new.

**Second-winter plumage:** Much as adult winter plumage, but with remnants of dark secondary bar, dark outer tail feathers (with broad whitish tips of 5-10 mm) and 4-5 juvenile outer primaries. After the last juvenile feathers have been exchanged, resembles adult.

## Moult

**Adult** has a complete moult to **winter plumage** after the breeding season. Birds in August-September normally have a 'winter head' (occasional individuals have a summer cap until October) and worn 4-6 outer primaries. Some have renewed all primaries by late September, but usually the primary moult is suspended during the autumn migration with 2-3 outer primaries worn, the latter being moulted in early winter/spring (outer primary growing end of March to mid April). The tail may be renewed in late September, but tail moult is not usually completed until winter to spring.

**Adult** has a partial moult to **summer plumage**. Birds in March-April (Costa Rica, USA) have a 'summer head' (C. Wilds & J. Alderfer *in litt.*; pers. obs.).

**Juvenile** has a complete moult to **first-winter plumage**. Mantle/back and coverts are presumably moulted from September-October; coverts are probably moulted earlier than in other similar terns. The tail is moulted from November, starting with t1 and then t4-5; t3 and t6 may be moulted as late as September-October of second calendar-year. The primary moult commences in (November) January-February: normally moults inner 4-5 primaries during spring, and suspends the moult in summer.

Moult to **second-winter plumage** is similar to the adult moult, but progresses more slowly. In August-September, remaining juvenile tail feathers (usually t6)

## PLATE 17

**Elegant Tern *Sterna elegans***
Similar to Lesser Crested Tern, but with on average longer and more drooping bill. The longest-billed (males) have a distinct slender appearance. Bill orange, often with paler yellow tip and darker/blood- or tomato-red base (most striking on males).

1 **Juvenile.** Similar to juvenile Lesser Crested Tern; some birds show dark line to upper mandible. Bill often more straw-coloured than shown.

2 **Juvenile.** A typical long-billed individual.

3 **First-winter/summer.** Separated from adult winter by dark lesser coverts and secondaries. Tail feathers grey, with slender pale tips on outer three pairs.

4 **Adult winter.** Similar to Lesser Crested Tern, but bill on average longer and more drooping.

5 **Second-summer.** As adult summer, but with darker outer primaries and sometimes traces of dark secondary bar (and possibly even sometimes grey in tail).

6 **Adult summer.** A long-billed individual, showing tomato-red base of bill.

**ELEGANT TERN** QUICK KEY TO IDENTIFICATION

1. **Red-billed Sandwich-type tern with slender bill (normally distinctly longer than head).**
2. **Bill long and narrow with drooping tip, generally slimmer than on similar species. Tip sometimes paler yellow and base sometimes darker red.**
3. **Has the longest crest of all terns; hangs down like hair tufts of a teenage punk.**
4. **White rump and tail contrast with pale grey upperparts.**
5. **In flight, very slim and elegant.**
6. **Except in adult summer plumage, has black mask which is broad and triangular. Covers the eye, so that narrow incomplete eye-ring is visible only at close range.**

and primaries are moulted. When 5-7 inner primaries have been replaced, a new series may begin (from June). The last juvenile outer primaries and their coverts are moulted in November-January. New inner tail feathers may be acquired in June (second calendar-year), but most often in September-December.

### Measurements

In mm. Own measurements, BMNH, NMNH, NNM.

WING LENGTH

| | | | |
|---|---|---|---|
| Ad | 300-328 | (312.7) | n = 34 |

• Ad ♂♂ 304-328, ad ♀♀ 300-323. Most skins examined had worn outer primaries. Four juvs 295-318. Van Halewijn (1990) gives ad ♂ 302-333 (317, n = 24) and ad ♀ 300-330 (314, n = 16).

TAIL FORK

| | | | |
|---|---|---|---|
| Ad | 35-85 | (69.1) | n = 27 |
| Juv/1st-winter | 29-63 | (46.2) | n = 7 |

BILL

| | | | |
|---|---|---|---|
| Ad | 53.2-68.6 | (62.3) | n = 31 |
| Juv/1st-winter | 55.8-63.6 | (59.1) | n = 7 |

• Ad ♂♂ 59.4-66.9, ad ♀♀ 55.8-64.2, but material limited. Van Halewijn (1990) gives ad ♂ 57.2-70.7 (64.3, n = 90) and ad ♀ 55.8-69.0 (60.8, n = 61).

BILL DEPTH AT GONYS

| | | | |
|---|---|---|---|
| Ad | 8.6-10.9 | (9.9) | n = 31 |
| Juv/1st-winter | 8.8-9.8 | (9.5) | n = 8 |

• Ad ♂♂ 9.0-10.9, ad ♀♀ 9.0-9.9.

BILL DEPTH AT REAR EDGE OF NOSTRILS

| | | | |
|---|---|---|---|
| Ad | 10.2-13.0 | (11.8) | n = 31 |
| Juv/1st-winter | 10.6-12.2 | (11.4) | n = 8 |

TARSUS

| | | | |
|---|---|---|---|
| Ad | 25.5-32.2 | (29.1) | n = 27 |
| Juv/1st-winter | 26.6-30.5 | (29.1) | n = 8 |

# Roseate Tern

*Sterna dougallii*

Photos **67-77**

### Identification in the field

The Roseate Tern is in identification terms the 'link' between Common/Arctic Terns and Sandwich Tern. The pale ground colour and the long and slender black bill lend the species an appearance approaching Sandwich Tern, but it is only the size of Arctic; compared with latter, it has shorter wings and even longer tail streamers. The head shape is similar to Common Tern's, but the profile is more elongate; long and narrow and elegant, reinforced by the narrow bill. The crown is flat, the highest point of the head usually being just above or behind the eye. The mainly black bill (see below) is as long as the head. It is both longer and more slender than Common Tern's. The shortest-billed individuals, however, are not strikingly long-billed and have a bill length as that of the longest-billed Arctic Terns; seen sideways on, such birds differ little from Common/Arctic, but head-on the bill is indeed narrow as the sides are convex.

The flight silhouette recalls Sandwich Tern's front-heavy appearance, especially if the outer tail feathers are broken off (K. Mullarney 1988 and *in litt.*). The flight is more steady and more purposeful than that of Arctic. With its quick wingbeats, the species can be reminiscent of a Little Tern. Upstrokes and downstrokes are similar to each other, whereas Arctic Tern has a more distinct upstroke than downstroke (Hume 1993). The species normally forages over deeper water than Common and Arctic Terns. It flies over long stretches at 8-15 m height and then dives at an acute angle directly towards the water's surface like a Gannet *Morus bassanus*. It has been recorded to remain longer under the water (2-2.5 seconds) than Common and Arctic Terns (Kirkham & Nisbet 1987). On the other hand, it is poorly adapted for hovering, and when it does hover it does so with rapid Little Tern-like wingbeats.

Perched birds are longer-legged than Common Tern (legs about 75% of bill length). The very long tail can project several centimetres beyond the folded wings. The white inner webs of the primaries form, on perched individuals, a characteristic white upper border to the hand, quite unlike that of Common and Arctic Terns (and rather as on Sandwich Tern of nominate race).

The call is a thick, upward-inflected 'cher-vrick', recalling Sandwich Tern's with a Spotted Redshank *Tringa erythropus* accent.

**Adult in summer plumage** is almost white, with black cap. The upperparts are very pale pearl-grey with no obvious contrast between back and tail. The long, normally black bill has a red basal area for only a short period during the breeding season; shows most red during brood-feeding period, when up to 50% of the bill is red (broadest on upper mandible). White wedge between gape and cap is generally narrower than on Common Tern. The cap can, as Common's, appear slightly angled in a tail wind.

Belly and breast are white with variable pink tinge. The upperparts are pale grey, as Sandwich Tern, in colour rather like Little Gull *Larus minutus* or Ross's Gull *Rhodostethia rosea*. In flight, secondaries and inner primaries are white and form a very narrow white trailing edge to wing, much as on adult Ross's Gull. The outer 2-3 primaries are darker (see below). The outer primary has a black outer web above. The underwing is white, with at most diffuse dark streaks on the outer 3-4 primaries. There is no solid dark trailing edge to the hand as on Common and Arctic Terns. Below, the outermost primary has a white outer web (note that it is black on upperside), contrasting with darker parts of inner web. The remiges (apart from the 3 outer primaries) are translucent against the light, making the wing appear narrow; the translucency is not, however, so obvious as on Arctic Tern.

The upperwing has a narrow dark wedge formed by dark inner webs to the 2-3 (4) outer primaries. This wedge is narrower and in summer is situated farther forwards on the hand than on Sandwich and Common Terns; with wear, it becomes rather like that of adult Little Tern, but the outer primary is normally paler. Dark outermost primaries are obvious during spring, and become almost black as summer progresses. The tail is pale grey to white, with white outer web on the outermost rectrix. The streamers are on average even longer than Arctic Tern's. When the tail is held closed, it forms a long point at the rear, not unlike that of a tropicbird. As on Arctic Tern, it seems to 'follow the bird about' and appears flexible and supple. The streamers are, however, so thin that they sometimes cannot be seen, so that the bird appears short-tailed! The outermost tail feathers are not uncommonly broken off, especially in late summer.

Perched individuals show a combination of Sandwich Tern's white underparts and Arctic's long tail (projects a good way beyond the stern, up to 10 cm). In summer there is a clear contrast between pale inner and dark outer primaries. The legs are bright red, very similar to, but often slightly brighter than Common Tern.

**Adult in winter plumage** retains long tail streamers. It has a white forehead, black loral streak and dark spots at the junction with the black mask, which generally extends farther forwards onto the forehead than on Common Tern. The underparts are white with variable pink tinge, especially on central areas (can be lacking). The upperparts are much as in summer plumage, but often with a faint dark bar on lesser coverts. The dark leading edge of the hand is obvious during autumn (before moult has reached the outermost primaries), but after moulting the hand becomes whitish. The bill is all black and the legs darker red than in summer plumage.

***PLATE 18***

**Roseate Tern *Sterna dougallii***

Size similar to that of Common Tern. In summer plumage much paler, with whitish underparts (showing varying rosy tinge), predominantly dark bill, long tail and broad pale inner webs to primaries. In flight, shows narrow dark leading edge to primaries but no clear dark trailing edge to primaries. Juvenile plumage and moult similar to Sandwich Tern (to which probably more related than to Common).

1 **Juvenile.** Note similarities to juvenile Sandwich Tern. Dark hood (with pale normally restricted to pale spot in upper part of lores), dark bill and dark legs.

2 **Juvenile moulting to first-winter (August-September).** Forehead becomes paler. In early autumn, shows mixture of juvenile and uniform grey feathers similar to Sandwich Tern.

3 **First-summer.** Similar to very pale Common Tern of similar age, but note dark legs and longer outer tail feathers.

4 **Adult moulting into winter plumage.** As with Sandwich Tern, winter head is developed near breeding places.

5 **Adult summer (April-May).** Note predominantly dark bill, rosy tinge to white underparts, long tail and broad white edges to inner webs of primaries.

6 **Adult summer (July-August).** At height of breeding season, up to 50% of bill may be red. Note Z-shaped division between black and red on bill, and typically most black on lower mandible (unlike congeners).

1
2
3
4
5
6

**Juvenile**, especially when perched, recalls a small, round-headed juvenile Sandwich Tern. The cap may appear all dark at a distance. The lores are extensively dark, with a pale spot above and in front of the eye. The forehead is greyish-brown. The palest-headed individuals have greyish lores and paler ground colour to the crown, causing the head to appear tritoned. From September the forehead becomes whitish (Oreel 1974; Mullarney 1988). The black cap is more irregularly demarcated behind the eye from the white neck sides than on Common and Arctic Terns; it has a black drop-shaped extension behind the eye and is angled at the rear.

The upperparts recall juvenile Sandwich Tern's. Mantle/back feathers and tertials have dark U-shaped markings and sandy-coloured bases; they contrast with paler coverts, most obviously on the darkest birds. Juveniles, too, have broad white edges to the upperside of the folded primaries.

The wing markings are something between those of Common and Arctic Terns, but dark tips to lesser and median coverts may form a more extensive dark fore area on the wing (as on some Arctic Terns). Inner greater and median coverts are normally dark-spotted, like the 'saddle' feathers, unlike typical Common and Arctic Terns. The secondaries have a dark bar, generally weaker than Common Tern's and most obvious on inner part of wing; it can sometimes be lacking (Kaufmann 1990). A broad pale central area may be present on the wing, as the outermost coverts are also pale and contrast with dark carpal and leading edge of wing. All remiges have white tips, forming a white frame to the wing, may be reminiscent of the wing markings of Little Gull, but much less prominent. The rump is grey. The tail is white with dark V-marks and edges near the tip (form rows of 3-4 dark spots on inner part of tail). Outermost pair of tail feathers essentially white, lacking dark outer webs of both Common and Arctic Tern (Mullarney *in litt.*).

The underside of the primaries lacks the dark rear edge of Common and Arctic, as only the 4-5 outer primaries have faint dark streaks. The outer primary has a dark inner web and white outer web. The rump is grey.

The bill is black; shorter than adult's. The brownish-black legs recall those of Sandwich Tern.

**First-winter plumage** is acquired soon after the breeding season (as with Sandwich and Forster's Terns, partly near the breeding site). White-mottled forehead and grey back are obvious features in September, but a few dark-patterned feathers plus juvenile wing and tail are retained. The legs gradually turn orange-red.

**First-summer plumage** is much as adult winter plumage. The cap resembles that of winter plumage, but is normally duller and brown-toned. The central parts of the crown are dark-spotted and the lores sometimes whitish. Lesser coverts and secondaries are normally dark and contrast with the rest of the upperparts. On more advanced individuals with uniform grey coverts, ageing is best based on dark juvenile primaries and their coverts. The tertials normally have diffuse darker centres. The tail is grey, but the outer feathers are white. The bill is black, and the legs darker blackish-red than in adult summer plumage, but with a white mottled forehead, faint carpal bar and red reduced on the bill (in July) compared to adults.

**Second-winter plumage** is much as adult winter plumage, but normally has more worn outer primaries and shorter tail streamers. The tail-coverts and central tail feathers are likely to be darker grey than on adults.

**Second-summer plumage** is unknown, but presumably is largely identical to adult summer plumage.

## Voice

A Sandwich Tern-like *cherr-rrick*, upward-inflected, like a rather coarse Spotted Redshank. Juvenile has softer call: a *k-r-r-rillee* resembling call of juvenile Sandwich Tern (Mullarney 1988).

**ROSEATE TERN** QUICK KEY TO IDENTIFICATION

1 **Adults are very pale, short-winged and long-tailed versions of Common Tern.**
2 **The bill is black for most of the year, at most with coral-red inner half in late summer.**
3 **Border between red and black on bill Z-shaped, with most red on upper mandible.**
4 **Upperparts pearl-grey, lacking obvious contrast between back and rump/tail.**
5 **Outer wing lacks dark trailing edge below, but has narrow dark leading edge above as on Little Tern.**
6 **Against the light, secondaries and innermost primaries are translucent, resulting in a broad pale area (rather like white rear edge of wing of adult Ross's Gull).**
7 **Flies with stiff rather rapid wingbeats.**
8 **Tail very long and thin, including on perched birds, when it clearly projects well beyond wings.**
9 **White inner edge to primary tips produce a broad white border to folded wing-tip.**
10 **Juveniles resemble small, juvenile Sandwich Terns.**
11 **Juveniles moult early to first-winter plumage, and in August often have mostly plain grey upperparts and white forehead.**
12 **Call similar to that of Sandwich Tern or Spotted Redshank.**

### Detailed description

Length 33-38 cm, wingspan 72-80 cm.

**Adult summer plumage:** Cap black. White wedge between cap and gape 2-3 mm. Uppermost mantle white, rest of upperparts pale pearly-grey; rump and uppertail-coverts are concolorous with or only slightly paler than back. Tail greyish-white, sometimes with white edges to feathers; t6 has white outer web. Primaries pale silvery-grey with broad white edges to inner webs. White primary tips 3-5 mm broad. Outer primary has black outer web on upperside, white on underside. Pale edges to secondaries broadest on inner webs. Worn primaries are darker, without silvery coloration. In spring, 2-5 outer primaries are dark with pale tips and inner edges.

Underparts white, with variable pink tinge early in breeding season (sometimes up to autumn). Breast and belly may be tinged pale grey.

Bill black, but during the breeding season inner part red to blood-red. Demarcation between black bill tip and red base angular (Z-shaped). Has most red on upper mandible. Red is acquired in Europe/North America from (mid May) early June, after completion of egg-laying. Red bill base is broadest (50-60% of bill; black tip 17-35 mm: west Europe) from brood-feeding period until leaving the breeding site. Birds in best condition acquire the most red (Donaldson 1968; Cormons 1976). The bill becomes all black in autumn, from July/August (in North America, latest birds with red bill base are seen in early September; from late September, almost 100% are black-billed). Bill narrow, lacking or with poorly marked gonydeal angle (40-50% out from base). From above, bill sides are more distinctly convex than on Common and Arctic Terns. Legs coral-red to orange-red, rather similar in colour to Puffin's *Fratercula arctica* (Harris *et al.* 1988).

**Adult winter plumage:** Forehead white, crown white with black spots and streaks merging diffusely into black mask from eye backwards. Mantle pale grey. Upperparts much as adult summer plumage, but sometimes has faint, mid-grey bar across lesser coverts (less conspicuous than on Common Tern). Contrast between outer and inner primaries dependent on moult: unmoulted outer 2-4 primaries dark in July-October; all primaries pale in November-April. Underparts white, sometimes with faint pink tinge. Bill black from August/September until May-June. Legs dark red.

**Juvenile:** Forehead and forecrown light brown, in fresh plumage dark-spotted and streaked, but with wear revealing paler feather bases; forehead may be white from July (Mullarney *in litt.*). Lores dark, rarely paler grey, with pale patch above central part of lores. Cap (eye to lower nape) black with pale yellowish-brown to greyish-white feather tips. Border with white neck sides curved. Has black drop-shaped patch behind eye and sharper black angle at rear than on Common and Arctic Terns. Head markings vary; pale-headed birds always have grey lores.

Mantle pale grey tinged buff when fresh and with very fine dark vermiculations (Mullarney *in litt.*). Back, scapulars and tertials pale grey with yellow-brown centres and black subterminal bars and U-shaped marks, normally most distinct on tertials. Upperparts vary: the palest individuals have only weak dark markings, while dark colour dominates on others, like a dark saddle (rarely, feathers of mantle and scapulars are sandy with fine dark mottling and just weakly marked dark subterminal bars; NMNH, 29740). Rump and uppertail-coverts pale grey with variable yellow-brown or brown spots (can be lacking).

Underparts white, on fresh birds sometimes with pale yellow-brown tinge on breast. Tail feathers pale grey with dark V-shaped subterminal spots near tip; t6 has white outer web.

Secondaries mid-grey with white tips; generally darker towards body. Secondaries are rarely pale. Inner primaries pale grey, outers darker grey; pri-

**PLATE 19**

**Roseate Tern *Sterna dougallii***

1 **Juvenile.** Newly fledged individual, showing dark hood with pale spot in upper lores as well as sandy-buff tinge to head and upperparts. Note dark tips to tail feathers.

2 **Juvenile moulting to first-winter (August-September).**

3 **First-summer.**

4 **Adult winter (August-September).** Similar to Common Tern, but in general with less contrasting bar on lesser coverts and pale secondaries.

5 **Adult summer (April-June).** Upperparts pale pearly-grey, showing at most a slight contrast between rump/tail and back. Note lack of clear dark trailing edge to undersurface of primaries.

6 **Adult summer (late summer).** Outer primaries become slightly darker, but does not show the typical wedge of Common and Sandwich Terns.

maries have white inner webs. Greater and median coverts pale grey with dark spots and variable yellow-brown tips. Innermost greater coverts patterned as back feathers, and normally contrasting with remaining coverts. Lesser coverts dark grey with white edges. Outer median coverts paler whitish-grey, greater primary coverts mid-grey.

Pre-fledged birds have paler dull pinkish bills, but almost all acquire an entirely dark bill well before fledging; black from fledging time. Legs black to brownish-black; tarsus distinctly scaly.

**First-winter plumage:** Much as adult winter plumage, but with juvenile tertials and tail feathers until December and juvenile remiges and greater primary coverts until April-May.

**First-summer plumage** much as adult winter plumage, but white forehead merges more diffusely into brown-tinted black facial mask. Vestiges of bars present on lesser coverts and secondaries. Primary coverts grey-brown. Outer primaries pale with usually the 5th and 6th primaries being darker (more worn) toward tips. Underparts occasionally white with faint yellow-brown to pink tinge. Tail pale grey with medium grey outer webs (most obvious on t3-5). Tail streamers 35-85 mm. T6 white. Legs dark red.

**Second-winter plumage:** Much as adult winter plumage, but lesser coverts and secondaries darker. Outer 4-5 primaries and their coverts grey-brown, relatively more worn than on adults. Tertials can be dark-centred with pale edges.

**Second-summer plumage:** Many are practically identical to adults (4 cal-yr+), but some at least show a tendency to have duller browner cap with white mottling on forehead, darker grey mottling in carpal region less extensive; clear cut red at base of bill. Some show all fresh-looking primaries in July (Mullarney *in litt.*).

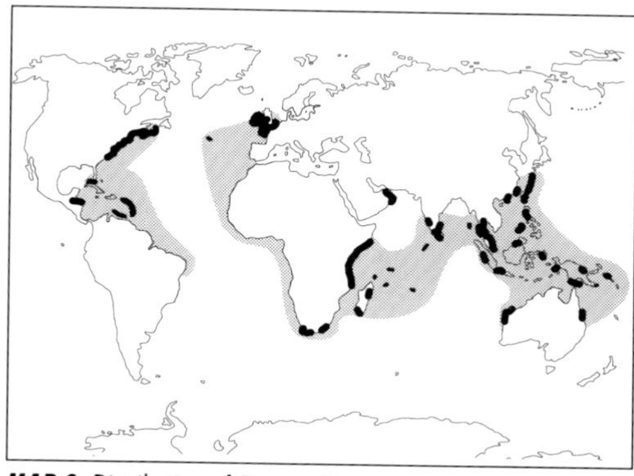

***MAP 8*** Distribution of Roseate Tern *Sterna dougallii.*

## Moult

Much as that of Sandwich Tern (in Western Palearctic).

**Adult** has complete moult to **winter plumage** from June-July. The moult commences with inner primaries while the young are being fed. In mid July moult of body and head begins; at same time tail moult commences, with t1 (followed by t2-6-3-4/5) (Glutz *et al.* 1982). Body moult completed in late autumn. Primary moult is resumed in midwinter.

Before primary moult is completed, a new moult series begins in autumn and early winter (normally after arrival in winter quarters). Sometimes a third moult series commences in late winter, so that three different moult series may be present on arrival at breeding grounds (Cramp 1985): series 1 complete with p10 (outermost), series 2 suspended at primaries 6-8, series 3 suspended at primaries 1-4. This strategy is common into September.

**Adult** has partial moult to **summer plumage** in February-April. The moult includes head, underparts and sometimes tail and parts of upperparts. In spring and summer, 5-7 (8) inner primaries are fresh.

**Juvenile** begins moult to **first-winter plumage** early. Feathers of forehead and back changed in August-September. Moult of remiges takes place in winter quarters, but retained juvenile remiges (up to 4-5 outer primaries) can be present up to spring of third calendar-year. Moults central primaries in first summer.

## Hybrids

Hybrids between Roseate Tern and Common Tern are known. See Common Tern.

## Geographical variation

Involves mainly bill colour. Intergrades merge into one another, making validity of the races unclear. Nominate *dougallii* from the West Indies generally have broader red bill base in the breeding season from late May. Black bill tip 15-22 mm (pers. obs.). Red can cover the inner two-thirds of the bill during the brood-feeding period (Donaldson 1968).

Eastern tropical populations have more red at the bill base, weaker pink tinge below and shorter wings. The race *korustes* (India to Burma) has darker upperparts than *dougallii*. Wing length 212-224 mm, bill 31-38.1 mm. Rump is grey, as upperparts (pers. obs.; Cramp 1985).

The race *bangsi* (Arabian Sea, and Indian Ocean to New Guinea) has up to

50% of the bill red during the breeding season, with at least 20-22 mm of black at bill tip. The smallest amount of black on the bill (9-20 mm of tip) is found on the form *ariidensis* (East Africa, Seychelles; skins, BMNH, NMNH), which can have an all-red bill. Wing of *ariidensis* 210-226 mm, bill 36.2-41.6; *ariidensis* has upperparts a shade darker grey than *dougallii*. Wing length (Java) 218-228 mm, bill 34.0-42.0 mm (skins, NNH).

The race *gracilis* (Australia and new Caledonia) has short wing (208-228 mm), and long bill (32.5-42 mm) (Cramp 1985; pers. obs.) with broader red base than *dougallii* in breeding season. Bill can be all red during breeding.

### Measurements

In mm. Own measurements, BMNH, NMNH, NNH, ZMA, UZM, ZMO, ZML. Race *dougallii* (Europe, North Africa, North America and Caribbean).
Adults May-August; juveniles August-September.

**WING LENGTH**

Eastern North America, Tunisia and west Europe

| | | | |
|---|---|---|---|
| Ad ♂ | 222-242 | (230.8) | n = 50 |
| Ad ♀ | 218-242 | (225.4) | n = 20 |
| Juv | 202-218 | (215.0) | n = 3 |

Caribbean

| | | | |
|---|---|---|---|
| Ad ♂ | 216-240 | (227.6) | n = 28 |
| Ad ♀ | 217-232 | (226.0) | n = 22 |
| Juv | 195-227 | (210.2) | n = 8 |

**TAIL FORK**

| | | | |
|---|---|---|---|
| Ad ♂ | 80-136 | (107.5) | n = 50 |
| Ad ♀ | 65-119 | (96.5) | n = 29 |
| Juv | 35-70 | (53.1) | n = 11 |

• In 1st-winter/1st-summer, 69-100 mm.

**BILL**

| | | | |
|---|---|---|---|
| Ad ♂ | 35.7-43.0 | (38.1) | n = 62 |
| Ad ♀ | 34.5-40.0 | (37.2) | n = 33 |
| Juv | 28.3-39.8 | (33.3) | n = 11 |

**BILL DEPTH AT GONYS**

| | | | |
|---|---|---|---|
| Ad ♂ | 6.1-7.8 | (6.5) | n = 57 |
| Ad ♀ | 5.5-7.4 | (6.5) | n = 34 |
| Juv | 5.7-6.5 | (6.2) | n = 10 |

**BILL DEPTH AT REAR EDGE OF NOSTRILS**

| | | | |
|---|---|---|---|
| Ad ♂ | 6.7-8.9 | (7.8) | n = 52 |
| Ad ♀ | 6.7-8.7 | (7.5) | n = 33 |
| Juv | 6.8-8.0 | (7.3) | n = 10 |

**TARSUS**

| | | | |
|---|---|---|---|
| Ad ♂ | 18.0-21.0 | (19.8) | n = 55 |
| Ad ♀ | 17.8-21.0 | (19.6) | n = 35 |
| Juv | 17.5-20.5 | (19.0) | n = 11 |

**WEIGHT** (in grams)

New York 96-128 (109.8) n = 144 (Glutz 1984)

• Average for British birds, May-July, 123.5.
• Juveniles at age of 22-27 days: 94.5-116 (105), n = 9.

# Common Tern

*Sterna hirundo*

Photos **78-96**

### Identification in the field

Common Tern is the 'classic' tern – well known for its black cap, red bill and forked tail.

Identifying Common and Arctic Terns is based essentially on differences in shape, wing markings, translucency of outer wing, colour contrasts of bill and leg length. During the breeding season the Common Tern is found both at lakes (in north Europe mostly associated with Black-headed Gull *Larus ridibundus* colonies) and on sheltered coasts, whereas Arctic breeds in more barren environments – in the south only on sandy shores. Differences in proportions are important when dealing with adults, but largely of no value for juveniles, which in autumn do not have fully developed wing and leg lengths.

Flying Common Terns have pointed wings and elongated outer tail feathers. Compared with Arctic Tern, the species is more angular and 'virile' in its entire emphasis, which, combined with the more uniformly broad wings, gives it more an appearance approaching that of a small gull. Inner and outer wing are fairly uniform in width. Against the light, only the inner primaries (at the break between arm and hand) are translucent, which easily distinguishes flying birds from Arctic Terns, which have the longer, narrower hand clearly translucent (torch on parchment paper!). The fact that the inner webs of the outer primaries on Common are pale (and therefore translucent) is not noticed because of the rapid wing movements – but shows well on photographs.

The body is elliptical. In flight, it seems somewhat distended, with centre of gravity around the rear edge of the wing; a good bit of the body projects behind the wings, but the tail streamers are rarely grotesquely long (on fresh adults, no more than the distance between rear edge of wing and undertail-coverts). Head, neck and bill are quite powerful, and can almost show features approaching Caspian Tern. The dagger-shaped bill accounts for 75-80% of the total head length; in flight it is often held pointing downwards (20°). On perched birds, forehead and crown are shallow and sloping, and the head appears slightly angular, with a 'break' at the junction between forehead and crown. The highest point of the head is behind the eye. In a tail wind the nape becomes angled, and a suggestion of a slight crest may then be visible. This rather powerful impression is emphasised by the fairly long legs, which are 75-90% the length of the bill. By contrast, the tail streamers do not project far beyond the rest of the tail.

Arctic Tern has a shorter body with deeper breast. The body does not extend much behind the wings, but the adult's tail streamers are generally longer, on some diagnostically grotesque and 'tropicbird-like'. The stern then appears 'pressed out' ('expressed'). Head, neck and bill, however, are short and appear 'compressed' compared with Common Tern's. Rounded shape and long and narrow rear end are pronounced on perched birds, which are, however, immediately revealed by their very short legs Arctic Tern looks as if it is perched right on the ground. The long, narrow stern is accentuated by the fact that the tail often projects several centimetres beyond the wings.

Common Tern's flight also gives a

pointer to its species-identity. It is slower, more 'normal' and gull-like and not so aggressively thrusting as Arctic Tern's. Common is better adapted to foraging in calm conditions, and easily drifts in head winds of over about 10 m/s.

**Adult in summer plumage** has a black cap and orange-red bill with sharply demarcated black tip; even at a distance the bill is clearly bicoloured. The upper mandible has more dark colour. Only rarely is the bill dark in spring or from August (it becomes dark in winter plumage), and exceptionally it is all red. White wedge between gape and cap is broader than on Arctic Tern, and its upper edge is straight, unlike on most Arctic and Forster's Terns. The breast is white and merges diffusely into the grey belly, which is a shade paler grey than the upperparts – normally distinctly paler than on Arctic; birds with grey breast and white cheek stripe have the cheek stripe less clearly demarcated than on Arctic Tern. Sometimes the belly is whitish or has a faint pink tinge. In flight, the belly is not so immediately and conspicuously dark against the white underwings as on Arctic Tern. Note that fresh summer plumage is darker and more bluish-tinged, underparts becoming gradually paler with wear.

The upperparts are mid-grey with contrasting white tail. The most important character distinguishing it from Arctic Tern is the dark wedge in the central part of the hand, formed by the darker central primaries (older than the inners in spring and summer). In spring, the 'wedge' is weak, and in most cases reduced to a narrow dark streak on the central primary, but in summer it becomes more and more obvious, as the outer primaries appear darker when their silver-grey protective powder coating is gradually worn off. The wedge is most obvious in late summer to autumn, when it can, on the most extreme individuals, recall the similar wedge of male Pallid Harrier *Circus* *macrourus*. The wedge is the flight character visible at greatest ranges, especially when seen diagonally from behind, and during autumn passage it is often this that reveals that the tern migrating past is a Common Tern. On rare occasions only, the wedge may be absent in one wing. The secondaries appear progressively darker from late summer, and often stand

***PLATE 20***

**Common Tern *Sterna hirundo***

One of the most widespread terns. A reference species in tern identification. Adult summer shows combination of grey underparts, black-tipped red bill and dark wedge on outer primaries. Rump and tail whitish in contrast to grey back. Wings never shorter than tail on standing birds. Adult winter shows darker lesser coverts, predominantly dark bill, white forehead and white underparts. Juveniles similar to those of Arctic Tern, but with darker secondaries.

1 **Adult winter.**
2 **Second-summer.** Variable. Typical birds look similar to adult summer, but with white feathers in forehead, darker outer primaries and white feathers on grey underbody. Some probably identical to adult summer; others close to first-summer, but with generally more adult-type bill and greater amount of grey on underbody.
3 **Second-summer/adult late summer.** In spring to beginning of August, birds showing pale feathering in forehead, some white on underbody and heavily worn outer primaries may be classified as second-summer type'. From late summer, adults starting their moult may look similar, and ageing is not recommended.
4 **Adult summer (April-May).** Note orange-red, dark-tipped bill, typically with most black on upper mandible. In fresh plumage, upper- and underparts appear rather dark grey; with wear, underparts become paler, and outer primaries typically darker.
5 **Adult summer (June-July).** Underparts wear a little paler than in fresh plumage, and outer primaries become darker, forming typical dark wedge in outer wing.
6 **Adult summer race *longipennis*.** Note dark bill, dark brown legs and darker underparts than in Western Palearctic *hirundo*.

2
3
4
6
5

out as dark (rather as on juvenile) before the moult. This is also visible from below. On perched adults, it is the contrast between inner pale and outer dark primaries that is seen.

The underwing is greyish-white with broad dark tips on the outer 5-6 primaries, rather diffusely demarcated from the feather bases but sharply so from the inner primaries. The outer tail feathers have dark outer webs. The legs are orange-red.

After the breeding season, the inner primaries are moulted. A Common/Arctic Tern with moult gaps in the outer wing is a Common Tern, as Arctic Tern does not moult until reaching winter quarters. But even if the bird is not in moult, the moult line stands out clearly through the dark wedge in the primaries. From July, white feathers may be growing in the forehead and underparts; the belly in particular then acquires an untidy appearance. The bill becomes darker from mid July, and from August can be all dark. The moult is, however, limited during the autumn migration in the area of the breeding sites, but is more pronounced at stop-over sites (in north Europe e.g. at the Wadden Sea and North Sea coasts, where large flocks gather in autumn to feed on spawning sandeels).

**Adult winter plumage** has features approaching the juvenile. It has a white forehead and lores contrasting with black mask and bill (sometimes with red base). The upperparts are pale grey with a dark bar on the lesser coverts. Unmoulted, dark primaries and their coverts are replaced in late autumn and winter. the legs are darker red than in summer plumage. Very rarely (see Moult), the summer plumage is largely retained.

**Juvenile** has more rounded wings, shorter tail and shorter bill than adults in the first weeks after leaving the nest site. Face and underparts are white. It shows rich contrasts of black, grey, white and brown. The upperparts are brown-scaled or barred. Dark lesser coverts contrast well with pale grey central part of wing (on perched birds like a dark U on the forewing). More important is the fact that the secondaries are dark as well. The dark bar thus formed can be weak, but means that the rear edge of the inner wing is never paler than the rest of the wing. In the field, this is the single most important character distinguishing it from juvenile Arctic, which has paler secondaries contrasting with the rest of the wing.

The upperparts, when fresh, have a yellow to mustard-brown tint to the face and on the scaly to barred mantle/back. In fresh plumage the feather fringes are brown, but the brown colour is lost relatively quickly and further into the autumn the 'saddle' becomes barred grey and white. Many have broader, almost triangular dark spots on the upperparts (especially scapulars and tertials). The rump is slightly greyer than the white tail.

The bill has an orange to light red base, which can appear as a pale streak in the middle of the bill, or a red inner part. As autumn progresses, the bill becomes dark. The legs are pale orange.

Newly fledged young have pale brown forehead and lores, merging diffusely with black mask. The crown has short dark streaks. Dark-headed birds are said to show a complete cap at a distance, but dark on the lores is always restricted to areas immediately in front of the eye. During the autumn the forehead becomes whiter and the mask better defined, and thus more like that of Arctic. In mixed flocks, however, both dark-headed types (often with distinct brown element above) and grey-toned birds with white forehead are seen, as their appearance depends on when the bird fledged: in September most are quite 'well developed', but late-fledging young are still like 'normal' birds in late summer.

**First-winter plumage** is much as adult winter plumage, but the upperparts are uniform grey (often darker than in adult winter plumage: Barthel 1991). Wing-coverts and some tertials are juvenile. Contrast between darker fore and rear edges and pale centre on upperwing becomes gradually more distinct in winter. The bill is black.

**First-summer plumage** is much as first-winter plumage – Common Tern in 'winter plumage' in summer is in its second calendar-year (previously known as '*portlandica*' variant). The forehead is white and the mask black. The bill is on the whole black, but can sometimes have a reddish inner part (up to half). Dark bars on lesser coverts and secondaries contrast with pale grey back. The 3-5 outer primaries are dark brownish, contrasting with pale inner primaries. The entire leading edge of the wing is dark, as the outer primary coverts are also dark. The underparts are white, often with scattered grey feathers. The rump and sometimes the tail are pale grey. The outer, dark-edged tail feathers are shorter than on adults.

The appearance at this age is variable. Typical individuals are similar to washed-out and worn juveniles, while 'more advanced' ones are said to acquire an adult-like summer plumage, though with darker secondaries, worn outer primaries and dark tail sides. The underparts are normally white (with scattered grey feathers), and a more or less white forehead blaze seems always to be present.

The following plumages also vary individually, and subadult birds are therefore best classed as 'second-calendar-year type' or 'third-calendar-year type'. Common Terns normally do not breed until their second summer (Austin 1938).

**Second-summer plumage** (third-calendar-year) is much as adult summer, and some in this plumage are indistinguishable from adults. Some can be identified as third-calendar-year summer plumage by a combination of the following features: (1) White forehead feathers (sometimes as white blaze). (2) Bill generally has broader area of black and more diffusely demarcated black tip. (3) Dark grey lesser-covert bar may be retained, though it is weaker than in first-summer plumage and often incomplete. (4) The outer primaries are generally darker than on adult, and often the primary coverts, too, are darker than adult's. (5) The underparts are grey, normally with a minor element of white (though grey predominates at this age, unlike in first-summer plumage; rarely, underparts are whitish). (6) Outer tail feathers are generally shorter than in adult summer plumage. (7) Often, inner and outer primaries are in moult, producing dark wedges in both middle and inner parts of hand.

Birds of known age have shown the characters referred to. A variant ('*pikei*') much as that described, but with strong red legs and inner bill, has previously (Austin 1938; Palmer 1941) been classed as at least tenth-calendar-year+. It is not, however, recommended that such birds be aged as anything but subadult or adult in moult (C. Wilds *in litt.*).

Note that the subadult types can be rather like adults in transitional plumage or in winter plumage. After mid August the proportion of adults in transitional plumages increases. Safe ageing then becomes almost impossible in the field.

### Voice

Sharp, hoarse and powerful. As a whole coarse and with plenty of 'y' and 'ä' notes, sounds big-voiced (Sundberg & Söderberg 1983). Most characteristic: *krrri-äääh*, drawn out and harsh, both syllables equal in length but second note lower. The time interval has been noted as a fourth (Jacobsen 1961). Longer and with more clearly separated notes than Arctic Tern's call.

*Hrrri-(a)*, first part stressed, whirring and high.

*Kirri-kirri*, rapidly repeated, with emphasis of 'r' sound.

**Detailed description** *Sterna hirundo hirundo* (west Europe and North America)

Length 31-35 cm, wingspan 77-98 cm.

**Adult summer plumage:** Cap black, brown-tinged with wear. The cap extends farther back on nape than on Arctic and Forster's Terns. Lower half of lores, head sides and neck sides white, hind-neck whitish-grey (palest on worn birds). Upper-parts mid-grey, with some white edges to scapulars and tertials. Rump to tail white to pale greyish-white, contrasting clearly with back. Some tail-coverts may be grey, rarely with yellow-brown shafts. Tail white, most feathers with grey outer webs, darkest on t6.

Throat to breast white to whitish-grey, diffusely demarcated from mid-grey belly. Belly paler than upperparts. A few per cent (adult males) have the breast grey, as belly, contrasting with white moustachial stripe which is broader and more diffuse than on Arctic. rarely, entire underparts are greyish-white or white (less than 1%, whitest with wear in late summer, before moulting). Some have a pink tinge to underparts in spring and early summer. Vent white.

Remiges pale grey with broad white inner webs. Fresh feathers have silver-grey tinge. 5-7 outer primaries have blackish tips (more than 4.5 mm broad on p10: Baker 1993) and white wedge on inner webs to a couple of centimetres from tip

**PLATE 21**

**Common Tern *Sterna hirundo***

1 **Juvenile.** Recently fledged, heavily marked individual. In fresh plumage, head and upperparts show brownish (typically warm) tinge, normally stronger than on similar juvenile Arctic.

2 **Juvenile.** An average individual. Note pale eye-ring, and dark lesser coverts contrasting with median and greater coverts. Bill normally bicoloured during late summer and autumn.

3 **Juvenile.** Heavily marked individual. Such birds are not infrequent (even in juvenile Arctic); the most strongly patterned may suggest Roseate, which, however, has all-dark bill and legs, broad white inner webs to primaries and dark lores.

4 **Juvenile (late summer/autumn).** With wear, upperparts lose brown tinge and forehead becomes white. When perched, best separated from Arctic by longer legs.

5 **First-summer.** Similar to adult winter. Probably much individual variation. The bird shown is similar to worn juvenile, and is identified in spring and middle of the summer by white forehead and underparts, darker lesser coverts and secondary bar and short tail streamers. Furthermore, primary coverts are dark. In first-summer, shows all-dark bill or variable reddish base of bill. May be inseparable from moulting adults in late summer/autumn.

6 **First-summer.**

(at acute angle). In spring, 5-6 outer primaries are pale grey or slightly darker than the others; central primaries darkest. In summer and early autumn, central and outer primaries gradually darken (light 'protective powder' is worn off and reveals dark outer webs of primaries). The majority acquire a dark primary wedge early, this accentuated by contrast with silver-grey inner primaries.

Worn birds in late summer may reveal white bases to feathers of forehead and lores. Underparts fade; throat to breast can become almost pure white. Often the secondaries become darker and form a faint dark secondary bar (silver-grey 'protective powder' is worn off, as on outer primaries).

Bill red to orange-red with black, sharply defined tip 12-19 (22) mm broad, sometimes only on upper mandible (seems to be commonest on western populations). Very rarely, the bill is uniform orange-red (Steinbacker & Goethe 1935; U.G. Sörensen *in litt.*). Extreme bill tip often paler, especially with wear. From July-August acquires black bill; the majority have a summer bill up to September (pers. obs., Scandinavia). Upper mandible blackens first. An infinitesimal percentage have a black bill up to April-May (Jukema 1984). Legs orange-red.

A moulting individual in its sixth calendar-year (England, August) had white forehead feathers, elements of white feathering on underparts and worn primary coverts (similar to first-summer plumage) (skin, BMNH).

**Adult winter plumage:** Forehead and lores white, mask black. Crown white with grey or dirty grey spots. Mantle, neck and underparts white. Upperparts much as in summer plumage, but with dark bar on lesser coverts and generally greyer rump.

Primary contrast depends on degree of wear and moult. In middle of winter the autumn moult is completed, and all remiges appear pale silver-grey (much as on Arctic Tern in summer).

Bill black with variable carmine-red base to lower mandible and on upper mandible to nostrils; often has narrow pale tip. Legs orange-red, red-brown or greyish-red.

**Juvenile:** Forehead and lores white, on newly fledged birds tinged yellowish-brown to grey-brown. Crown has white, brown or black streaks or spots; when newly fledged only diffuse contrast with forehead, but later in autumn contrast between forehead/crown and black mask (from in front of eye to ear-coverts and nape) becomes more distinct. White eye-ring normally visible as white crescents above and below eye.

Throat, hindneck and underparts white. Upperparts pale grey with yellow-brown, brown or whitish-grey feather tips. Grey feather centres demarcated from pale tips by brown to black crescent-shaped spots, most obvious on scapulars and tertials. The palest birds have predominantly pale grey feathers, with obvious suggestion of dark only on tertials. Some have white tips to lower scapulars. Brownish-yellow to mustard-brown shade on upperparts is worn off a few weeks after leaving the nest site.

Uppertail-coverts and rump pale grey with white feather tips (rump white on palest individuals). Fresh feathers can have yellow-brown tips or shading.

Tail pale grey with black outer webs to outer 2-3 (occasionally all) feathers, white tips and white edges to inner webs. Tail feathers are variably tinged yellowish-brown or have yellow-brown tips, or are grey in centre.

Upperwing contrasty, with dark bars on lesser coverts (up to 1.5 cm broad) and secondaries. Secondary bar varies from dark grey to weak grey-brown, and on the palest individuals is uniform in colour with the coverts. Primaries dark grey with white tips and inner webs to up to 7-8 inner primaries. In September-January, remiges are worn and brownish.

Bill pink to orange, with broad black tip and upper edge to upper mandible. The bill turns black from a couple of weeks after leaving nest site (Palmer 1941). In September the majority have a black bill. Legs yellowish-orange to pinkish-orange; lacks obvious scaling. Legs become black into autumn.

**First-winter plumage:** Much as adult winter plumage, but retains juvenile coverts until January/February. Primaries are replaced from January/February; inner 5-8 are renewed up to first summer.

**First-summer plumage:** Rather like adult winter plumage. Forehead, lores and crown white, sometimes with scattered dark feathers. Mask black. Underparts white, occasionally with some grey feathers. Upperparts grey with dark lesser-covert and secondary bars, these often standing out clearly against pale back and remaining coverts. Inner primaries pale grey, contrasting with dark brownish-tinged 2-4 outer primaries (exceptionally until November). Retained juvenile primary coverts dark. Tail greyish-white, generally darker than on adults, with dark grey outer webs and pale grey inner webs; t5-6 can have up to a couple of millimetres of pale tips. Tail streamers 35-65 mm.

Bill black, sometimes with reddish-orange base (up to 50%) or base of lower mandible. Legs sometimes greyer than adult's.

In August-December, moults to second-winter plumage.

**Second-summer plumage:** Varies. Some are much as first-summer plumage, but white is restricted to the forehead (sometimes as white spots or white blaze). The bill is normally as adult's, but generally has broader black tip (can cover over 50% of bill). As with adult, the bill is rarely uniformly orange-red.

Some have a dark bar on the lesser coverts (weaker than in earlier plumages). The underparts are much as adult summer plumage, but with elements of white; rarely, white with scattered grey feathers. Secondaries and unmoulted primaries generally darker than adult's. Primary moult usually active in May-July, when adults have arrested moult. Because of different moult, the outer wing can be contrasty, with dark wedges in both inner and outer parts of hand. Outer primaries can be relatively fresher and paler than adult's (USA; Wilds 1993). Tail streamers 50-70 mm.

Others are much as adult summer plumage, but have white feathers in grey underparts, white feather edges in cap and generally darker outer primaries and primary coverts. Worn adults and adults moulting to winter plumage rather similar (see Adult summer plumage).

**Third-summer plumage** as adult summer plumage. Some have white-flecked lores and forehead (Cramp 1985). Certain ageing of second-summer plumage and older cannot be recommended.

## Moult

**Adult** has a complete moult to **winter plumage**. The moult begins in July and is suspended to a varying degree during the autumn migration. Primary moult may commence after the breeding season from late July, starting when the previous moult is arrested. Inner primaries are moulted rarely in May-June (pers. obs.; Hume 1993). In the Baltic, about 10% moult the inner primaries during autumn migration in late July to early August, but in the Wadden Sea region (western Denmark to the Netherlands) many are in a more advanced stage of moult. The majority in August have a moult limit at primaries (3) 4-5. Primary moult is normally resumed in September or on/after arrival in winter quarters, and is completed in January to early March. A new moult series may commence during the winter, when primaries 6-7 have been replaced.

The secondaries are moulted in autumn and winter in two groups: 1-13 are moulted from the outer most inwards, secondaries 14-20 are moulted twice (at beginning and end of primary moult) (Ginn & Melville 1983).

The tail is moulted after the breeding season. First to be replaced is t1, then t2 (may be moulted before t1: Cramp 1985); t3-6 are moulted in December-January sometimes immediately after t1-2. In January-February the tail is normally new. Active tail moult unusual in Scandinavia (pers. obs.). Ginn & Melville (1983) state that the entire tail may be renewed before the autumn migration.

Body moult before autumn migration is limited. The majority in north Europe (Scandinavia, Britain) have a limited moult until mid August: from mid July a few per cent have white feathers in lores and forehead; in August to mid September the percentage of adults with white forehead does not exceed 5% (pers. obs., Sweden, England). Cramp (1985) gives one-third as having white forehead in August-September (west Europe), which agrees with 35% of birds in the Netherlands in late August to early September being white-foreheaded (pers. obs.). The higher proportion is due to the fact that the moult is mostly carried out in food-rich stop-over sites in the North Sea and the Wadden Sea. The majority (75-80%) in west France in late August to early September, however, were largely as north European birds (probably from southerly breeding populations). From late July, elements of white feathering on the underparts and active moult of coverts can be seen. The percentage in transitional plumage gradually increases in August. The majority (50-75%) in the Netherlands in late August to early September had acquired dark lesser coverts of winter plumage and had a predominance of white on the underparts, but an overwhelming proportion of adults in both north Europe and France at the same period were in summer plumage (pers. obs.). Among those populations with a limited moult prior to autumn migration, most of the body moult takes place in winter quarters in October-January.

Geographical variation in moult is considerable. North American birds possibly moult earlier than European ones; birds in California are in winter plumage during autumn migration, though no (or very restricted) moult is seen in autumn in eastern and northern parts of USA (C. Wilds, pers. comm.). Birds from Maine replace lesser coverts and outer rectrices before migration (Palmer 1941). Wilds (1993) states that 4-5 (7) inner primaries may be changed prior to autumn migration. The body moult is completed in November-December, and primary moult has reached the outer primaries in January-February (Wilds 1993).

**COMMON TERN** QUICK KEY TO IDENTIFICATION

1. **Compared with Arctic Tern, broader-winged and shorter-tailed, with heavier body and slimmer but more powerful head and bill.**
2. **Perched birds have clearly visible legs, at least 50% length of bill.**
3. **Adults in summer plumage have black cap and orange bill with black tip.**
4. **Adults have distinct dark wedge on central primaries, this becoming increasingly more obvious and broader in summer and autumn.**
5. **Only innermost part of hand is translucent against the light. Dark rear edge to outer wing fairly broad and diffuse.**
6. **Underparts paler than upperparts on adults.**
7. **Juveniles have dark bands on both rear and fore edges of primaries. Rear edge of secondaries darker than coverts or concolorous, never paler.**
8. **Juveniles have bicoloured bill.**
9. **In first-summer plumage, dark bars are visible on both fore and rear edges of inner wing. Plumage similar to adult winter plumage.**
10. **Second-summer plumage adult-like, but with white forehead, dark lesser-covert bar and white-flecked underparts.**

Failed breeders may moult some feathers of upperparts, breast and belly from June. In August, about 50% moult the underparts and some upperwing-coverts. Exceptionally, there is no moult to winter plumage: A bird from Madagascar in January had pure adult summer plumage (photo R. Prys-Jones, BMNH). An overwintering bird in the Netherlands was in summer plumage apart from dark grey secondaries and shorter tail streamers (Maasen & van der Meulen 1983), which may have been due to wear.

**Adult** has a partial moult to **summer plumage**. The moult includes head, body, tail, upperwing-coverts, outer secondaries and inner (plus unmoulted outer) primaries. The moult begins with innermost primary and tail in December-February, and is arrested during migration in March-April, when head, body, tail and 3-5 (6-7) inner primaries have been renewed. Ginn & Melville (1983) state that all primaries may be replaced (birds from South Africa). Often returns to breeding site with three generations of primaries (Baker 1993).

**Juvenile** moults to **first-winter plum-**

**age** in winter quarters in (October) November-March. Rarely, some feathers are moulted from August. Head, body, tail and most coverts have been replaced in February-March.

Primary moult commences with the inner primaries in (December) January-February, and is suspended during summer with (4) 5-7 (8-9) inner primaries renewed. Birds in late September (Israel) had not replaced 3-4 outer primaries; many up to January-February have 2-4 outer primaries very worn. Juvenile outer primaries are present rarely until April (third calendar-year). Tail moult normally begins in October-November, with t1 first, followed by t6; last to be moulted are t4-5, which in midwinter are darker from wear.

In May-June (second calendar-year) a new moult series may begin (when first moult series has reached primary 8). It is slow, and is suspended in summer with 1-3 inner primaries replaced. The moult is resumed in winter quarters, and is finished in March-April of the second summer.

Moult to **second-winter plumage** takes place in June-August, and includes head, body and tail. In December-February a new moult series begins in the primaries. This is arrested with (4) 5-7 (8) inner primaries new to those birds visiting breeding sites, but is continued by those in winter quarters in the third summer. The tail is moulted from November-December, beginning with t1.

**Second-summer plumage** is acquired in February-June. The moult includes 40-90% of head and body feathers (Wilds 1993), but less on upperparts, upperwing-coverts and tail. In July-August, can have two active moults in inner and central primaries. The subsequent moults are as for adults.

---

***PLATE 22***

**Common Tern *Sterna hirundo***

1 **Juvenile.** Recently fledged individual.

2 **Juvenile (late summer/autumn).** With wear, back and middle part of wing become paler, contrasting with darker lesser coverts and secondary bar - the latter the main character distinguishing it from juvenile Arctic Tern.

3 **Juvenile.** Note bicoloured bill and dark secondary bar.

4 **First-summer.** Similar to juvenile, but upperparts uniform grey. Retained juvenile outer primaries, primary coverts and secondaries much worn. Normally shows dark sides of tail. Such winter-type birds in spring and summer are first-years.

5 **First-summer (autumn).**

6 **Adult winter (from end of September; majority October).**

7 **Second-summer/adult moulting into winter plumage.** As adult summer, but typically shows combination of pale feathering on forehead, white feathers on underbody, traces of dark lesser-covert bar and even darker unmoulted primaries. When adults start moult into winter plumage (normally beginning of August), they quickly become inseparable from second-summer type'.

8 **Adult summer (spring).** In spring, dark primary wedge is indistinct on the majority, but becomes gradually clearer through wear. Wedge in combination with grey underbody is diagnostic - Arctic Tern does show even darker underbody, but has pale primaries without dark wedge.

9 **Adult summer (late summer).** Dark primary wedge striking. Worn birds often show darker secondaries. Bill may begin to darken from early August.

10 **Adult summer.**

11 **Adult moulting from summer to winter plumage (August/September).** When worn and in moult often looks irregularly patterned, with underbody a mixture of grey and white, darker outer primaries and secondaries, new and older coverts admixed and white forehead.

12 **Adult summer race *longipennis*.** Note dark bill and greyer upperparts than in *hirundo*. Intergrades with latter in Central and East Asia. See text.

1
2
3
4
5
6
7
8
9
10
11
12

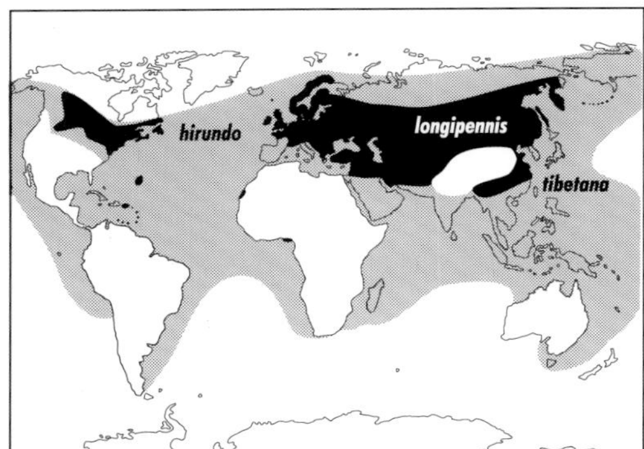


***MAP 9*** Distribution of Common Tern *Sterna hirundo.*

### Geographical variation

Nominate *hirundo* (Europe, North Africa and Asia to west Siberia and Kazakhstan, and North America to the Caribbean) described above.

Geographical variation within this race small; American birds have shorter wing than West Palearctic ones (see Measurements). Black bill base of adults in summer plumage (skins): North America 10-18 mm, Britain 10-18 (20) mm (a few black only on upper mandible), south Scandinavia 12-19 mm, Finland 16-22.5 mm (tendency for darker coloration on upper mandible to nostrils than in west Scandinavia), west Siberia (12) 16-21 mm (own measurements, skins, BMNH, UZM, ZMH, NNH, ZMA).

Race *longipennis* (central Siberia to Alaska and China) in adult summer plumage has black bill, darker red-brown legs and darker grey body. Bill shorter but wings longer than in *hirundo*. Underparts grey with white cheek stripe; underparts rather as Arctic Tern's, but cheek stripe generally broader and shorter, normally ending immediately behind eye. Cheek stripe can be as narrow as on adult Whiskered Tern (especially male) (M. Ullman *in litt.*). T1-2 have paler (grey) outer webs than *hirundo*.

A broad intergrade zone occurs in Siberia/central Asia, where birds with red basal 50% of bill predominate (red generally darker than on European birds). Westernmost individuals with black bill occur in the Ob basin, Yenesei and Kazakhstan (pers. obs.; M. Ullman *in litt.*). The percentage of black-billed birds increases progressively eastwards. In Kamchatka and in east Siberia the bill is black, but a few per cent have red bill base. Moult similar to that of nominate *hirundo*, but only a few per cent in summer plumage in mid April.

Race *tibetana* (Himalayas to Mongolia and China) recalls *hirundo*, but the bill is shorter (see Measurements) and black bill tip is comparatively broader (14-21 mm). Plumage and moult as nominate *hirundo*.

### Hybrid Roseate x Common Tern

Hybrids between Common Tern and Roseate Tern are known from breeding populations in USA (Hays 1975). Adult hybrids have upperparts, underparts and secondaries intermediate between the two species, and black cap (not brown-tinted with wear as on Common Tern). T6 has grey outer web. Outer 5-7 primaries have black outer webs and inner part of inner webs, but white inner webs to tips, or black, square-cut tips (not acutely angled against inner part as on Common). Bill much as on Common, but generally with broader black tip. Call intermediate. Wing 255-256 mm, tarsus 20.0-24.3 mm, bill 36.3-39.9 mm.

Possible hybrid pairs in Britain had Common Tern-like young, but copulation between hybrid parents was not observed (Robbins 1974).

**Juvenile**s of hybrid parents had upperparts much as Common Tern, but with traces of Roseate Tern pattern. Forehead to crown dark with pale streaks, palest on forehead. Primaries have pale edges on inner webs to tip. Tail as Common Tern, but with suggestion of dark V-markings on t3-5; t6 has grey outer web. Legs brown to black with distinct scaling (Hays 1975).

A hybrid juvenile Roaseate x Common Tern in the Netherlands has been described (Bijersbergen 1988; Walhout 1988; Mullarney 1988). Resembles juvenile Common Tern with several divergent characters. Cap diffusely demarcated, with heavy dark streaks on lores and mid crown. Lores grey-flecked. Ear-coverts white-spotted, eye-ring visible. Back and wing-coverts much as juvenile Roseate, but inner greater coverts much as juvenile Common. Outer primaries as Common Tern, lacking broad white edges to 3 outer primaries. Some dark colour on outer web of t6. Bill black with pink base to lower mandible and along cutting edges. Legs pink.

**Measurements**

In mm. Own measurements, BMNH, NMNH, NNH, ZMA, UZM, MN, NRM, ZML, ZMO, ZMU, ZMH. Race *hirundo* (north and west Europe, Finland, North America). Race *longipennis* (east Siberia, Java). Race *tibetana* (Kashmir, Ladakh, Tibet). Adults May-September; juveniles August-October.

WING LENGTH

| | | | |
|---|---|---|---|
| *hirundo* (Scandinavia, Finland, west Europe) | | | |
| Ad ♂ | 256-289 | (271.9) | n = 201 |
| Ad ♀ | 248-292 | (270.1) | n = 111 |
| Juv | 228-273 | (252.5) | n = 152 |
| *longipennis* | | | |
| Ad ♂ | 263-299 | (276.7) | n = 55 |
| Ad ♀ | 262-287 | (274.8) | n = 32 |

• American *hirundo* ad ♂ 255-284 (268.1, n = 28), ad ♀ 255-284 (268.3, n = 9).

• According to Hario (1986): west European ads 250-288 (271, n = 459). Dutch birds (own measurements, ZMA, NNH): ad ♂♂ average 270.0, ad ♀♀ average 267.3. Scandinavian birds: ad ♂♂ average 273.1, ad ♀♀ average 271.9.

• 1st-winter *hirundo* (December-February): 230-262 (250.4, n = 12).

• Outer primary often very worn at tip.

TAIL FORK

| | | | |
|---|---|---|---|
| *hirundo* | | | |
| Ad ♂ | 58-92 | (73.2) | n = 198 |
| Ad ♀ | 64-93 | (74.9) | n = 102 |
| Juv | 28-56 | (41.9) | n = 155 |
| 1st-winter | 33-70 | (52.1) | n = 15 |

• One ad ♂ (Finland, ZMH) had tail fork of 109; one ad ♀ (Netherlands, ZMA) had tail fork of 99.

• Serventy *et al.* (1971) give 51-114 for *longipennis* (ad summer).

• Ad winter 55-85. Two 2nd-summer types 43 and 72.

BILL

| | | | |
|---|---|---|---|
| *hirundo* | | | |
| Ad ♂ | 32.2-40.3 | (36.8) | n = 201 |
| Ad ♀ | 32.1-39.6 | (35.7) | n = 103 |
| Juv | 26.4-35.6 | (30.9) | n = 155 |
| 1st-summer | 32.8-37.4 | (35.7) | n = 17 |
| *longipennis* | | | |
| Ad ♂ | 31.8-39.9 | (35.2) | n = 55 |
| Ad ♀ | 31.9-37.4 | (33.5) | n = 37 |
| *tibetana* | | | |
| Ad ♂ | 30.4-36.7 | (33.8) | n = 41 |
| Ad ♀ | 29.9-35.2 | (32.2) | n = 42 |

BILL DEPTH AT GONYS

| | | | |
|---|---|---|---|
| *hirundo* | | | |
| Ad ♂ | 5.6-8.0 | (7.0) | n = 198 |
| Ad ♀ | 5.4-7.7 | (6.7) | n = 110 |
| Juv | 5.0-7.4 | (6.3) | n = 152 |
| 1st-summer | 6.0-7.3 | (6.7) | n = 17 |

BILL DEPTH AT REAR EDGE OF NOSTRILS

| | | | |
|---|---|---|---|
| *hirundo* | | | |
| Ad ♂ | 7.6-10.0 | (8.2) | n = 201 |
| Ad ♀ | 7.2-9.5 | (8.3) | n = 111 |
| Juv | 6.3-8.7 | (7.4) | n = 157 |
| 1st-summer | 7.3-8.8 | (8.0) | n = 17 |

TARSUS

| | | | |
|---|---|---|---|
| *hirundo* | | | |
| Ad ♂ | 17.5-22.0 | (19.6) | n = 199 |
| Ad ♀ | 17.4-21.5 | (19.4) | n = 111 |
| Juv | 17.7-21.6 | (19.3) | n = 152 |
| 1st-summer | 18.1-20.4 | (19.4) | n = 16 |

WEIGHT (in grams)

| | | | |
|---|---|---|---|
| May-June, Netherlands | | | |
| Ad ♂ | 112-137 | (124) | n = 5 |
| Ad ♀ | 110-141 | (126) | n = 6 |
| August-September, Netherlands and Shetland | | | |
| Ad | 89-165 | | n = 79 |
| Juv | 80-160 | | n = 42 |

• For USA, spring and summer, 103-145 given for ads (Cramp 1985).

# Arctic Tern

Photos **97-107** *Sterna paradisaea*

### Identification in the field

The Arctic Tern is a 'sister-species' to the Common Tern. Field identification of the two species represents a well-known problem, which comes to the fore especially during migration, when the two often appear together. Differences in shape and proportions, together with the translucency of the wing, are important in separating the species.

At all ages the Arctic Tern's primaries are clearly translucent. This is most obvious when the bird is seen diagonally against the light, when the hand becomes almost luminous (as when a torch is shone onto parchment paper!). The narrow, but distinct black rear edge to the outer 7-8 primaries then becomes very prominent. Common Tern has only the junction between arm and hand translucent; the underside of the primaries then appear darker, with more poorly demarcated – though broader – black rear edge.

**Adult** Arctic Terns over a sandbank in summer are, with their graceful and delicate flight, almost tropicbird-like. At such times, their grey underside to the body, the translucent, almost gleaming white underwings and the very long tail streamers give them a highly characteristic appearance.

The Arctic Tern is in every way more extreme than the more gull-like Common Tern: all tern characters are intensified and sublimely adapted to a life on the wing. Compared with the Common Tern, Arctic is more compact, with shorter, oval-shaped body which is deepest at the breast but extends only minimally behind the wings, but on the other hand the extremely long and narrow outer tail feathers (streamers) give the species a protracted appearance. The wings are narrower, with longer, more pointed hand, and appear to be situated farther forwards owing to the shorter head and bill and the long and narrow, elongated rear end, created by the very long tail (up

***PLATE 23***

**Arctic Tern *Sterna paradisaea***
Similar to Common Tern, but differs in more rounded head, shorter bill and especially much shorter legs, often making perched birds appear 'legless'.

1 **Juvenile.** Heavily marked individual. Normally, very recently fledged birds show red at base of bill. Note lack of conspicuous eye-ring, less contrast between lesser and median coverts than on Common Tern and shorter legs. Brown tinge to upperparts on fresh birds typically colder than on Common.
2 **Juvenile.** A typical bird, lacking warm brown colour tones. White forehead typically shows better contrast with black mask than on Common. Bill becomes all dark a few weeks after fledging.
3 **Juvenile.** Pale, less marked individual.
4 **First-summer.** Like juvenile, but with paler, uniform upperpart feathers. Bill black, mask well marked. Note all primaries of same generation (unlike Common).
5 **Second-summer.** As adult summer, but forehead white, traces of dark lesser-covert bar present and underparts show mixture of grey and white feathers. At this age, often shows traces of dark at tip of upper mandible. Some birds are probably indistinguishable from adults, but the combination mentioned is typical for 'second-summer type'.
6 **Adult summer.** Rather uniform grey with white cheeks and uniform, blood-red bill. Note just narrow area of white on lores. All primaries of same generation.

1
2
3
4
5
6

to 2.5 times the wing breadth) which undulates in the wind like that of an adult Long-tailed Skua *Stercorarius longicaudus*. On summer-plumaged adults, the ratio between the part projecting in front of the wing and that extending behind is 1:1.8-2.5 (1:1.5-2 on Common Tern) (Malling Olsen 1982).

The Arctic Tern has a very elegant flight, especially in strong winds, when the body clearly moves during the stiff, well-balanced wingbeats, which are deeper than those of Common Tern. They attack the wind steadily with more angled wings than Common, and are obviously better adapted for foraging in blustery weather. At sea it plunges vertically from several metres' height, but in calm weather and near the coast it forages like Common Tern with oblique dives. Prey is also snatched up directly from the water's surface. Overall, the Arctic Tern is an excellent flier; note that it undertakes the longest migration of all the world's birds.

When perched, the Arctic Tern is neckless, attenuated and very short-legged. It has an evenly rounded head with highest point immediately above the eye. The adult's tail can project several centimetres beyond the wings, but wings and tail can, as on Common Tern, fall level. The legs are clearly shorter than the bill. Perched birds appear to be sitting right on the ground, like huge porcelain figurines. Experienced tern-ringers say that there is just room around the tarsus to fit a ring! In strong winds more leg is revealed, but even then the Arctic Tern still appears disproportionately short-legged. The bill is normally slimmer and narrower than Common Tern's.

**Adult in summer plumage** has a black cap and coral-red bill (rarely, dark red, especially in April-May and August). The bill is normally uniform in colour, but can have some dark coloration on the tip of the upper mandible, often combined with black at the bill base. Any dark colour, however, is diffuse, and black on both upper and lower mandibles is exceptional.

The black cap appears depressed in front of the eye, revealing only a narrow white wedge between cap and gape. The cap is shorter than Common Tern's. Rounded head and short, 'fitted-on' bill give typical individuals a 'good-natured' expression.

The cheeks are white, normally well demarcated from pale grey breast. The most-marked birds (males) have a white moustachial stripe not unlike that of Whiskered Tern. The blue-grey underbody contrasts well with white underwings (whiter than on Common, intensified in certain lights when the whole underwing is translucent). The 7-8 outer primaries have narrow black tips, forming a sharply defined black line along the rear edge of the hand – very obvious against the light. This is, however, less well demarcated from the inner primaries, as the innermost dark-marked primary has a reduced amount of black compared with the others. The upperwing is silver-grey, a shade bluer than Common Tern's and with only primary tips dark. The hand often looks paler than the arm. The mantle and back contrast with the white rump and tail; the outer tail feather has a narrow dark outer web. On perched birds, the upperparts and the underbody appear fairly uniform in colour.

The Arctic Tern lacks Common's dark primary wedges. On the one hand all primaries are of the same generation (acquired in rapid succession in winter quarters), and on the other the primaries are really pale (even with wear stand out as pale; dark on Common). Only exceptionally are moult gaps visible, presumably on birds which have been weakened during the winter moult. The legs are coral-red.

**Adult in winter plumage** has a black bill and white face. The black mask is narrow, like a black band from behind the eye and across the nape. The transition between mask and white crown can lack sharpness owing to narrow dark streaks. The upperparts are much as in summer plumage, but a dark bar across the lesser coverts may be present (Pizzey 1980). Since the winter plumage is borne only in winter quarters around Antarctica, it is poorly known. It is possible that parts of the plumage are retained and that the species moults directly into new summer plumage in late winter. During the rapid moult, several primaries are growing out simultaneously.

**Juvenile** Arctics have more rounded wings and shorter bill and tail than adults. They are paler and more cleanly marked than juvenile Commons, and have a grey-brown to sandy-coloured tinge only to completely fresh feathers and for a period of a few weeks after leaving the nest site. The most important point is that the secondaries are white (or faintly pale grey) and appear the palest part of the upperparts. The bill is all black, but on leaving the nest site it has a red base. The white forehead and forecrown are clearly demarcated from the black mask. The mask covers the eye and extends farther down on the neck sides than on adults. The eye-ring is lacking or is very weak, so that the eye is normally disguised by black.

The upperparts are a shade darker than on adults. At close range white feather edges produce a slightly scaly appearance, but at a distance the upperparts appear uniform grey. Dark lesser coverts create a variable covert bar, which can sometimes be almost as distinct as on young Common Terns, but normally appears weaker. Some look at a distance as if they have uniform grey lesser and median coverts, like a grey triangle on the forewing next to white secondaries and inner primaries. In this case a contrast arises which may be compared with the wing pattern of Sabine's Gull *Larus sabini*. The white secondaries are accentuated against the light, when they are translucent and a broad white, almost luminous region is produced, but even in poor lighting this panel is obvious. The median coverts normally have a row of dark spots (tend to be more distinct than faint dark spots on back). The white rump contrasts well with the grey upperparts.

Young Common Terns have darker secondaries (only on the most poorly marked are they uniform with the middle part of the wing) and pale grey rump. The wing's translucency is a good character on juveniles, too. Juvenile Common have, in addition, generally broader pale feather edges above, bicoloured bill and white eye-ring. The head and wing shapes together with bill length are, however, of less significance during the autumn.

**First-winter/first-summer plumage** is much as juvenile, but has whiter crown and uniform grey mantle/back. The black mask appears triangular, as it gradually broadens towards the nape. With wear, a dark covert bar often stands out clearly. The plumage varies less than the corresponding plumage of Common Tern.

The bill is black or has a red base. The legs are black, greyish or red.

Arctic Terns in 'winter plumage' during summer are in all likelihood second-calendar-year birds. The majority remain in winter quarters in their first summer, but a small proportion migrate north and appear in late spring and summer in north Europe (less than 1% of migrating birds at Falsterbo in summer/autumn 1991 and 1992: Malling Olsen 1993). The percentage of second-calendar-year types in north Europe is greater than that of other breeding species, and this is to be expected since the species breeds farther north and more 'commuters' turn up compared with the more southerly breeding terns.

The Arctic Tern, besides its proportions and wing translucency, differs from second-calendar-year Common Tern in also

1
2
3
4
5
6
7

**PLATE 24**

**Arctic Tern *Sterna paradisaea***

In flight, silhouette is compact, with smaller and more rounded head and shorter bill than on Common. Tail long and slender. All flight feathers translucent, making narrow dark trailing edge to primaries stand out very contrastingly.

1 **Juvenile.** Newly fledged individual. Similar to Common Tern, but with broad whitish triangle on hindwing, created by white secondaries.
2 **Juvenile (autumn).** Plumage black, white and grey, typically lacking brown elements.
3 **First-summer.** Similar to juvenile. Note all flight feathers of same generation. White secondaries distinguish Arctic from Common Tern even at this age. Normally shows larger amount of white on crown than Common. Mask therefore often looks more restricted, as broad dark triangle behind eye.
4 **Adult winter.** Probably similar to first-summer. In middle of winter, moults several flight feathers simultaneously. Plumage poorly known.
5 **Second-summer.** Similar to adult summer, but with variable pale forehead, traces of darker lesser-covert bar and some white feathers on underbody. Often shows dark tip to bill (normally restricted to upper mandible) and dark base of bill.
6 **Adult summer.** Uniform grey upperwing, often with outer wing paler than inner wing. Bill and legs coral-red. Note rounded body shape and very long tail streamers.
7 **Adult summer.** In spring and late summer, sometimes shows dark tip to upper mandible.

having white secondaries and broader white crown. As with adults, the wing is moulted in the winter quarters, so all primaries are of the same generation. Common Terns in their first summer have the outer 2-5 primaries worn and contrasting with paler inners.

**Second-summer plumage** is much as adult summer plumage, but the majority have a white forehead, either as scattered feathers or as a white blaze immediately above the bill base. Occasionally, the lores or a broader wedge between gape and cap are also white (rather like Common Tern in summer plumage). The black cap can be tinged brown. The plumage is otherwise much as adult summer, but the breast is sometimes whiter and showing a slight transition into the grey belly (can have a few white feathers), and darker bar on lesser upper-wing-coverts normally visible. The bill is generally darker red than the adult's, and can have a dark tip.

Several plumage characters, especially the underparts and the bill, recall adult Common Tern. Differences in proportions and the translucency of the wing are in this case of great value for separation from Common Tern.

Birds in the plumage described have been seen mostly in summer. It is not established whether these involve second-summer plumage or 'retarded' adults which have retained parts of their winter plumage. They most often appear in mid-summer away from the colonies, which makes it likely that subadults rather than adults are involved. The uncertainties described, however, mean that they are best referred to as 'second-summer-plumage types'.

## Voice

Higher, clearer, shorter and more rattling than Common Tern's (Sundberg & Söderberg 1983). Can sound almost nasal and is more muffled than Common's. The commonest call is *kriii-ä*, with emphasis on first syllable and shortened second syllable. A three-note version may be heard during display.

Another call, *ki-aaarrhhh*, with short first syllable and open, almost restrained second syllable with quite long time interval, noted as about a seventh (Jacobsen 1961). The first syllable may be omitted.

### Detailed description

Length 33-35 cm, wingspan 75-85 cm.

**Adult in summer plumage:** Cap black, shorter than Common Tern's, and 'depressed' in front of the eye. Narrow (1-3 mm) white area between

**ARCTIC TERN** QUICK KEY TO IDENTIFICATION

1. **Streamlined body with rounded head, pointed hand, and very long outer tail feathers (adult) which undulate in the wind.**
2. **Perched birds very short-legged, can appear legless.**
3. **Summer-plumaged adults have black cap which appears 'squashed down' in front of the eye and coral-red bill lacking clear black tip.**
4. **Adults have uniform grey upperparts with, at most, black rear edge to primaries (no wedge!).**
5. **All remiges translucent: primaries appear luminous against the light, with distinct black rear edge.**
6. **Underbody clearly darker than underwings, and concolorous with upperparts.**
7. **Juveniles have dark lesser-covert bar but white secondaries. Appear purer silver-grey than Common Terns.**
8. **In summer of second calendar-year resembles washed-out juvenile with latter's whitish rear edge to inner wing. Crown often whiter than in other plumages.**
9. **Juveniles normally have black bill.**
10. **First-summer plumage resembles adult winter plumage. Has white secondaries.**
11. **Second-summer plumage adult-like, but with white forehead, white-mottled upperside and sometimes dark bar on lesser coverts. Best distinguished from Common Tern by different proportions and translucent wing.**

gape and lower edge of cap. Throat and cheek stripe white, especially on males, contrasting well with blue-grey breast and belly. Breast rarely white (a few per cent, especially females). The grey underparts have a weak bluish tinge, and are almost uniform in colour with the upperparts. With wear (late summer), paler. Vent white.

Upperparts blue-grey, rump to tail white. (T4) t5 (t6) has pale grey outer web, t6 rarely darker as on Common Tern. Tail-coverts and central tail feathers may have yellowish-brown to pale orange-brown shafts.

Remiges pale grey above, white below. Outer 7-8 primaries have 1.5-2.5 mm of black at the tips; least on primaries 7-8. Secondaries pale grey with broader white tips than Common Tern. Worn secondaries rarely slightly darker than rest of upperparts.

Bill coral-red, rarely (late spring and late summer) with diffuse black area of up to 1 cm in length at tip of upper mandible or at bill base. Bill sometimes darker red, especially in April-May and August (pers. obs.). Dark tint or black areas possibly remnants of winter plumage. Legs coral-red.

Occasional individuals have white forehead at age of up to 6 (12) years – possibly a regular feature on certain birds in summer plumage (Cullen 1957; pers. obs.). See Common Tern (*pikei* variant).

**Adult winter plumage:** Lores, forehead and crown white. Crown has black spots or short streaks creating diffuse transition into narrow black mask from eye to nape. White neck sides can extend onto nape. Mantle and underparts white. Upperparts as adult summer plumage, but with dark grey bar on forewing formed by dark lesser coverts and primary coverts. Pale grey outer webs to outer tail feathers often restricted to t1-4. Uppertail-coverts sometimes grey-toned and contrasting with white rump. Tail streamers 55-75 mm. Bill black, sometimes with red base or edges. Legs dark brownish-red to black, occasionally with carmine-red soles.

**Juvenile:** Head and body much as on juvenile Common Tern, but upperparts are less brown-tinted. Brown element is retained for only a few weeks after leaving nest site (exceptionally, until late September).

Forehead and lores greyish-white to yellow-brown, lores in front of eye sometimes black. Pale eye-ring lacking or weak. From late July/early August, forehead and lores become white. Mask (crown to nape) black. Back, scapulars and tertials pale grey with greyish-white (rarely, pale grey-brown to sandy-coloured) edges and dark grey subterminal spots (especially on tertials). Tips of median coverts often darker (forming row of dark spots). Upperpart pattern normally weaker than on Common Tern. Rump and uppertail-coverts white.

Underparts white. Breast sides and flanks can be tinged grey-brown or yellow-brown.

Tail feathers have grey outer webs and white inner webs and tips, sometimes grey inner webs and dark subterminal spots. Tips of tail feathers (especially t1, but occasionally all) may have tinge of yellow-brown. Upperwings pale grey with mid-grey bar across lesser coverts, generally narrower and paler than similar bar on Common Tern. The palest birds have lesser and median coverts uniform in colour. Coverts (especially medians) can have diffuse dark subterminal spots and narrow white edges. Secondaries white to greyish-white; form broad pale panel on rear inner wing. Primaries adult-like. Dark rear edge to outer part of hand as on adult, but sometimes with only 4-5 outermost primaries dark-tipped (Malling Olsen & Danielson 1989; pers. obs.).

Bill orange-red with black culmen and tip when newly fledged. From early August black. Bill base is exceptionally red until November (Malling Olsen & Danielson 1989). Legs orange-red, dark red or greyish-red, but black from early autumn.

**First-winter/first-summer plumage:** Much as adult winter plumage after moult in January-February. This plumage is exhibited in first summer, and recalls a pale juvenile. Has white forehead and crown (sometimes with a few dark streaks), dark bar on lesser coverts and black bill (sometimes with dark red base). Upperparts pale grey, with contrasting white rump and tail. Underparts white, sometimes with isolated grey feathers. Primaries are fresh in summer; moulted in January-April and October-December. Does not moult until arrival in winter quarters; delayed summer visitors become very worn and can acquire almost a white crown to nape in October-December, though with some black spots on the nape (pers. obs., skins, BMNH; Gordon 1986).

**Second-summer plumage:** Much as adult summer plumage, but the cap normally duller and more brown-toned, with variable white in forehead and lores (sometimes as white blaze). White wedge between gape and cap generally broader than on adults (2-3 mm). Some have darker grey bar on lesser coverts (11% of 90 individuals: Cramp 1985). Underparts generally paler than on adults, with whiter breast and often with an element of white feathers. Tail streamers shorter than in adult summer plumage. May retain some old tail feathers. Primaries adult-like, but some have replaced innermost 1-2 (5) during spring. Rarely, a Common Tern-like wedge may then be produced, though less well marked and shorter.

Bill dark red, sometimes with diffuse dark elements. Legs dark brownish-red.

Possibly the primary moult is arrested in midsummer with the innermost 1-2 (5) primaries new (Cramp 1985; pers. obs.).

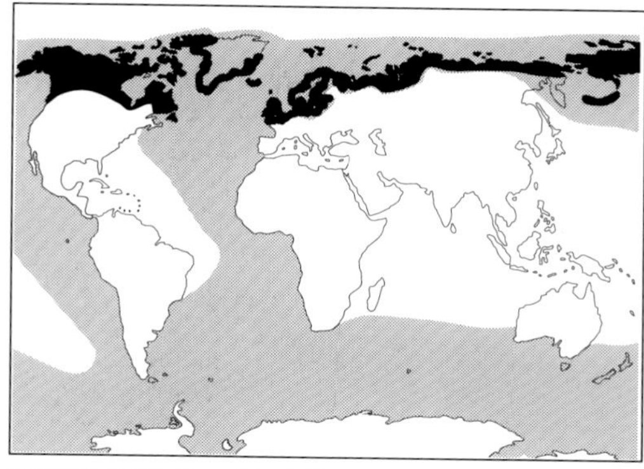

***MAP 10*** Distribution of Arctic Tern *Sterna paradisaea.*

## Moult

Moults more rapidly than other *Sterna* terns, resembling other long-distance migrants such as South Polar Skua *Stercorarius maccormicki.*

**Adult** has a complete moult to **winter plumage**. Moult takes place in the winter quarters. Rarely, a few feathers of forehead and body are moulted in late summer and early autumn (presumably nonbreeders or failed breeders), but otherwise shows no or only very limited moult before arriving in winter quarters. In late October-November (South Atlantic), the majority are in worn summer plumage. Inner primary, t1-2, head and underparts are moulted immediately after arriving in wintering area in (late September) October to early November.

Most of the moult takes place within a concentrated period in the pack-ice belt during the antarctic summer. Head, body, tail and wing-coverts have been moulted in January, t3 and t6 sometimes later (up to late February). The primaries are renewed in 2-3 (5) months (Ginn & Melville 1983). Birds from the South Atlantic had replaced 8 inner primaries in January-February (skins, ZMA, ZMO). Primary moult terminates from early February to early March. Birds from late February had p10 growing (skins, ZMA). Unlike Common Tern, moults all primaries once annually. Moult is poorly known, however, and probably just partial; old summer plumage may be partly moulted directly into new summer plumage in late winter.

**Adult** has partial moult to **summer plumage** before spring migration in early February-March. The moult includes head, body, tail (sometimes t6 and t1) and upperwing-coverts. In late February, 75-100% have summer-plumaged head and body (skins, ZMA). Rarely, 1-2 inner primaries are moulted before breeding.

**Juvenile** has a complete moult to **first-winter plumage** on arrival in winter quarters. Parts of the head, body and scapulars may be moulted during the final stage of the migration (from late October, exceptionally from late August). The moult is completed in February. Primary moult commences in December-January, and is completed in April-May. Possibly, birds in good condition may moult at the same time as adults. A bird from the Netherlands (January) had not started the moult (skin, NNH).

The subsequent moults are as for adult. A second-calendar-year individual from the North Atlantic in December had not begun the moult (skin, BMNH).

Moult to **second-summer plumage** possibly starts later than that of adults. Only partial summer plumage may perhaps be acquired, since typical second-summer plumage has the underparts a mixture of grey summer and white winter feathers, and some head feathers and coverts replaced. Like Common Tern, may arrest the primary moult, with 4-5 inner primaries renewed, before spring migration.

## Geographical variation

The species is monotypic. Geographical variation non-existent (Cramp 1985); see comments under Measurements.

### Measurements

In mm. Own measurements, Scandinavia, Finland, Netherlands, North Atlantic and Greenland, BMNH, NNH, ZMA, UZM, MN, NRM, ZML, ZMO, ZMU, ZMH. Juveniles August-September, 1st-summer birds North Atlantic June-August.

WING LENGTH

| | | | |
|---|---|---|---|
| Ad ♂ | 257-295 | (277.7) | n = 194 |
| Ad ♀ | 260-293 | (276.5) | n = 125 |
| Juv | 218-252 | (237.7) | n = 60 |
| 1st-summer | 245-269 | (255.5) | n = 28 |

• Birds from Finland (28 ♂♂, 11 ♀♀, ZMH) generally had shorter wing: average ad ♂ 274.2, ad ♀ 272.0 (own measurements).

TAIL FORK

(difference between t1 and t6)

| | | | |
|---|---|---|---|
| Ad ♂ | 78-133 | (105.3) | n = 186 |
| Ad ♀ | 72-126 | (98.7) | n = 125 |
| Juv | 28-62 | (48.1) | n = 68 |
| 1st-summer | 42-81 | (69.2) | n = 29 |
| 2nd-summer | 63-82 | (73.3) | n = 10 |

BILL

| | | | |
|---|---|---|---|
| Ad ♂ | 28.9-35.8 | (32.5) | n = 186 |
| Ad ♀ | 26.5-35.0 | (31.6) | n = 125 |
| Juv | 23.9-32.3 | (26.5) | n = 68 |
| 1st-summer | 28.3-32.5 | (30.8) | n = 29 |

BILL DEPTH AT GONYS

| | | | |
|---|---|---|---|
| Ad ♂ | 6.0-7.9 | (6.8) | n = 186 |
| Ad ♀ | 5.8-7.5 | (6.7) | n = 125 |
| Juv | 4.7-6.6 | (5.7) | n = 71 |
| 2nd-cal-yr | 5.3-7.2 | (6.5) | n = 26 |

BILL DEPTH AT REAR EDGE OF NOSTRILS

| | | | |
|---|---|---|---|
| Ad ♂ | 7.2-9.1 | (8.0) | n = 186 |
| Ad ♀ | 6.8-8.7 | (7.7) | n = 125 |
| Juv | 6.1-8.2 | (7.0) | n = 68 |
| 2nd-cal-yr | 6.9-8.7 | (7.7) | n = 29 |

TARSUS

| | | | |
|---|---|---|---|
| Ad ♂ | 13.2-17.0 | (15.1) | n = 185 |
| Ad ♀ | 13.1-16.9 | (15.0) | n = 125 |
| Juv | 12.9-18.0 | (14.9) | n = 69 |
| 2nd-cal-yr | 13.3-16.9 | (15.0) | n = 22 |

WEIGHT (in grams)

• May-August: ad ♂ 87-118, ad ♀ 99-119 (Cramp 1085)

• Juvs in north and west Europe: 76-110.

• Murmansk coast, breeding birds: ad ♂ 93-134 (107.3, n = 67), ad ♀ 89-129 (106.1, n = 31).

• Weddell Sea, antarctic winter, during moult: ad ♂ 116-154 (131.5), ad ♀ 121-133 (127).

# Aleutian Tern

*Sterna aleutica* Photos **108-111**

## Identification in the field

The Aleutian Tern breeds on islands and coasts in the northern part of the Pacific between east Siberia and Alaska. Surprisingly, however, the species has been found once in Britain (Weir 1983).

The proportions of this tern are much as those of Common Tern, but the black bill is longer and narrower, the wings generally longer and broader and the tail streamers shorter (stern shorter than on Common). It often looks bigger than the Common Tern, possibly because of its darker plumage (M. Ullman *in litt.*). The legs are at least as long as those of Common. Perched birds often lift their wings by 30°, so that head and wings are on the same level.

It is very elegant in flight and flies with slower and deeper wingbeats than Common and Arctic Terns, this especially noticeable on downstroke. The body rises and falls clearly with the wingbeats. Against the light, only the inner primaries are translucent.

**Adult in summer plumage** resembles something between Common Tern and Bridled Tern. The upperparts are dark grey (with very faint brown tinge at close range), with contrasting white rump, tail, fore and rear edges of wings and inner primaries. As on Common Tern, the darker outer primaries form a dark wedge against the paler inner primaries. The underwing is white with a dark bar across all the secondaries (the feature visible at longest range), but with a pale gap on the pale inner (translucent) primaries. The 5-6 outer primaries have broader dark tips than on Common Tern. When perched, the white leading edge to the inner wing is striking owing to the grey remainder of wing and body.

Bill, lores and crown are black. The forehead and a narrow line to behind the eye are white (as Little Tern or Bridled Tern). The throat is white, but the underparts are otherwise mid-grey. The legs are blackish.

**Adult winter plumage** has underparts white. Mask similar to that of Arctic Tern, and crown and some upperpart feathers white-spotted. Best separated from similar species by dark bar on secondaries. Tail grey with white sides.

**Juvenile** has dark brown cap, which is somewhat paler in front of the eye (reflecting adult's head markings). The bill is blackish with greyish-yellow base to lower mandible. Neck sides and breast sides and sometimes breast may be warm yellow-brown, and in such cases contrast with the otherwise white underparts.

The upperparts are scaly, as the dark grey-brown feathers have broad, warm sandy- to rusty-coloured edges. Narrow white leading edge to wing and white area across secondaries contrast with the rest of upperparts. Tail-coverts to tail are pale grey, but the central tail feathers have dark subterminal spots and pale edges. The primaries are dark, but paler inner primaries form a pale wedge as e.g. on young Herring Gulls *Larus argentatus*.

The subadult plumages are similar to adult winter, but upperparts generally paler and with more striking dark lesser coverts.

## Voice

Soft, far-carrying staccato *chif-chif-chu-ak*. The call is wader-like (N. Kjellén pers. comm.). Also a short, sharp *chit*, similar to

***MAP 11*** Distribution of Aleutian Tern *Sterna aleutica.*

**PLATE 25**

**Aleutian Tern *Sterna aleutica***

Size as that of Common Tern. In summer, easily distinguished by combination of dark grey upperparts and underbody, head pattern recalling Bridled Tern, black bill and legs and dark bars across under secondaries.

1 **Juvenile.** The darkest medium-sized *Sterna.* Note strong cinnamon tinge to most of upperparts and sides of breast.
2 **Juvenile.**
3 **Juvenile.**
4 **Adult winter (and probably even first-summer) (September).** Similar to first-summer Arctic Tern, but with darker secondaries.
5 **Adult summer.** Note white forehead, dark grey upperparts and underbody and dark secondary bar.
6 **Adult summer.** Upperparts show characteristic combination of medium-grey wings and back, white rump/tail and white front.
7 **Adult summer.**

call of Red-necked Phalarope *Phalaropus lobatus.*

### Moult

Probably similar to that of Common Tern, but later on average.

Moult to summer plumage includes inner 5 primaries (thus shows contrast in summer; *contra* Cramp 1985). Moult to winter plumage seemingly starts at end of August away from breeding grounds; birds at that time (Hong Kong) showed summer plumage, but single new feathers in upperparts, and some had moulted inner primaries and t6. Earlier birds in winter plumage in mid September (when most are in active moult) (Kennerley *et al.* 1993).

Immature and juvenile moults poorly documented. Lee (1992) mentions birds (first-summers?) moulting outer primary.

#### Detailed description

Length 32-34 cm, wingspan 75-80 cm.

**Adult summer plumage:** White forehead and line to above or behind eye, contrasting with black lores and mask over crown, ear-coverts and central parts of nape; white forehead 7-13 mm broad, 20-24 mm long. Upperparts medium-grey, possibly paler when fresh. Rump to tail white, but central tail-coverts and t1 can be grey. Leading and trailing edges of wing and tips of tertials white. Throat to upper breast white, with variable transition into grey breast and belly, which on fresh birds may have tinge of pink.

Underwing white with dark bar across secondaries. Secondaries have mid-grey outer webs and darker grey inner webs. Inner primaries mid-grey, outer primaries dark grey with faint silvery tint on outer webs. The inner webs of primaries have broad white bases to 5 cm from the tip. Leading edge of wing white. Bill and legs black.

**Adult winter plumage:** Much as adult summer, but head shows poorer contrasts as crown and lores are white or have fine white streaks. Winter head similar to that of Arctic Tern. Pale collar may be conspicuous against grey mantle.

Back feathers dark grey with variable white edges. Upperwing grey, lesser coverts darker. Contrast between back and rump/tail weaker than in summer plumage. Underparts white.

**Juvenile:** Forehead, lores and crown dark grey-brown to yellow-brown. Dark spot in front of eye. Ear-coverts and rearmost part of crown dark-streaked. With wear, head markings become whiter. Underparts white, with variable yellow-brown to grey-brown neck sides and breast sides (sometimes nape) which can form incomplete neck band. Secondaries dark.

Upperparts blackish-brown with sandy to rusty-coloured edges 1-3 mm broad, broadest on tertials. Greater wing-coverts mid-grey with diffuse

white edges. Primary coverts dark grey with narrow yellow-brown edges. Back sometimes a touch paler. Uppertail-coverts medium-grey with broad, but diffuse, white to yellow-brown edges and tips. Leading edge of wing white. Tail feathers pale grey with black V markings inside yellow-brown tips. Inner webs to t2-5 mostly grey, t6 white apart from grey tone to tip of inner web, yellow-brown tip and black subterminal spot on outer web. Primaries dark grey (darkest at tip) with silvery tinge and narrow yellow-brown tips (broadest on inner webs). Secondaries blackish-grey with broad white tips to inner webs and white fringes.

Yellow-brown feather tips are abraded during the autumn or 'whiten'.

**Measurements**

In mm. Own measurements, Alaska, Sakhalin, BMNH, NMNH.

**WING LENGTH**

| | | | |
|---|---|---|---|
| Ad ♂ | 262-282 | (271.8) | n = 20 |
| Ad ♀ | 260-281 | (271.5) | n = 21 |
| Juv | 260-277 | (269.6) | n = 12 |

**TAIL FORK**

(difference between t1 and t6)

| | | | |
|---|---|---|---|
| Ad ♂ | 70-115 | (92.7) | n = 20 |
| Ad ♀ | 70-113 | (86.7) | n = 17 |

**ALEUTIAN TERN** QUICK KEY TO IDENTIFICATION

1 **Black bar across underside of secondaries is visible even at a distance.**
2 **In adult summer plumage, black bill and white forehead combined with grey underbody unique.**
3 **Upperparts grey with white rump and tail.**
4 **Juvenile contrastingly patterned, with darker coloration on breast and belly and pale wedge on inner primaries.**

BILL

| | | | |
|---|---|---|---|
| Ad ♂ | 31.0-34.6 | (33.3) | n = 23 |
| Ad ♀ | 30.8-34.8 | (32.9) | n = 21 |

BILL DEPTH AT GONYS

| | | | |
|---|---|---|---|
| Ad ♂ | 5.5-6.7 | (6.2) | n = 23 |
| Ad ♀ | 5.3-6.6 | (6.2) | n = 22 |

BILL DEPTH AT REAR EDGE OF NOSTRILS

| | | | |
|---|---|---|---|
| Ad ♂ | 6.7-7.4 | (7.0) | n = 23 |
| Ad ♀ | 6.8-7.7 | (7.2) | n = 12 |

TARSUS

| | | | |
|---|---|---|---|
| Ad ♂ | 18.0-20.3 | (18.6) | n = 22 |
| Ad ♀ | 17.5-20.7 | (18.9) | n = 21 |

# Forster's Tern

*Sterna forsteri*

Photos **112-120**

### Identification in the field

Forster's Tern breeds in North America. It is nowadays an almost annual visitor to the British Isles in late autumn and winter (Alström *et al.* 1992).

Forster's Tern resembles the Common Tern, but is bigger, with relatively shorter wings, larger, more angular head with heavier bill and clearly longer and stronger legs. Apart from in adult summer plumage, it has a white head with black mask restricted to an oval-shaped patch on the ear-coverts. These head markings are unique among medium-sized terns, but are found again in the Gull-billed Tern, which is easily identified by its more powerful 'gull-breadth' bill and even longer, black legs. Note that subadult Arctic Terns often have a white crown, but invariably have a black band from eye to eye.

The flight silhouette recalls Common Tern, but the heavier head gives a front-heavy appearance, with shorter wings. Has elongated (cigar-shaped) body and long tail streamers (similar to Arctic Tern's). Against the light, only the inner primaries are translucent, less obviously so than on Common Tern. Larger head and bill together with deeper breast give a centre of gravity farther forward than on Common Tern.

Forster's Tern forages by plunging from a few metres' height, usually obliquely or vertically, rather like Arctic and Little Terns' persistent and aggressive diving. It is very manoeuvrable in strong winds, when dense flocks are reminiscent of Little Gulls *Larus minutus* or Kittiwakes *Rissa tridactyla* as they continuously 'attack' the wind. Compared with the Common Tern, Forster's copes better with strong head winds, and at sea appears to be as well adapted to strong winds as the Arctic Tern. It does, however, often catch flying insects using a much slower flight, in which it is buoyant and more elegant. Flight action is obvious at sheltered waters.

When perched, it recalls a long-legged Common Tern with paler primaries. The legs are longer and sturdier than those of both Common and Roseate Terns. The tail streamers often extend several centimetres beyond the stern, though this is just as much a result of the fact that the wings are shorter as that the tail streamers are long. Many, however, have substantially longer streamers than Common Terns in summer, comparable in length with those of Arctic and Roseate Terns.

The call is nasal and low, a deep 'zarrp' interspersed with a clicking note 'gik-gik' (unlike that of Common and Arctic).

**Adult in summer plumage** resembles Common Tern with white underparts and generally paler grey upperparts, on which fresh silver-grey primaries are the palest part; in spring, especially, the hand looks remarkably gleaming white. In sheltered surroundings (e.g. with inland breeders) the primaries suffer only minimal wear during the summer, but even worn primaries become only slightly darker. Adult Forster's Tern lacks Common Tern's distinct dark primary wedges. The rump is white to whitish-grey, contrasting with the back and the pale grey tail. Teh contrast may be striking in poor light, the impression is then rather like that of a male Hen Harrier *Circus cyaneus*, whereas strong sunlight gives rump and tail the same colour. The tail is pale grey with white outer web to the outer primary (Common and Arctic Terns have a white tail with black outer web to outer rectrix). At a distance the upperparts become rather uniformly pale. The tail streamers can approach those of Arctic in summer; on perched birds they project up to 3 cm beyond the tail (Wilds 1993). The underwing is similar to that of Common Tern, but the dark rear edge to the hand is paler, rather like that of Sandwich Tern in colour; the hand is framed by black outer webs to the outer primaries.

The head is much as that of Common Tern, but the cap is shorter and the white wedge between cap and gape broader; in addition, the dividing line is more uneven, with a dark area extending down in front of the eye. In total, the cap appears to 'sit higher up on the head' than on Common and Arctic Terns. The bill is orange-red in colour (and generally more orange), but generally has a broader black tip, covering up to 30%. Compared with Common's bill, it is more powerful and more characterful, with more obviously curved upper mandible and better-marked gonydeal angle. The long, sturdy legs are orange.

Perched birds are best distinguished from Common Terns by proportions, white underparts and silver-grey primaries, which are often paler than the upperparts. Identification is straightforward in spring, but as Common Tern gets paler with wear, and outer primaries of Forster's darken, identification in late summer is less easy. Note, however, that Forster's never shows dark webs in wing but just darker tips to outer primaries. In spring, Roseate Tern may create bigger problems, but note Roseate's slimmer, darker bill and even paler upperparts.

Adults moult into winter plumage early, and in September the vast majority bear the characteristic winter plumage.

**Adult in winter plumage** has a white head with black ear-coverts, the latter forming a well-demarcated, oval 'bandit's mask'; latter recalls that of Gull-billed Tern, but is normally more solidly black. Crown and nape are greyish-white with faint dark spots. Rarely, the nape is darker grey, which at a distance gives the effect of a complete black mask rather like that of Common Tern, but the crown is then contrastingly paler.

In autumn, new primaries are obviously paler than the coverts and back, and the rump generally paler than in summer plumage.

The bill is black, sometimes with paler base. The legs are red-brown to reddish-orange.

**Juvenile** is the palest and the most lacking in contrast of all juvenile *Sterna*. From September it resembles adult winter, but in the period immediately after leaving the nest site back and crown are tinged brown, though this is soon lost. During autumn, the upperparts are silver-grey with faint darker grey secondary bar and

---

**PLATE 26**

**Forster's Tern *Sterna forsteri***

Similar to Common Tern, but with longer, heavier bill and legs and larger head. In juvenile and winter plumages, head is white with a black 'bandit's mask' behind the eye, a feature shared only with the larger, heavier-billed and longer-legged Gull-billed Tern. In appearance a typical *Sterna*.

1 **Juvenile.** Recently fledged individual. For short period after fledging shows pale cinnamon tinge to head and mantle.

2 **First-winter.** Similar to adult winter, but with darker-centred tertials and coverts.

3 **Adult winter.** Very pale, with characteristic head pattern.

4 **Second-summer.** Similar to adult summer, but with white (or partly white) forehead and darker outer primaries.

5 **Adult summer.** Similar to adult summer Common Tern, but with white underparts, paler grey upperparts, silvery primaries and more orange bill and legs. Black bill tip typically broader. Unlike Common, outer tail feathers often penetrate some centimetres beyond wings.

1
2
3
4
5

bar on primary-covert tips. The lesser coverts can also be darker. The tertials have dark centres – often the only obvious age character in the field. The back feathers have at best faint dark subterminal spots. The head is similar to adult winter, but the nape is on average darker (Wilds 1993).

The inner tail is dark grey and contrasts with white outer tail feathers. The bill is much as adult winter plumage; legs brownish-red.

Like the adults, juveniles moult early in autumn. Thereafter they are most easily aged by dark-centred tertials, faint dark bars on secondaries and lesser coverts, and darker inner part of the tail.

**First-winter/first-summer plumage** is much as adult winter plumage, but the nape is often darker and, together with the ear-coverts, can form a mask similar to winter-plumaged Common Tern's. Of importance is the fact that the black oval behind the eye is the darkest part of the head. Most safely aged by darker secondary bar, sometimes dark bar across lesser coverts and paler mid-wing panel. The primaries are darker than the adult's; the outer primaries gradually darken, and in its first summer the bird can have a really dark hand. Tail often shows one or two darker grey feathers. In active moult during spring. Combination of winter head with darker 4-5 primaries is age-diagnostic in first summer. The bill is black, perhaps with slightly paler red base. The legs are more orange than on adults (J. R. Hough *in litt.*).

**Second-winter/second-summer plumage** is rather like adult, but in winter to spring has darker, more worn primaries. Typically the 4-5 outer primaries are darker than the rest of the wing in spring and early summer. They are replaced as autumn approaches. In second summer the head is variable. Some have an adult cap, but the majority have a white-flecked forehead (Wilds 1993) or white feathers in the crown. The bill is normally as that of the adult. Outer 4-5 primaries contrastingly darker than rest of wing.

## Voice

Typical call is a *keerr*, recalling Black-headed Gull *Larus ridibundus*, deeper and harsher than that of Common/Arctic, and a harsh *zaarrp* (like a higher version of Caspian Tern's). On breeding grounds, latter call often followed by two or three hard metallic notes, *gik-gik*.

### Detailed description

Length 33-36 cm, wingspan 73-82 cm.

**Adult summer plumage:** Cap black (shorter than Common Tern's, with wear showing brownish-black tinge). White wedge of 3-6 mm between gape and cap is narrowest in front of eye, broadest in centre of lores. Upperparts pale blue-grey, generally paler than on Common (but some are the same colour). Rump and uppertail-coverts white to whitish-grey, contrasting with grey back and tail; centre of tail rarely white. Fresh rectrices have diffuse whitish fringes. Outer tail feather has white outer web and tip. Remiges silver-grey, in fresh plumage contrasting with darker grey coverts and back; remiges have narrow white edges and inner webs, broadest on secondaries. Outer primaries have silvery-grey streak along shaft on inner webs, remaining primaries have grey inner webs with diffuse pale grey crescent at base. Leading edge of wing white. Underparts white, rarely (1.1%) with weak pale grey tinge to, especially, breast; exceptionally, with a very slight rosy tinge. Underwing markings similar to those of Common Tern, but dark tips to outer primaries dark grey rather than blackish.

With wear, upperparts, including remiges, become darker grey, outer primaries acquire more obviously dark tips above, tertials become browner, secondaries darker (can form narrow dark secondary bar) and nape grey-toned. The exposed parts of the primaries and tail feathers become darkest, reducing the contrast between remiges and back. On birds breeding in more sheltered environments, such as inland lakes, the primaries wear more slowly than on those from coastal localities (C. Wilds *in litt.*). White outer web of t6 contrasts well with narrow dark edge to inner web and remaining grey rectrices.

Bill orange to orange-red with black tip (15-25 mm on upper mandible); extreme tip occasionally pale. Summer bill is present April-August. Legs orange-red.

**FORSTER'S TERN** QUICK KEY TO IDENTIFICATION

1 **In all plumages except adult summer, white-headed with distinct black oval 'highwayman's mask' around eye.**
2 **Primaries often paler than rest of upperparts.**
3 **Tail grey with white outer webs to outermost feathers.**
4 **White rump contrasts with grey back and tail, creating pattern not unlike that of adult male Hen Harrier.**
5 **In adult sumer plumage, like a powerful, angular, long-billed and long-legged Common Tern with white underparts.**
6 **Perched adults have pale wingtips. Tail projects several centimetres beyond wings.**
7 **Juveniles are weakly marked; resemble winter-plumaged adult, but have dark-centred tertials and faint dark secondary bar, as well as shorter tail.**

**Adult winter plumage:** Head white with distinct, black 'highwayman's mask' through eye and ear-coverts. Nape greyish-white, sometimes with faint darker spots. Crown may have short, narrow dark streaks.

Wing markings depend on wear. In early autumn outer primaries are worn, but they are moulted during autumn and in September-October the hand is pale, with only the outer primary worn. The tail is moulted in summer, when contrast between new (pale) and worn (darker) rectrices can be distinct. In late autumn and midwinter all flight feathers are pale and fresh, apart from odd inner secondaries and rectrices.

Bill black, sometimes with brown to grey, orange-grey or reddish-grey base to lower mandible; extreme tip can be pale. Legs red-brown to reddish-orange, occasionally greyish-orange.

**Juvenile:** Feathers of forehead, crown, mantle, back, scapulars, tertials and short inner wing-coverts have pale grey to white tips and edges. Fresh crown and upperpart feathers have grey to yellow-brown or pale cinnamon-brown wash. Rump white to whitish-grey, occasionally with brown feather tips. Tail feathers grey with yellowish-brown or dark grey, diffusely marked tips; t6 has dark grey inner web and white outer web. Upperwing grey with faint dark secondary bar (and sometimes lesser-covert bar). Tertials and primary coverts have dark centres to outer part and narrow white to pale sandy edges. Primaries dark grey.

Underparts white. Nape to breast sides can be brown-toned or have faint grey-brown spots.

In late summer, the brown elements (which rarely can be seen up to October) are worn off and replaced by grey-brown or greyish-white.

Bill blackish horn-brown to black, with greyish-yellow or orange to pink base. Legs yellow-brown to orange-brown.

**First-winter plumage:** Much as adult winter, but forehead and crown more heavily dark-spotted. Tertials, secondaries and sometimes lesser coverts have dark centres. New inner primaries pale grey, gradually contrasting with dark, faded outer ones, which are moulted in the first summer. Legs generally more orange than on adult.

**First-summer plumage:** Much as first-winter plumage, but sometimes with black feather tips in crown, forehead and nape. Tail streamers shorter than adult's. Legs orange.

**Second-winter/second-summer plumage:** Much as adult, but 4-5 outer primaries dark and worn in autumn to midwinter. In March-April the next primary moult series commences, and towards May-June replaces inner 5-6; in late summer, 2-3 outer primaries are dark and worn. T4-5 darker than remaining rectrices. Has some dark-centred lesser and median coverts. Forehead feathers may show white bases (most obvious with wear). Bill base and legs paler orange-yellow than adult's.

**Third-winter plumage** and subsequent plumages as adult.

## Moult

**Adults** have a complete moult to **winter plumage**. The moult is earlier than Common Tern's, and commences in mid July to mid August with inner primaries. Feathers of the forehead and crown may be moulted from mid June, but majority still show a summer head in July. Moult of head, body and tail progresses rapidly. From September almost 100% have a winter head (eastern USA, end September to early October, pers. obs.); a few dark feathers are often retained in forehead and lores until end of October. The moult is completed in November-December, earlier than with Common Tern. Last to be moulted are the secondaries and t4-5. The primaries are moulted between July and October; 1 (2) outer primaries mostly unmoulted in September-October (over 90% in late September to early October in eastern USA had p10 worn); latest in growth up to November.

**Adults** have a partial moult to **summer plumage** in (January) February-March (mid April). The moult includes head, underbody, parts of mantle, back and scapulars and some tail feathers (t6 February/March to early April). Last to be

1
2
3
4
5
6
7

**PLATE 27**

**Forster's Tern *Sterna forsteri***

Flight silhouette similar to that of Common Tern, but relatively larger-headed with heavier bill. In most plumages head pattern is typical. Furthermore, white rump often stands out against pale grey upperparts and central parts of tail.

1 **Juvenile.** Recently fledged individual.

2 **First-winter.** Similar to adult winter, but with slightly darker secondaries and tertials.

3 **First-summer.** Similar to adult winter, but secondaries and unmoulted juvenile outer primaries dark.

4 **Adult in late stages of moult to winter plumage (September-October).** Moults early to winter plumage, head and body normally moulted August-September. Outer primaries moulted September-October.

5 **Adult winter.** After primary moult in autumn, appears very pale.

6 **Second-summer.** As adult summer, but with variable amount of white on forehead and darker tips to outer primaries. Never shows the typical dark wedge on primaries of Common Tern.

7 **Adult summer.** Similar to Common Tern, but underbody white and upper primaries as pale as - or paler than - inner wing. Note white rump against grey central areas of tail and back. Pale plumage as well as long tail streamers also recall Roseate Tern, which shows predominantly dark or all-dark bill, rosy or pale grey tinge to underbody, even paler grey upperparts, dark outer primaries and no dark trailing edge to primaries.

***MAP 12*** Distribution of Forster's Tern *Sterna forsteri.*

moulted are forehead feathers. Moult of inner primaries begins anew in January-February (Wilds 1993), and is arrested in spring when the innermost (2) 3-5 (8) primaries have been replaced.

**Juvenile** has a complete moult to **first-winter plumage** in autumn to midwinter. The earliest feathers moulted are in mantle and median coverts. Tail moult begins in December with t1; t4-5 (6) often not moulted before April-June. Retained juvenile lesser coverts and tertials are moulted in the following spring and summer (tertials sometimes in winter). Primary moult commences in November-January, and 3 inner primaries may be replaced by late January; in spring up to 5-6 inner primaries are moulted. A second primary moult series begins in April-September (Cramp 1985). The wing can be fully moulted by July-August (Wilds 1993), but many retain juvenile 4 (5) outer primaries and some secondaries in their first summer to second autumn.

Subsequent moults as for adult, but birds in **second-summer plumage** show active primary moult in April-September. Moult averages later than that of adults, e.g. primaries 4-5 in moult when adults are moulting 7-9 (August-September).

## Geographical variation

Monotypic. Populations from south-central USA have been described as '*litoricola*' (Oberholster 1874), said to be smaller (especially wings and tail) and paler than other Forster's. Although wings are on average shorter (♂ averages 259.3, ♀ 258.8), the differences are hard to discern; validity of subspecies seems dubious).

### Measurements

In mm. Own measurements, eastern and southeastern USA, BMNH, NMNH, NNH, NRK, UZM, ZMA.

WING LENGTH

| | | | |
|---|---|---|---|
| Ad ♂ | 245-275 | (261.2) | n = 70 |
| Ad ♀ | 255-277 | (260.8) | n = 41 |
| Juv/1st-winter | 236-262 | (252.2) | n = 54 |

TAIL FORK

(difference between t1 and t6)

| | | | |
|---|---|---|---|
| Ad ♂ | 79-137 | (102.8) | n = 54 |
| Ad ♀ | 74-121 | (95.3) | n = 39 |
| Juv/1st-winter | 38-58 | (45.0) | n = 46 |

• Tail fork ad winter 50-70, 2nd-summer 63-85.

BILL

| | | | |
|---|---|---|---|
| Ad ♂ | 35.9-43.0 | (39.9) | n = 76 |
| Ad ♀ | 35.4-41.3 | (38.4) | n = 46 |
| Juv/1st-winter | 30.0-41.0 | (37.3) | n = 51 |

BILL DEPTH AT GONYS

| | | | |
|---|---|---|---|
| Ad ♂ | 7.4-8.5 | (7.8) | n = 74 |
| Ad ♀ | 6.8-8.3 | (7.8) | n = 53 |
| Juv/1st-winter | 6.7-8.1 | (7.4) | n = 50 |

BILL DEPTH AT REAR EDGE OF NOSTRILS

| | | | |
|---|---|---|---|
| Ad ♂ | 9.0-11.0 | (9.4) | n = 81 |
| Ad ♀ | 7.7-10.8 | (9.2) | n = 47 |
| Juv/1st-winter | 7.8-10.0 | (8.9) | n = 51 |

TARSUS

| | | | |
|---|---|---|---|
| Ad ♂ | 21.5-25.8 | (23.8) | n = 67 |
| Ad ♀ | 21.3-25.6 | (23.0) | n = 46 |
| Juv/1st-winter | 21.2-25.7 | (22.5) | n = 50 |

# White-cheeked Tern

*Sterna repressa*

Photos **121-129**

### Identification in the field

The White-cheeked Tern breeds in the Red Sea, the Persian Gulf and in the northern part of the Indian Ocean. It is somewhat smaller than Common Tern, with relatively shorter and more slender wings and legs but longer Roseate Tern-like bill often drooping at tip. It is the darkest of the medium-sized *Sterna* species. The upperparts are dark grey with grey rump and tail. In flight, the underwing is characteristic: all remiges have a dark rear edge, creating a continuous dark trailing edge contrasting with pale central part of the wing, this accentuated by greyer lesser coverts. The paler mid-wing region can be visible through a telescope at a range of a couple of kilometres (Hirschfeld 1990).

The flight is powerful, with faster and deeper wingbeats than Common Tern's, and the body clearly moves up and down with the wingbeats. It forages most frequently by making short dips to the water's surface, and hovers and plunges less than other *Sterna* species; when it does hover, it does so low above the surface with raised wings.

**Adult in summer plumage** recalls a long-billed and long-tailed Whiskered Tern with attenuated rear end and shorter legs. It has a black 'tern cap', white cheek stripe and dark smoky-grey upperparts and underparts. The cheek stripe normally contrasts well with the black cap and grey underside. The stripe recalls that of adult Whiskered, but is often broader at the front (can extend over throat) and terminates farther forward on the neck sides. The grey underparts may have an element of white or be paler grey; the palest birds are close to the darkest Common Terns (especially of race *longipennis*). The tail may project some centimetres beyond the wings.

The underwing markings are conspicuous against the dark underparts and axillaries. The dark secondaries have a narrow but distinct white trailing edge.

The upperparts are uniform ash-grey, showing only poor contrast with the rump and tail. Back and rump have pale sides, and this is obvious when seen sideways on. Fresh primaries are a paler silver-grey than the rest of the upperparts, but they wear relatively quickly (an effect of strong sunlight?) and then become darker than the rest of the wing. Sometimes a dark bar may be seen on the lesser upperwing-coverts, especially the innermost ones. In sharp sunlight, the upperparts appear paler than the underparts. Dark line at the tips of the outer primaries is broader than on Common Tern.

The bill is red with black tip. It recalls Common's, but is longer and narrower, and generally with broader dark tip. Some, however, have an almost all-red bill.

The legs are red to orange with a brownish tinge, relatively shorter than those of Common Tern.

**Adult in winter plumage** has uniform grey upperparts with contrasting paler, silvery-grey primaries (darker on worn birds). The underparts are white, contrasting well with the darker upperparts. The head recalls that of Common Tern, but the mask is broader and more diffusely demarcated from the grey-spotted forehead and crown. The bill is black. The grey tail and rump, as dark as the back, are the most important character distinguishing it from similar species.

The underwing is as in summer plum-

1
2
3
4
5

**PLATE 28**

**White-cheeked Tern *Sterna repressa***
Size and structure similar to Common Tern, but with on average longer and slightly drooping bill. In all plumages has darker grey upperparts - lacking contrast between rump/tail and back.

1 **Juvenile.** Upperparts darker and more patterned than on Common Tern. Often shows darker centres to feathers of mantle, scapulars and tertials than shown.
2 **First-summer/adult winter.** Similar to Common Tern, but upperparts slightly darker with rump/tail concolorous with back. Black mask often broader than on Common Tern.
3 **Second-summer.** Similar to Common Tern of same age, but grey on both under- and upperparts darker.
4 **Adult summer plumage.** Similar to Common Tern, but underparts darker grey than on congeners, on darkest birds approaching adult summer Whiskered Tern, with similar white cheek stripe. This individual shows bright red legs and bill similar to Common Tern.
5 **Adult summer.** A dark-billed and dark-legged individual, looking similar to certain Common Terns of race *longipennis*. Note longer, slightly drooping bill.

age, but lesser coverts, too, may be pale, and pale mid panel is fainter.

**Juvenile** is reminiscent of a dark juvenile Common Tern, but, as adults, has a grey tail concolorous with the back. The mask is heavier and broader than on Common, less well demarcated from pale forehead and lores. The lesser coverts normally have darker centres than those of Common, and dark secondary bar is broader and more obvious than on most Common Terns. Upperpart contrast weak, as all coverts are dark grey (especially basal part). In fresh plumage, all upperparts have cinnamon fringes. The upperparts are dark grey-brown with narrow, pale feather edges. On perched birds, the dark-centred tertials contrast with paler primaries.

The bill is black; orange-red base present only on newly fledged young. The legs are yellowish-brown.

**First-winter plumage** recalls juvenile, but the mantle and back are uniform grey from the first autumn. Distinguished from adult winter by dark bar on lesser coverts and secondaries. In late spring and summer 4-5 outer primaries become blackish-brown, contrasting with new inner ones.

**First-summer plumage** is much as first-winter, but blackish-grey areas may be likely to appear on the underparts. Dark lesser-covert and secondary bars contrast well with the grey upperparts, which typically are paler (and browner?) than on adults. The bill is black, sometimes with red base. Legs dark. Similar to Common Tern, but upperparts uniform grey.

**Second-summer plumage** resembles adult summer plumage, but the cap is black with white forehead bar (often as a narrow white bar above bill base), and the dirty grey underparts have an element of white feathering. The upperparts are much as on adult, but with vestiges of dark bar on lesser coverts and secondaries. The bill varies from all black to much as adult summer.

## Voice

Recalls that of Common Tern, but a diagnostic, hoarse *kee-errr kerrit* or *kee-ceek* with accent on second syllable (on first syllable in Common) has been described (Britton 1982).

### Detailed description

Length 32-34 cm, wingspan 78-83 cm.

**Adult summer plumage:** Cap black (in fresh plumage glossy blue-black, with wear brownish). White area between lower lores and gape 1.5-3 mm. White moustachial stripe broadest in front of eye; can terminate behind eye but often continues to rear edge of cap. Throat grey to white (joining with moustachial stripe). Underparts including axillaries dark smoky-grey, darkest on belly. Underparts can be paler grey or white-flecked; in fresh plumage they often have a faint vinaceous tinge.

**WHITE-CHEEKED TERN** QUICK KEY TO IDENTIFICATION

1. **The darkest *Sterna* with black cap. Bill is slender and long.**
2. **Summer-plumaged adults have dark grey upperparts and underparts, and silver-grey primaries.**
3. **Black cap is separated from grey breast by broad white cheek stripe.**
4. **Bill red with black tip.**
5. **Underwing diagnostic: dark secondaries show good contrast with whitish median and greater coverts.**
6. **Lesser coverts and axillaries darker than median and greater coverts.**
7. **In all plumages, uniform grey upperparts lacking obvious contrast between grey back and tail distinguish this species from its congeners.**
8. **Facial mask in winter plumage is broader than that of Common Tern.**
9. **Juveniles rather like dark Common Terns, but with grey rump and tail, and also more uniformly dark back and tertials contrasting with paler grey primaries.**

Undertail-coverts pale grey. Underwing-coverts whitish-grey; lesser coverts darkest, pale mid panel contrasting with lesser coverts and especially with dark grey secondaries and primary tips. Primaries have broad Common Tern-like dark tips on underside.

Upperparts dark smoky-grey. Inner part of upperwing concolorous with back, but lesser coverts can be slightly darker. Secondaries dark grey with white tips. Primaries on fresh birds pale silvery-grey (paler than inner part of wing), but on worn birds darker brownish-grey and uniform with or darker than inner wing. Rump and tail grey; rump has white sides. Outer tail feathers have dark grey outer webs and up to 4 mm of pale colour at tips.

Bill orange to dark red with black tip (13-23 mm). Legs red to orange. 'Summer bill' acquired in March to early April (Arabia, north part of Red Sea) and retained until (September) October/November.

**Adult winter plumage:** Forehead and lores white, merging diffusely into dark-grey-streaked or -spotted crown, which is darkest at rear. Nape and ear-coverts black. Underparts white, sometimes tinged grey. Upperparts much as in summer plumage, but generally with more distinct dark bar on lesser coverts. Primary contrast depends on wear. Bill black from July to early spring (in some populations to May), any red being limited to base of lower mandible. Legs black with red tinge.

**Juvenile:** Head as adult winter plumage, but recently fledged young have yellow-brown to greyish-brown areas in forehead. Mantle, back, scapulars and tertials smoky-grey with broad white edges and yellow-brown to grey-brown subterminal spots. Rump, uppertail-coverts and majority of upperwing-coverts white-edged with slightly darker grey to grey-brown centres. Lesser upperwing-coverts darker grey with narrow yellowish-brown fringes. Fore edge of wing white. Greater coverts and remiges adult-like, but with tinge of brown. Fresh feathers have narrow white tips.

Tail feathers dark smoky-grey (darkest on outer webs) with brown-toned centres, broad white tips and narrow white inner webs. Underparts white. Bill black with pale orange to red base. Legs pale orange. Bill and legs soon become all black.

**First-winter/first-summer plumage:** Much as adult winter plumage, but with dark brownish-grey bar on lesser coverts (can be retained until following plumage). Outer 4-5 primaries worn and dark brown in first spring to autumn (July-August). Outer primaries have pale inner webs.

**Second-summer plumage:** Much as adult summer plumage, but cap is duller and browner, and forehead to bar above bill base is variably white. The crown, too, may be white-flecked. Underparts as adult, but normally with some areas of white. Occasional individuals at this age probably have pure grey underparts. Darker bar on lesser coverts generally more distinct than in adult summer plumage. Secondaries dark. Bill and legs much as adult, but bill generally has broader black tip, and can be all black. Tail streamers generally shorter than in adult summer plumage. Primary moult active during breeding season, when adults suspend the moult.

## Moult

**Adults** have a complete moult to **winter plumage**. The moult starts after the breeding season. Birds with a later moult cycle (e.g. October in Red Sea, Oman) have a correspondingly later moult and are in summer plumage up to September-October. Head, upperparts and underparts are moulted from September, beginning with forehead, some back feathers and scapulars. Tail is moulted in August-February (May), t1 first and t5-6 last.

Suspended primary moult (5-6 inners replaced prior to breeding) is resumed from mid July to late August or in September-October, depending on breeding season. At the same time a new moult series may begin in the inner primaries. Outer primaries are moulted in late December to early February; wings appear fresh in April-June.

**PLATE 29**

**White-cheeked Tern *Sterna repressa***

In flight, always separated from congeners by darker, uniform grey back, rump and tail. Underwing often striking, showing pale mid-panel against darker lesser coverts and secondaries.

1 **Juvenile.** Similar to Common Tern, but darker and less contrasting.

2 **First-summer.** Similar to Common Tern; note broader black mask and grey rump/tail.

3 **Adult winter.**

4 **Second-summer.**

5 **Adult summer (late breeding season).** This individual shows fresh, silvery-grey inner primaries. After primary moult cycle, all primaries may appear silvery in contrast to darker grey inner wing, but the contrast is soon lost through wear.

**Adults** have a partial moult to **summer plumage**. Moult includes head, body, 4-5 inner primaries and part of tail (usually t1-4). Remiges and rectrices are moulted from late December/January. First to be moulted are inner primary (plus retained

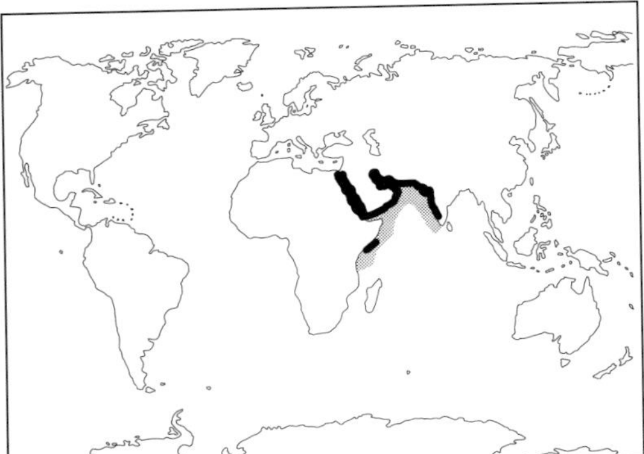

***MAP 13*** Distribution of White-cheeked Tern *Sterna repressa.*

outer primaries from previous moult) and t1. Primary moult is suspended late February to early April with inner (2-3) 4-5 primaries replaced. Head and body are moulted in February to early April. Cap is largely complete from late March, but a few white feathers may be present up to early April.

**Juvenile** has a complete moult to **first-winter plumage**. The moult commences with head, body, tertials and central tail feathers in September-November. Wing-coverts, remainder of tail and remiges are moulted from January-February (March). Primary moult slower than with adults. In first winter/spring, 4-5 (6) inner primaries are replaced. In summer, the moult may be suspended for periods of time. The moult is completed in August-November at the earliest, but normally in December-March (third calendar-year). A new moult series in the primaries may begin at about one year of age. Central tail feathers are replaced in June.

During summer of second calendar-year, the plumage is replaced directly by **second-winter plumage**. Later moult series presumably much as those of adults.

### Measurements

In mm. Own measurements, BMNH, NNM, Red Sea, April-July.

**WING LENGTH**

| | | | |
|---|---|---|---|
| Ad ♂ | 232-251 | (243.0) | n = 20 |
| Ad ♀ | 229-262 | (245.5) | n = 22 |
| Juv/1st-winter | 218-237 | (228.2) | n = 5 |

• Birds from Persian Gulf (May-June) average longer-winged: ad ♂ 241-252 (247, n = 5), ad ♀ 246-258 (250, n = 5) (Cramp 1985).

**TAIL FORK**

(difference between t1 and t6)

| | | | |
|---|---|---|---|
| Ad ♂ | 65-90 | (72.9) | n = 20 |
| Ad ♀ | 62-92 | (72.6) | n = 23 |
| Juv/1st-winter | 24-50 | (37.9) | n = 5 |

• Total tail length (Cramp 1985) in May-June: Red Sea, ad ♂ 131-154 (142, n = 9), ad ♀ 132-140 (136, n = 4); Persian Gulf, ad ♂ 145-157 (151, n = 3), ad ♀ 144-167 (152, n = 4).

**BILL**

| | | | |
|---|---|---|---|
| Ad ♂ | 34.4-38.0 | (35.9) | n = 23 |
| Ad ♀ | 33.7-36.7 | (35.1) | n = 22 |
| Juv/1st-winter | 28.6-34.1 | (32.2) | n = 5 |

• Birds from Persian Gulf, May-June: ad ♂ 36-39 (37.4, n = 4), ad ♀ 34-37 (35.7, n = 5) (Cramp 1985).

**BILL DEPTH AT GONYS**

| | | | |
|---|---|---|---|
| Ad ♂ | 5.9-7.0 | (6.4) | n = 23 |
| Ad ♀ | 5.6-7.0 | (6.3) | n = 22 |
| Juv/1st-winter | 5.5-6.6 | (6.2) | n = 5 |

**BILL DEPTH AT REAR EDGE OF NOSTRILS**

| | | | |
|---|---|---|---|
| Ad ♂ | 6.9-8.0 | (7.6) | n = 23 |
| Ad ♀ | 6.7-8.0 | (7.3) | n = 22 |
| Juv/1st-winter | 6.1-7.7 | (7.2) | n = 5 |

**TARSUS**

| | | | |
|---|---|---|---|
| Ad ♂ | 17.5-20.4 | (18.8) | n = 23 |
| Ad ♀ | 17.5-19.8 | (18.7) | n = 22 |
| Juv/1st-winter | 17.4-20.3 | (18.7) | n = 5 |

• Birds from Persian Gulf, May-June: ad ♂ 19-21 (19.7, n = 4), ad ♀ 18-20 (18.8, n = 5) (Cramp 1985).

**WEIGHT** (grams)

From Urban *et al.* (1986), Egypt

| | | | |
|---|---|---|---|
| Ad ♂ | 78-105 | (90) | n = 9 |
| Ad ♀ | 87-92 | (90) | n = 3 |

• Cramp (1985) gives ad ♂♂ with weight of 142 and 3rd cal-yr at 113, Laccadive Islands, India, February.

# Bridled Tern

*Sterna anaethetus* Photos **130-138**

### Identification in the field

The Bridled Tern is a tropical species which has been recorded occasionally in Europe, most often in summer.

It superficially resembles a large, long-winged and long-tailed juvenile Black Tern, but on perched birds the tail projects up to a few centimetres beyond the wings. It is the size of Common Tern, but heavier and longer-winged. The longer bill is black and as long as – or a little shorter than – the length of the head. The sturdy legs are black.

It has a purposeful and elegant flight, the body clearly moving with slow and elastic wingbeats. This species forages both by dipping towards the water's surface in Gull-billed or Black Tern fashion and by making short plunge-dives. It is marine and adapted to a life at sea, but is sometimes seen along coasts and in harbours.

**Adults** have black-and-white head markings, pale grey nape band and grey-brown upperparts. This tricoloured pattern quickly distinguishes the species from the larger Sooty Tern, the only species that presents a confusion risk.

**Adult in summer plumage** has head similar to Little Tern's. The white forehead comes to a point on each side halfway between bill base and the highest point of the crown, and forms a white triangle which gradually narrows towards the eye. It normally extends up to 1 cm behind the eye, but can end above the eye. The triangle contrasts clearly with the black lores and mask. The black loral stripe is uniformly broad between upper mandible and eye. Behind the eye, the lower edge of the black cap continues to the nape, leaving a pointed white wedge between the cap and the usually grey-toned breast (see Geographical Variation).

Cap and upperparts are separated by a whitish-grey nape band, though this can be difficult to see (Holman 1982; Harris 1988) and is usually absent in eastern populations. The upperparts are mid-brown, but the flight feathers somewhat darker. The contrast is, however, slight, and is most easily seen on perched birds. In flight, it has been noted at up to a few hundred metres' range (pers. obs.). The tail is grey-brown with white outer feathers, the latter variable (see Geographical Variation).

Breast and belly are white to greyish-white, normally darkest on the belly. Underwing-coverts are white, the bases of the primaries pale grey and the tips of secondaries and primaries, together with outer web of outermost primary, dark grey (Lithner 1982; Harris 1988). White inner webs to the 3 outer primaries form a white 'fan' at leading edge of wing, contrasting somewhat with the greyer inner primaries – a character unique among *Sterna* species (Cramp 1985; Harris 1988). The contrasts on the underwing are more diffuse compared with Sooty Tern's black/white.

The black bill is a little shorter than the length of the head. The legs are black and fairly sturdy.

**Adult winter plumage** is paler and more diffusely patterned than summer plumage, as crown and lores are pale-spotted and less well demarcated from the forehead. The white supercilium is often broader behind the eye. The mantle feathers, and sometimes the scapulars, have pale edges, giving a white-peppered appearance.

**PLATE 30**

**Bridled Tern *Sterna anaethetus***

1 **Juvenile.** Variable. This individual is rather typical. Others have much darker and more uniform upperparts and just weakly marked pale supercilium.

2 **Adult summer.**

**Juvenile** has a greyish-white forehead and crown, diffusely separated from black mask from eye to nape. Often the broad white supercilium contrasts with the grey lores (latter occasionally as a rounded spot in front of eye). The rear crown is spotted black, and the pale nape band may be lacking altogether. The head markings vary. Some have predominantly pale crown, while others have the face similar to adult winter plumage. Mantle, back and upperwing-coverts are brown with cream-coloured to white feather edges, which are broader than in adult winter plumage. The upperwing is brown with darker bar on lesser coverts and blackish-brown remiges. Tail and tail-coverts are brown; the rectrices have greyish-white tips, but lack the adult's white outer webs.

The underparts are greyish-white to white. Breast sides and sometimes flanks are usually grey-brown. Bill and legs are black, but can have a blue tinge.

Certain individuals are all dark on upperparts and have a dark head, with only weak pale supercilia.

**First-winter plumage** is much as adult winter plumage, but juvenile wing and tail are retained. Compared with adult, the crown is more clearly white-streaked, and contrast between dark lesser coverts and paler remaining coverts is sometimes obvious.

**First-summer plumage** is much as adult summer plumage, but outer tail feathers are shorter, and lacks adult's white on outer feathers. The head markings are more diffuse than in adult summer plumage. Adult plumage is said to be acquired within 22 months (Alström *et al.* 1992).

## Voice

Most typical call is a yapping *wep-wep*,

like that of Black-winged Stilt *Himantopus himantopus.*

**Detailed description** *Sterna anaethetus melanoptera* **(West Indies and Atlantic)**

Length 30-32 cm, wingspan 77-81 cm.

**Adult summer plumage:** Forehead to halfway between bill base and highest point of crown, and extending to eye, white; white may terminate at eye but normally continues as a narrow line 1-9 (10) mm behind eye. Forehead patch 5.5-7 mm deep from bill base to centre of forehead, 20-29 mm from bill base to behind eye. Black loral stripe from base of upper mandible to eye is uniform in width. Crown, ear-coverts and upper nape raven-black.

Lower nape and uppermost mantle pale grey to greyish-white, normally contrasting with cap and upperparts, especially on worn birds.

Upperparts mid-brown, often tinged olive on scapulars, tertials, and median and greater coverts. Lesser coverts and primary coverts black, leading edge of wing white. Mantle, back and up-

## PLATE 31

**Bridled Tern *Sterna anaethetus***

Size close to that of Common Tern. Upperparts dark and contrasting with black hood, often separated by pale neck-bar. White frontal patch similar to that of Little Tern.

1 **Juvenile.**

2 **Winter plumage.**

3 **Adult summer.** Note white front contrasting with darker upperparts. Tail pattern (white only on outer tail feather) as well as absence of pale neck-bar are features of eastern race *antarctica* and *anaethetus.* Atlantic *melanoptera* shows larger amount of white (including two outer tail feathers) and broader pale neck-bar.

4 **Adult summer.** Underwing pale with broad dark trailing edge, but paler bases to primaries (compare Sooty Tern).

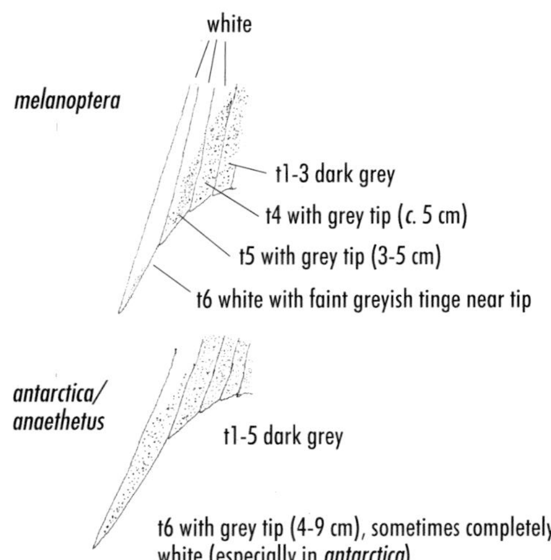


***FIGURE 6*** Bridled Tern *Sterna anaethetus.* Tail pattern in different subspecies.

pertail-coverts brownish-grey to mid-grey, showing at best a weak contrast with remaining upperside. In fresh plumage, upperparts tinged grey.

Underparts white to greyish-white, darkest on belly, and greyest in fresh plumage. Tail feathers mid-grey with white bases and inner webs to t2-3; t4 normally has white outer web; t5 white with grey near tip; t6 white. Worn tail feathers have more obvious grey tips.

Remiges black, fresh feathers with grey tinge. Secondaries have narrow white tips and broad white edges to inner webs. Primaries have white 'crescents' at base, gradually decreasing towards inner feathers. White inner webs to at least 3 outer primaries form white area on underside of hand. Underwing-coverts and axillaries white.

Bill and legs black.

**Adult winter plumage:** As adult summer plumage apart from following. Lores spotted white (sometimes all white) and crown white-streaked. White supercilium up to 1 cm behind eye, generally broader than in summer plumage. Nape band white with some dark streaks and spots. Upper mantle pale grey with white feather bases and tips. Scapulars, tertials and new median and greater wing-coverts dark olive-grey with narrower greyish-white edges. Lower mantle, back and rump mid-grey with white edges, tips and sometimes visible white bases. Underparts white. Tail as in summer plumage, but outer feathers have greyer tips and 5-6 cm of grey at tips of t5-6.

In worn plumage, upperparts may be very pale (Cramp 1985).

**Juvenile:** Forehead patch and crown greyish-white, crown becoming gradually dark-spotted towards rear. Broad white supercilium reaches behind eye. Lores white or grey with black spots and black crescent in front of eye. Ear-coverts blackish-brown to black with narrow white streaks. Head markings vary: some have black U-shaped band from behind eye to nape (similar to winter-plumaged Whiskered Tern). With wear, mask becomes blacker and more distinct.

Mantle medium-grey with white to pale grey feather bases. Upperparts otherwise mid-grey to grey-brown with up to 5 mm of cinnamon-brown to yellow-brown or white feather edging, broadest on back; feather centres can be darker grey-brown. Lesser coverts uniformly dark, darker than remaining coverts. Rump and uppertail-coverts dark brown with narrower pale edges.

Birds with more uniformly dark upperparts and narrower pale feather edges are regular – in extreme cases, the upperparts are entirely dark, and the head dark with only weak pale supercilium. Such birds also have broader dark grey breast sides.

Tail dark grey-brown with up to 2 mm of brownish-white to white at tips, and variable narrow white outer web to t6, or with grey-brown to yellow-brown mark near tip. Inner web of t6 grey-white to 3-5 cm from tip. Remiges adult-like but lack grey tinge. Secondaries darker, sometimes with narrow white edges.

Underparts white, tinged grey in fresh plumage. Neck sides and throat sides variably grey to yellow-brown, can form diffuse 'Black Tern patch' (according to Cramp 1985, most obvious on individuals with broadest dark nape band). Flanks sometimes grey.

Bill and legs adult-like, but bill shorter and sometimes with blue-grey base.

**First-winter plumage:** Much as adult winter, but pointed and very worn outermost primaries, secondaries and some coverts juvenile until age of 9-12 months (Cramp 1985). This plumage is replaced directly by **second-winter plumage**, which is identical to adult winter.

## Moult

**Adult** has a complete moult to **winter plumage**. The moult begins towards end of breeding season with innermost primary, sometimes with odd feathers in head and on back. The moult intensifies after breeding season. After about two months, inner 2-4 primaries plus most of head and body have been renewed. Primary moult lasts 6-7 months, and is followed by a new moult series (in parts of the tropics, every 7th-8th month). Last to be moulted are a number of tertials, tail, mantle/back, tail-coverts and some wing-coverts. Tail moult begins at same time as primary moult and is carried out rapidly: Cramp (1985) mentions that the tail is normally completely moulted when the central primaries are moulting, but sometimes later; one specimen (ZMA) had replaced t6 while p 10 was in growth. Tail-moult sequence is t1-t6-t3-t2-t4-t5, sometimes with t6 before t1.

**Adult** acquires **summer (breeding) plumage** in a partial moult, which, for birds which breed every 12 months, includes head and neck, mantle and at least parts of the tail. In addition, a variable number of other body feathers are moulted. For details on birds with shorter moult cycles, see Cramp (1985).

**Juvenile** has a complete moult to **first-winter plumage**, 3-6 months after fledging. Head, mantle and t1 are moulted first. Primary moult begins at the age of 4-7 months.

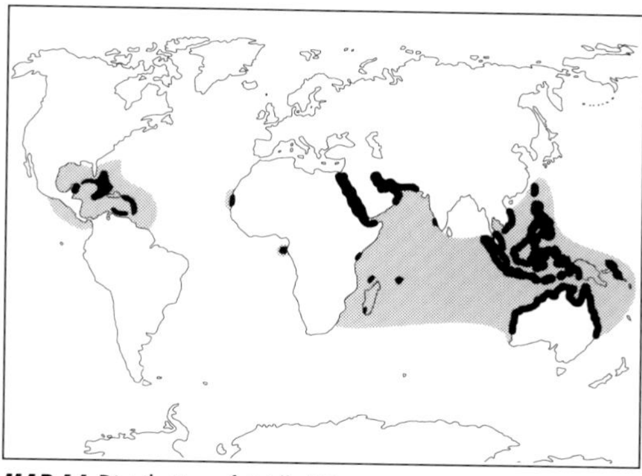

***MAP 14*** Distribution of Bridled Tern *Sterna anaethetus.*

**BRIDLED TERN** QUICK KEY TO IDENTIFICATION

1. **Dark tern with tricoloured upperside: black mask, pale grey nape band and brown upperparts.**
2. **Triangular white forehead patch continues up to 1 cm behind eye.**
3. **Bases of underside of primaries pale and contrasting diffusely with dark edges and tips.**
4. **In juvenile and winter plumages, more diffuse head markings with broader white supercilium and pale-patterned lores, crown and upper mantle.**
5. **Younger birds have suggestion of a dark 'Black Tern patch' on neck sides.**
6. **Outer 1-2 tail feathers predominantly white.**

## Geographical variation

The race *melanoptera* (West Indies and Atlantic) is described above. It normally has breast and belly uniformly white. The upperparts are normally browner than in the race *anaethetus* (see below). Grey nape band normally shows good contrast with cap and upper mantle. Bill generally more powerful than in other races (see Measurements).

Most constant differences are in the tail. Race *melanoptera* has t6 white (sometimes with slight grey tip to inner web); t5 is white with 3-5 cm of grey at tip (broadest on inner web); t4 has about 5 cm of grey at tip, but can have some white at base of outer web.

Races *antarctica* (Red Sea to Indian Ocean) and *anaethetus* (Sunda islands to Australia) have darker upperparts, in particular darker mantle, concolorous with coverts. Pale nape band is narrower than in *melanoptera,* and normally absent. Belly generally greyer than that of *melanoptera,* contrasting with breast. The tail has less white than *melanoptera*: t6 has white base of outer web, but 4-9 cm of tip grey; on some t6 is pure white (especially in *antarctica*); remaining tail feathers dark.

Racial differences involving the body are most distinct during the breeding season; for the tail, throughout the year.

**Juvenile**s almost identical, but white on t6 extends up to 5-7 cm from tip on *anaethetus* and 3-5 cm from tip on *melanoptera.*

### Measurements

In mm. From Cramp (1985) and own measurements, NNH, NRK, UZM, ZMA, ZMO. Race *melanoptera* (Caribbean and West Africa); *antarctica* (Red Sea to Madagascar); *anaethetus* (Indonesia and northern Australia).

WING LENGTH

| | | | |
|---|---|---|---|
| *melanoptera* | | | |
| Ad ♂ | 255-274 | (265.3) | n = 11 |
| Ad ♀ | 253-263 | (259.0) | n = 8 |
| *antarctica* | | | |
| Ad ♂ | 245-266 | (267.1) | n = 15 |
| Ad ♀ | 242-262 | (254.0) | n = 14 |
| *anaethetus* | | | |
| Ad ♂ | 245-289 | (268.6) | n = 24 |
| Ad ♀ | 249-282 | (263.3) | n = 15 |
| All races | | | |
| Juv ♂ | 235-258 | (252.0) | n = 15 |
| Juv ♀ | 235-252 | (243.8) | n = 9 |

TAIL FORK

| | | | |
|---|---|---|---|
| *melanoptera* | | | |
| Ad ♂ | 80-95 | (85.9) | n = 12 |
| Ad ♀ | 80-101 | (87.8) | n = 8 |
| *antarctica* | | | |
| Ad ♂ | 73-110 | (87.2) | n = 9 |
| *anaethetus* | | | |
| Ad ♂ | 78-113 | (93.4) | n = 11 |
| Ad ♀ | 90-108 | (102.3) | n = 7 |

• In winter plumage, 60-80.

BILL

| | | | |
|---|---|---|---|
| *melanoptera* | | | |
| Ad ♂ | 39.5-43.0 | (40.8) | n = 10 |
| Ad ♀ | 37.6-40.1 | (38.4) | n = 11 |
| *antarctica* | | | |
| Ad ♂ | 39.0-46.6 | (42.3) | n = 15 |
| Ad ♀ | 38.0-41.1 | (40.2) | n = 8 |
| *anaethetus* | | | |
| Ad ♂ | 38.5-44.2 | (42.0) | n = 29 |
| Ad ♀ | 37.5-42.0 | (39.8) | n = 17 |

• Juv 36.0-40.5 (37.5, n = 4).

BILL DEPTH AT GONYS

| | | | |
|---|---|---|---|
| *melanoptera* | | | |
| Ad ♂ | 8.0-9.6 | (8.6) | n = 10 |
| Ad ♀ | 7.6-9.0 | (8.3) | n = 8 |
| *antarctica* | | | |
| Ad | 6.3-7.2 | (6.7) | n = 11 |
| *anaethetus* | | | |
| Ad ♂ | 6.3-7.2 | (6.7) | n = 10 |
| Ad ♀ | 6.4-7.5 | (7.1) | n = 8 |

BILL DEPTH AT REAR EDGE OF NOSTRILS

| | | | |
|---|---|---|---|
| *melanoptera* | | | |
| Ad ♂ | 9.0-10.7 | (9.5) | n = 10 |
| Ad ♀ | 9.0-9.5 | (9.3) | n = 8 |
| *antarctica* | | | |
| Ad | 7.9-9.4 | (8.6) | n = 8 |
| *anaethetus* | | | |
| Ad ♂ | 7.9-9.4 | (8.5) | n = 10 |
| Ad ♀ | 7.6-8.4 | (8.1) | n = 8 |

TARSUS

| | | | |
|---|---|---|---|
| *melanoptera* | | | |
| Ad ♂ | 18.9-22.1 | (20.6) | n = 12 |
| Ad ♀ | 19.2-22.0 | (20.6) | n = 8 |
| *antarctica* | | | |
| Ad ♂ | 17.3-22.1 | (20.6) | n = 15 |
| Ad ♀ | 19.0-21.1 | (20.0) | n = 14 |
| *anaethetus* | | | |
| Ad ♂ | 18.7-23.0 | (21.5) | n = 24 |
| Ad ♀ | 18.3-22.0 | (20.8) | n = 17 |

# Sooty Tern

*Sterna fuscata*

Photos **139-146**

### Identification in the field

The Sooty Tern is a black and white tropical tern the size of a Sandwich Tern. It is normally seen far from land, and is a characteristic bird of coral islands and atolls in the tropics: flocks of almost green-glossed Sooty Terns against a blue sky and a green-blue, salt-scented sea are the quintessence of what is genuinely tropical!

Sooty Tern is a big, heavy, long-tailed and long-billed tern with long tail streamers. It has a powerful flight with deep, sometimes almost skua-like, driving wingbeats. It spends most of its time in the air, and is normally seen on land for any longer periods only in the breeding season. It often soars high in the sky. Foraging is usually in huge flocks, which prefer to snatch up fish from the water's surface rather than plunge-dive.

**Adult** is highly characteristic and generally speaking can be confused only with Bridled Tern. It is, however, somewhat bigger, longer-winged and more black-and-white with distinctly blackish upperparts: in very sharp sunlight, it can, it is true, appear somewhat paler, but a warm brown tinge can then be seen (Harris 1988). Black cap continues directly into black upperparts and upperwings via a narrow stripe through the nape. Very striking, too, is the underwing: all remiges are blackish-grey, contrasting clearly with white coverts. The underwing is then more obviously bicoloured and contrasty compared with that of Bridled Tern.

**Adult in summer plumage** has a black cap contrasting with a broad white forehead patch, the latter as a rounded white blaze. The white reaches to the middle of the forehead, and ends roundly or at an acute angle in front of the eye; it does not extend behind the eye as on Bridled Tern. The black loral stripe is broadest at the eye, and becomes progressively narrower towards the gape. The black facial mask often bulges behind the eye, where it is broader than on Bridled. The mask joins directly with the uniformly black/brown-black upperparts through a narrow, consistently black nape band. The upperparts are uniformly dark, but with white outer tail feathers. The upperside contrasts greatly with the white underside, which in sharp sunlight over a blue-green sea (e.g. at coral reefs) acquires a bluish-green coloration! It is normally, however, difficult to perceive the faint grey tinge to the belly. Worn birds become more brown-toned on the upperparts.

**Adult winter plumage** is as summer plumage, but the upperpart feathers have variable white fringes.

**Juvenile** is quite unlike the adult, though equally characteristic. It is sooty-brown with very distinct white to sandy-coloured spots at the tips of the upperpart feathers (creating obvious pale-spotted pattern). Forehead is sometimes a shade paler and contrasts with a black patch in front of the eye, which is visible only at close range. The leading edge of the wing is dusted white. The underparts are grey-brown with pale grey lower belly, vent and underwing-coverts, the latter contrasting well with dark remiges. Lesser coverts and sometimes axillaries are normally darker, and a broad pale central panel is then produced on the underwing. The remiges are in principle the same colour as on adults, but can be a shade paler.

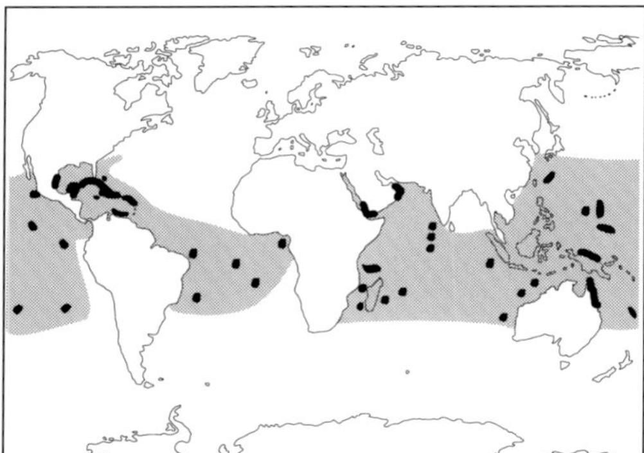

***MAP 15*** Distribution of Sooty Tern *Sterna fuscata.*

Under certain conditions, the juvenile recalls a big, long-winged Black Tern, but is easily distinguished by size, longer wings and slower flight, pale panel on wing-coverts and obvious tail streamers.

**First-winter plumage** is much as juvenile, but forehead, nape and underparts are paler.

**First-summer plumage** is something between juvenile and adult plumages. The underbody is variably brown- or grey-patterned, especially on breast and flanks, the crown is white-flecked and the outer tail feathers are grey.

The subsequent plumages are adult-like, but can have dark spots on white areas of the plumage.

## Voice

Noisy, a seething racket being heard from colonies. The call is a characteristic *wide-a-wake*, or *kerr-wack-a-wack*, loud and piercing.

### Detailed description

Length 33-36 cm, wingspan 82-94 cm.

**Adult summer plumage:** Forehead patch white, broadest and most rounded at the sides (seen head-on, sometimes like two white blazes, rather like males of *Ficedula* flycatchers). The blaze is rounded or angled in front of the eye; it is 8-11 mm deep, and 18-25 mm long from bill base to rear edge. Black loral stripe from base of gape to eye broadens gradually towards eye (broadest on males, on which it can be up to 6-7 mm in front of eye). Loral stripe continues into black mask over crown and ear-coverts, and via narrow black stripe on nape to black upperparts. In fresh plumage, cap is glossy blue-black.

Leading edge of wing white. Underparts white, with faint grey tinge on flanks and belly in fresh plumage. Tail feathers have black outer webs and blackish-grey inner webs; t6 has white outer web and inner part of inner web, while up to 9 cm of outer part of inner web is mid-grey. Remiges black with grey base to inner webs of primaries, most obvious on the outermost; underside of remiges blackish-grey. Underwing-coverts and axillaries white. Tips of greater primary coverts sometimes grey-toned. Bill and legs black.

In worn plumage, white feather bases are revealed in central nape and upper mantle and can form a faint white neck band. The upperparts become brown-tinged, and white on outer tail feathers is reduced. May retain black outermost primary (with white tip) from winter plumage.

**Adult winter plumage:** Much as adult summer plumage, but lores, crown and mantle spotted white, hindneck and uppermost mantle sometimes greyish-black with narrow white feather edges and bases. Back, tertials and rump black to grey-black with broad white edges of up to 2 mm (may be lacking). Underparts white.

T6 black with white tip (up to 6 mm) and grey base to inner web and sometimes with grey tinge to outer web. Upperwing-coverts often a mixture of black and brown feathers (palest at tips). New feathers can have narrow white tips. Sometimes does not acquire a winter plumage, but summer plumage is moulted into the following summer plumage.

**Juvenile:** Blackish-brown with white to yellow-brown feather tips on upperparts, broadest on scapulars and tertials. Forehead can be slightly paler. Rear lores black. Underparts dark grey-brown; lower belly, vent and underwing-coverts pale grey. Lesser underwing-coverts and sometimes axillaries normally darker, sometimes dark grey-brown. Pale underwing-coverts usually appear as a pale central area in the wing. Tail black with yellow-brown tips to central feathers.

Leading edge of wing white to greyish-white. Remiges greyish-black (fresh feathers are greyest) with narrow white tips to secondaries and inner primaries. With wear, upperparts become browner and pale feathers tips more obvious, especially on scapulars. A suggestion of pale feather bases may be visible on head and body.

> **SOOTY TERN** QUICK KEY TO IDENTIFICATION
>
> 1 **Very characteristic long-winged and long-tailed tern with black upperparts and white underside.**
> 2 **Rounded or slightly angled white forehead patch does not extend behind eye.**
> 3 **Underwing shows good contrast between white coverts and black remiges.**
> 4 **Juveniles are dark with white-peppered upperparts and pale lower belly and underwing-coverts (especially medians and greaters).**

Bill and legs black. Recently fledged young sometimes have greyish-red base to upper mandible and a greyish-red tinge (on photographs).

**First-winter plumage:** Much as juvenile apart from following. Forehead, lores, throat and to a lesser extent crown are spotted brown or grey. Throat has black spots and streaks, most obvious on lower throat, where a dark throat bar may be formed. Pale areas contrast weakly with black facial mask (as on adult). Upperparts dark brown or blackish-grey with white feather tips to scapulars and tertials. Some grey-tipped feathers may be present on upperparts. Belly dark grey with an element of paler grey. Underwing-coverts and tail-coverts pale grey.

Tail as adult winter. Juvenile remiges present until age of 9-10 months, gradually wearing to brown. Bill and legs black.

**First-summer plumage:** Much as first-winter plumage, except throat, lower belly and undertail-coverts paler, sometimes greyish-white.

**Second-winter/second-summer plumage:** Much as adult, but with dark-spotted underside, especially on breast and flanks (until up to 5 years of age on a few per cent) (Cramp 1985).

## Moult

Varies according to breeding season. Populations may, depending on water temperature, nest twice annually (but probably different individuals).

Following data from birds with 12-month breeding cycle.

**Adults** moult to '**winter plumage**' at end of breeding season, when innermost primary and parts of head, mantle/back and tail are changed. When the 2-3 innermost primaries are new, the body is normally in winter plumage. Failed breeders may moult earlier, and replace up to 4-5 inner primaries on the breeding grounds. Primary moult lasts about 7.5 months.

**Adults** have a partial moult to '**summer plumage**' soon after the moult to the previous plumage has ended. The moult includes head, body, tail and some inner primaries. The tail is moulted in the following sequence: t6-t1-t2-t5-t4-t6-t1-t2-t5-(t3-t4); sometimes t1 is moulted before t6.

Birds with a shorter moult cycle acquire only partial winter plumage, as a rule including some feathers of head, mantle/back and scapulars. Primary moult as given above. In the tail, normally only t6 and t1 are moulted (sometimes also t2 and t5) twice annually. Birds breeding every half-year do not acquire winter plumage, but summer plumage is instead replaced by another summer plumage and breeding takes place with primary moult suspended (Cramp 1985).

**Juvenile** moults to **first-summer plumage** at the age of about 6 months. The moult commences with head and upperparts and is followed by primaries and underparts. When 2-4 inner primaries have been replaced, the rest of the plumage has been renewed. Tail and tertials are moulted last.

## Geographical variation

Slight. Races *fuscata* (Caribbean, Atlantic and West Africa) and *nubilosa* (Red Sea to Southeast Asia) are the same size. Nominate *fuscata* has white underparts (including underwing-coverts). Race *nubilosa* has a grey tinge to belly and underwing-coverts in fresh plumage, the grey being lost with wear.

### Measurements

In mm. Own measurements, NNH, NRK, UZM, ZMA, ZML. Combined measurements from *fuscata* (Caribbean and West Africa) and *nubilosa* (Indian Ocean from Yemen to Australia and New Zealand).

**PLATE 32**

**Sooty Tern *Sterna fuscata***

Distinct, black and white sea tern. Larger than Bridled Tern, with cap and upperparts concolorous, shorter, more rounded white forehead patch and more contrasting underwings (primaries blackish). In flight, elegant.

1 **Juvenile.** Rather pale-patterned individual. Others are almost uniform sooty-brown with buff rather than white tips to upperpart feathers.

2 **Adult summer.** Note black cap concolorous with rest of upperparts. Rounded white frontal patch does not reach behind eye.

WING LENGTH

| | | | |
|---|---|---|---|
| Ad ♂ | 280-305 | (294.0) | n = 22 |
| Ad ♀ | 276-302 | (289.0) | n = 17 |
| Juv ♂ | 276-291 | (284.4) | n = 10 |
| Juv ♀ | 270-285 | (278.9) | n = 19 |

• Race *nubilosa* (Southeast Asia to Australia): ad ♂ 293-305 (297.3, n = 12), ad ♀ 270-302 (291.8, n = 6). Nominate *fuscata* (south Caribbean): ad ♂ 277-297 (288.3, n = 10), ad ♀ 280-291 (283.7, n = 3). Own measurements, NNH, NRK, UZM, ZMA.

TAIL FORK (difference between t1 and t6)

| | | | |
|---|---|---|---|
| Ad ♂ | 85-124 | (101.5) | n = 7 |
| Ad ♀ | 98-124 | (111.0) | n = 3 |
| Juv ♂ | 39-43 | (41.7) | n = 7 |
| Juv ♀ | 37-55 | (46.3) | n = 8 |

**PLATE 33**

**Sooty Tern *Sterna fuscata***

1 **Juvenile.** Dark, with varying pale underwing-coverts and central hindbelly. Superficially resembles odd-patterned, large and slender marsh tern *Chlidonias*, but with longer and more pointed wings and clearly forked tail.

2 **Juvenile.** Upperparts beautifully patterned dark and pale.

3 **First-summer.**

4 **Adult summer.** Note contrasting black and white plumage.

5 **Adult summer.**

6 **Adult summer.**

• Measurements given are from breeding season. In 'winter plumage' tail difference is smaller: 55-87 (70.8, n = 19).

• Race *nubilosa* (Southeast Asia to Australia): ad ♂ 83-101 (92.0, n = 11), ad ♀ 60-120 (74.0, n = 4). Nominate *fuscata* (south Caribbean): ad ♂ 89-124 (96.0, n = 4), ad ♀ 71-97 (85.0, n = 4).

BILL

| | | | |
|---|---|---|---|
| Ad ♂ | 40-46 | (42.3) | n = 23 |
| Ad ♀ | 38-43 | (40.9) | n = 13 |
| Juv ♂ | 35.6-39.0 | (37.7) | n = 4 |
| Juv ♀ | 34.4-40.2 | (37.1) | n = 4 |

• Race *nubilosa* (Southeast Asia to Australia): ad ♂ 39.8-48.9 (43.0, n = 11), ad ♀ 37.3-43.2 (41.3, n = 9). Nominate *fuscata* (south Carib-

bean): ad ♂ 37.2-45.0 (41.4, n = 10), ad ♀ 43.3-46.7 (44.6, n = 3).

**BILL DEPTH AT GONYS**

| | | | |
|---|---|---|---|
| *nubilosa* (Southeast Asia to Australia) | | | |
| Ad ♂ | 7.3-9.2 | (8.0) | n = 11 |
| Ad ♀ | 6.8-8.0 | (7.4) | n = 8 |
| *fuscata* (south Caribbean) | | | |
| Ad ♂ | 7.4-8.4 | (7.9) | n = 10 |
| Ad ♀ | 7.3-8.0 | (7.7) | n = 8 |

**BILL DEPTH AT REAR EDGE OF NOSTRILS**

| | | | |
|---|---|---|---|
| *nubilosa* (Southeast Asia to Australia) | | | |
| Ad ♂ | 8.9-10.5 | (10.0) | n = 11 |
| Ad ♀ | 8.1-9.9 | (9.2) | n = 6 |
| *fuscata* (south Caribbean) | | | |
| Ad ♂ | 9.4-10.4 | (9.8) | n = 8 |
| Ad ♀ | 9.2-10.0 | (9.5) | n = 8 |

**TARSUS**

| | | | |
|---|---|---|---|
| Ad ♂ | 21-25 | (23.4) | n = 25 |
| Ad ♀ | 22.1-28.0 | (25.1) | n = 16 |
| Juv ♂ | 20.4-24.4 | (22.6) | n = 4 |
| Juv ♀ | 19.9-21.7 | (20.6) | n = 4 |

• Race *nubilosa* (Southeast Asia to Australia): ad ♂ 21.0-24.8 (22.9, n = 16), ad ♀ 21.7-24.0 (22.7, n = 10). Nominate *fuscata* (south Caribbean): ad ♂ 20.4-23.2 (22.4, n = 7).

**WEIGHT** (in grams)

• Florida, spring, mean weight 179-205, dependent on condition. Of 8,700 individuals, Dry Tortugas, Florida, average 189. Juvs weigh about 175 on leaving nest site (Cramp 1985).

# Little Tern

Photos **147-155**

*Sterna albifrons*

### Identification in the field

Little, Least and Saunders's Terns are the smallest terns. The Little Tern is only the size of a ringed plover *Charadrius*, and in shape resembles a half-sized Sandwich Tern. Little Tern gives the impression of a small, white, over-active and almost aggressive coastal bird which flies fast and purposefully – like a bird in a hurry moving over the water in almost tern-like or ringed-plover-like flight! In the breeding season it also shows periods of slower, elegant flight.

The Little Tern hovers at a few metres' height with downward-pointing bill (when it recalls a white Great Grey Shrike *Lanius excubitor* or a gigantic butterfly) and plunge-dives directly towards the water's surface, rising again after a few seconds. It usually forages over shallow water near the shoreline, but sometimes several hundred metres out, where it may hover at heights of up to 10 m.

The Little Tern is large-headed, with a long and narrow bill about the same length as the head. The pointed wings, especially seen against the light, appear narrow, with the remiges (except the dark outer primaries) translucent. Arm and hand on a bird in active flight are almost uniform in width. The body is streamlined and slender, with no obvious centre of gravity. The tail is shorter than that of other native terns, especially when seen against a light background, when the tail streamers disappear. During the summer, the tail length has been estimated at 1.2-1.5 times the breadth of the wings at their base.

Perched birds are short-legged and compact, with flat head drawn down between the shoulders and the long bill held horizontally.

The Little Tern is in itself very characteristic. Great difficulties arise, however, when separating the closely related species (races?), Saunders's and Least Terns. Identification in winter and immature plumages is normally not possible even in the hand.

**Adult in summer plumage** has a black cap and white forehead, the latter narrowing gradually in a triangle towards the eye. The loral stripe is black, broadest on males, on which it gradually becomes broader towards the eye. The yellow bill has a black tip and looks like a matchstick stuck on to the head. The upperparts are pale blue-grey with black outer 1 (2-3) primaries, which form a distinct black leading edge to the outer wing. The rump is paler grey and the tail pure white. The legs are yellow to orange-yellow.

From July-August the inner primaries are moulted, and elements of white appear in the crown. The bill can darken from August.

**Adult in winter plumage** has a dull black, grey-spotted mask which is diffusely demarcated from the white-flecked crown. Black spot in front of eye stands out against white lores and face. The upperparts are much as in summer plumage, but lesser coverts become darker and the tail greyer. The wing markings depend much on degree of wear and moult.

In midwinter the bill is black. The legs are grey or brown, sometimes tinged yellow.

**Juvenile** is smaller and more compact than adults, with more rounded wingtip; in the period immediately after leaving the nest site it recalls a pale-winged ringed plover, as it has a more uncertain and flapping flight than adults. In plumage it is rather like juvenile Sandwich and Roseate Terns. The upperparts are tricoloured, with darker leading edge to wing (lesser coverts and outer primaries), pale grey or yellow-brown mantle/back and coverts and white secondaries and inner primaries. Mantle/back have black V markings, which as early as late summer are replaced by pure grey feathers. Rump and central tail feathers are grey, but outer tail feathers white. Dark tips to the tail feathers can form a faint dark tail band.

Forehead and crown initially have a yellowish-brown to cinnamon-brown tinge, but soon (from July-September) become white. From the central crown backwards, grey-brown streaks merge into the dark, very narrow facial mask. At close range the big eye is clearly accentuated by a white eye-ring, but at a distance they become one with a black triangle from in front of the eye backwards. The underparts are white, sometimes with a faint brown-toned 'Black Tern patch' on breast sides.

The bill is brownish-black, with variable paler yellowish base or edges after fledging. The legs are greyish-yellow, sometimes orange-toned.

**First-winter plumage** is much as adult winter, but the head is darker, as the crown is more distinctly spotted dark. The bill is black and the legs orange-red. Ageing of Little Terns apart from in juvenile and adult summer plumages is, however, risky.

**First-summer plumage** recalls adult winter plumage, but shows features approaching summer plumage. Dark grey lesser coverts, grey greater primary coverts and worn, grey-toned outer primaries are retained from juvenile plumage. The head can be much as in winter plumage, but some have a more summer-like head. Bill and legs have a tinge of yellow. Not uncommonly the central primaries are in active moult in summer, creating a 'notch' or gap between new inner (pale) and worn outer (dark) primaries.

**Second-winter plumage** recalls adult winter plumage, but can probably be distinguished by a combination of dark lesser-covert bar and good contrast between new inner and worn outer primaries (Chandler & Wilds 1994).

## Voice

Harsh; a monosyllabic *ket* or *ket-ket*, or *kweek*, which is heard frequently from foraging birds. Often uttered as a double-note.

**Detailed description** *Sterna albifrons albifrons* **(Europe eastwards to central Asia, and North Africa)**

Length 22-24 cm, wingspan 48-55 cm.

**Adult summer plumage:** White triangular forehead patch to above centre of eye 8-12 mm broad (broadest on females) above bill base, 15-20 mm long (from bill base to behind eye). Crown, ear-coverts and loral stripe black. Males generally have broader black loral stripe, which becomes progressively broader towards eye and terminates squarely around bill base; depth at bill base 2.5-3.5 mm, at eye 4.5-6 mm. Females have more uniformly broad and usually narrower black loral stripe (3-4 mm). Upperparts pale blue-grey. Blue tinge, together with white edges to larger scapulars and tertials, soon abraded. Greater primary coverts sometimes brownish. Rump white, in fresh plumage (spring) with faint pale grey tinge. Tail white or with variable pale grey tinge: t1 can be grey, t2-3 can have faint pale grey tinge on outer webs; about 10% have faint grey tinge to outer webs of t4-5; t6 normally white. Even on the most grey-toned individuals, however, there is always some contrast between paler rump/tail and darker grey back, or white inner part of tail feathers contrasting with grey tinge to outer part. T1-2 rarely almost as dark as back. Extremely rarely, the tail is grey like the back (Denmark, May, UZM 45073). Underparts white, sometimes with grey tinge to body, especially on individuals with grey-tinged rump and tail (Cramp 1985). Alula dark grey.

Outer (1) 2-3 primaries dark grey to black, contrasting well with rest of upperwing, forming blackish leading edge to hand. Up to three generations of primaries may be present. In north Eu-

rope, the majority have 3 old (outermost) primaries but a number have 2-4 (5); 1-2 old primaries in the breeding season is more common farther south. A few per cent in north Europe have only the outermost primary dark (see Cramp 1985). Secondaries pale grey with white tips. Leading edge of wing, underwing-coverts and axillaries white.

Bill yellow with (2) 4-11 mm of black at tip. A few per cent have pure yellow bill; only exceptionally is black bill tip lacking within European populations (Glutz *et al.* 1982). Cramp (1985) states that 15% lack black tip (especially during late summer). From early August the bill blackens from the base; from September birds are seen with all-black winter bill. It is not rare for the upper mandible to be shorter than the lower mandible, presumably through having been broken off. Legs yellow to orange-yellow, deepest in colour in the breeding season. Males have on average a more obviously orange bill.

**Adult winter plumage:** Forehead, lores and crown white with variable grey tinge and dark spots. Narrow black mask from eye through ear-coverts is broadest at the nape. Nape feathers are white-fringed, on the most marked individuals forming a white central area on the nape. White feather edges wear off during the autumn. Upperparts much as in summer plumage, but dark lesser

***PLATE 34***

**Little Tern *Sterna albifrons*, Saunders's Tern *Sterna (a.) saundersi* and Least Tern *Sterna (a.) antillarum*.**

Three small terns, very closely related (may be all races of same species). In all plumages other than adult breeding almost identical, and probably not safely identifiable in the field. These are the smallest of all terns, appearing just half the size of Sandwich Tern. The flight action is decidedly forced, at times appearing almost wader-like (especially in recently fledged juveniles, which have blunter wings).

1 **Little Tern, juvenile.**

2 **Little Tern, adult winter/first-summer.**

3 **Little Tern, adult summer.** White frontal patch triangular, frequently reaching just behind eye.

4 **Least Tern, adult summer.** Head pattern identical to that of Little Tern.

5 **Saunders's Tern, adult summer.** White frontal patch shorter and squarer than on Little Tern, not reaching behind eye.

**PLATE 35**

**Little Tern *Sterna albifrons*, Saunders's Tern *Sterna (albifrons) saundersi* and Least Tern *Sterna antillarum*.**

1 **Little Tern, juvenile.** Superficially like Sandwich Tern in miniature. Typical individual with whitish secondaries and scaled upperparts.

2 **Little Tern, juvenile moulting into first-winter.** From late summer, upperside is a mixture of juvenile and uniform pale grey feathers.
Note: Individuals with dark secondaries are not infrequent, although they may occur relatively more frequently among Saunders's Tern. More research is needed.

3 **First-winter/adult winter.** Most are inseparable after December-January. First-summers retain winter plumage.

4 **Little Tern, adult summer.** Note white forehead patch, narrowing behind eye, and white rump.

5 **Little Tern, adult summer.** Characteristic, with long and slender yellow bill with dark tip, pale grey upperparts, and narrow dark line on leading edge of wing created by worn outer (1)2-3 primaries. White rump and tail positively identify this individual as Little Tern *albifrons*, but individuals with greyish tinge to rump and middle parts of tail occur. These areas are rarely concolorous with back, as bases of rump feathers normally are whiter (see Saunders's and Least Terns).

6 **Least Tern, adult summer.** As Little Tern, but note rump and most of tail grey, concolorous with back. Adult male has a distinct call, *ki-riik*, similar in tone to Little Tern's, but with rhythm and pitch as call of European Oystercatcher *Haematopus ostralegus*.
May show slightly grey tinge to underparts (especially breast) (very rare in Little Tern).

7 **Saunders's Tern, adult summer.** Typical individuals may be identified by combination of shorter (rounded) white frontal patch, not reaching behind eye, paler and uniform grey upperparts and blacker (broader) area on primaries than on Little Tern. Many intergrades occur in breeding areas of Saunders's Tern, making safe field identification very difficult.

**LITTLE TERN** QUICK KEY TO IDENTIFICATION

1 **Only half the size of other terns.**
2 **Forehead white in all plumages, extending very narrowly to behind eye.**
3 **Bill yellow with black tip.**
4 **Tail and rump white, sometimes tinged grey, especially on t1-3; t5-6 normally white (see Saunders's and Least Terns).**
5 **White rump contrasts with grey back and any grey tail feathers.**
6 **In breeding season, 2-3 outer primaries are blackish-grey, contrasting with grey of rest of upperwing.**
7 **Juveniles and first-winters resemble half-sized Sandwich Terns.**

coverts form a dark covert bar. Rump to tail grey-toned, and usually contrasting less with back, though t6 always white. Underparts white.

Appearance of primaries depends on moult/wear. Up to September-October outermost primaries are blackish and contrast with paler central and inner ones. After moult in November-December outer primaries are pale grey with silver-grey tinge, but towards spring they become darker and from February-March they show contrast with grey central and pale grey inner primaries.

Bill black to horn-coloured with black tip from September; in winter black. Acquires 'summer bill' from mid February, at same time as moult to summer plumage. Legs dark greyish-yellow or brown-toned.

**Juvenile:** Lores, forehead and crown pale yellowish-grey. Crown has brownish-grey to black streaks. Mask from in front of eye to ear-coverts and nape blackish-brown, in fresh plumage with narrow sandy-coloured fringes; nape sometimes white in centre. Mantle/back, scapulars and tertials pale grey to yellowish-brown with white edges and black to blackish-brown U-shaped spots, creating scaly pattern. Lower back to tail pale grey with white feather edges and tips. Tail feathers pale grey with black spots and V markings near tips; t6 (5) normally white. Tail-coverts pale grey with broad white edges; appear pure white at a distance.

Underparts white, with faint yellowish-brown tinge to breast and flanks when fresh, sometimes as breast-side patches rather like those of juvenile and winter-plumaged Whiskered Tern. Secondaries and inner primaries pale grey to whitish-grey. Outer primaries blackish-grey with narrow white edges, latter broadest (about 1 mm) on innermost feathers. Upperwing-coverts grey with pale yellow-brown to greyish-white edges and with black V-shaped subterminal spots on inners and sometimes longest lesser coverts. Lesser coverts and primary coverts greyish-black with narrow grey tips.

From late July yellow-brown tinge disappears, and the face becomes whiter.

Bill brownish-black, with paler greyish-yellow base on fledging; occasionally only tip and edges are dark. Legs greyish-yellow, often with orange tinge.

**First-winter plumage:** Much as adult winter apart from juvenile primaries, tail and some wing-coverts, which can be replaced in October-November. Distinguished by fresh, grey-toned outer primaries showing poor contrast with rest of primaries (on adult, clear contrast exists between black outers and paler inners). In November-January outer primaries are worn (fresh on adults), in February-April new or growing in. Second moult series begins in inner primaries (normally 1-3 innermost new; 3-5 on adults).

**First-summer plumage:** Much as adult winter/first-winter plumage apart from scattered black feathers in crown and a few grey mantle feathers. Primary moult may continue in summer, or be suspended with innermost 1-2 new (from third moult series), while primaries 2-4 are worn.

**Second-winter plumage:** Much as adult winter plumage apart from relatively fresher outer primaries.

**Second-summer plumage:** As adult summer plumage, but with element of grey-brown in primary coverts. In addition, some white-tipped crown feathers and remnants of dark on lesser coverts may probably be present in this plumage.

## Moult

Complex; from age of barely one year, three different generations of primaries are present. All moult series commence with replacement of inner primary, but outer 2 (3) primaries are renewed only once per year (winter). The moult is arrested at beginning of the breeding season. This moult is very unusual among West Palearctic terns, but occurs also with Saunders's and Least Terns, Roseate Tern and the *Chlidonias* terns.

**Adult** has a complete moult to **winter plumage**. Primary moult begins in late June to late August with inner primaries: in mid August-September inner 1-5 (7) primaries are renewed. The moult is suspended during the migration, but is resumed in winter quarters, when it terminates with outer primaries in December-January. In October-December (before the worn, outer primaries have been replaced) a new moult series commences with inner primaries.

Moult of body and head starts in mid July (exceptionally, from early July). In Scandinavia this includes only scattered feathers in the crown (sometimes lores). Feathers of central forehead and very front of crown are moulted first. Most of the moult is said to take place at stop-over sites during the autumn migration. In the Netherlands about 50% had a dark bill and almost fully moulted head in mid August to early September. Lesser coverts may be changed from early August (skins, ZMA). The earliest birds in winter plumage have been noted near the winter quarters in early September. Tail moult begins with t1 at the same time as the inner primaries are replaced; t1-2 are replaced in late summer, t3-5 normally in September-October; t6 may be renewed before t3-5, but may also be moulted in midwinter. A new moult series in the tail may begin in late winter and spring.

**Adult** has a partial moult to **summer plumage** from late February to erly April. The moult includes head, body, wing-coverts and some tail feathers. Inner primaries are moulted once more in February to mid March. The moult is arrested before nesting, with inner (1) 2-4 (5) primaries replaced (when 7-9 have been renewed from the first series). In the breeding season, the outer 2 (3, exceptionally 4) primaries are 5-7 months old and therefore very dark from wear. Inner primaries may be replaced in July, so four generations of primaries can be present in midsummer.

**Juvenile** has a complete moult to **first-winter plumage**. The moult starts in late July with mantle/back and scapulars. In August-September head and body, tertials and some wing-coverts are moulted. During early part of autumn migration mantle/back and scapulars are a mixture of juvenile and first-winter feathers. In mid to late August normally 50-75% of

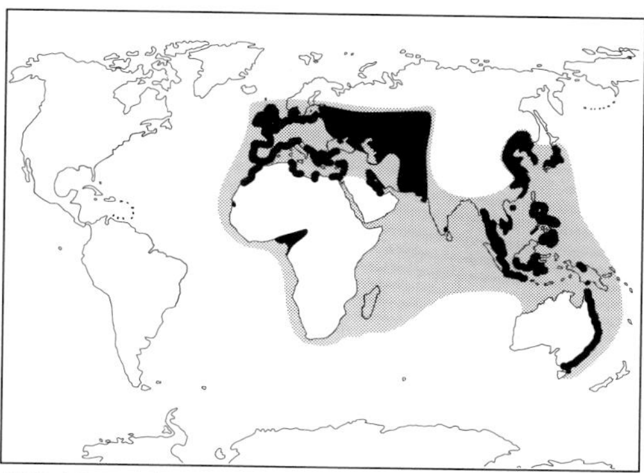

***MAP 16*** Distribution of Little Tern *Sterna albifrons.*

the upperpart feathers have been replaced, but birds with entirely juvenile upperparts appear up to the end of August to mid September. The majority, however, are in first-winter plumage in September-October, apart from remiges and rectrices and some wing-coverts, which are moulted late September-December beginning with central tail feathers and inner primaries (can be replaced from late August; in October up to 4 inner primaries may have been replaced: Baker 1993; Serra 1993). The first primary moult ends in April-May, but is arrested at primaries 7-8. Second moult series begins with inner primaries in February-March and is arrested in mid May, when (1) 3-5 inner primaries have been replaced.

A **first-summer plumage** is not normally acquired, but odd black feathers may appear in the crown and some grey feathers in the upperparts. Some begin a third primary moult during summer of second calendar-year (from May), when second series has reached outer 7th-8th primary. This series is suspended around the middle of the hand before the autumn migration. In June three generations of primaries: inner 1-3 are new, 3-5 central ones are moderately worn, but the outers (up to 50%) are juvenile. Some second-calendar-year birds have four different generations of primaries, as inner primaries may be moulted again in July. For full details on moult, see Cramp (1985).

## Geographical variation

Slight. Birds from southern Mediterranean and Middle East average smaller and narrower-billed than those from northwest Europe. More often lack black bill tip than do north European populations.

Race *guineae* (West Africa) is generally smaller than nominate race. Bill more commonly wholly yellow. Rump and tail often grey, t6 white. Tail can be darker grey than on Saunders's Tern. Some are inseparable from nominate; validity of the race possibly dubious. Populations from the Persian Gulf often have grey rump and tail.

Race *sinensis* (including *'pusilla'*) (India and east Asia) has grey rump and t1-3, and may show white rump/tail (especially eastern populations); t4-5 white, often with grey tinge to outer webs and outer part; t6 white (grey on fewer than 1%). Bill yellow with up to 6 mm of black at tip. Wing 161-193 (176.4, n = 56 skins, BMNH, NMNH). Unlike other races, *sinensis* shows whitish primary shafts. Tail streamers generally longer than on Saunders's Tern, up to 68 mm. Many are intermediate between Little and Saunders's, e.g. having Little Tern's head markings and grey rump and tail (skins, BMNH). In structure and size, *sinensis* seems close to Fairy Tern *S. nereis* of Australasia and Yellow-billed Tern *S. superciliaris* of South America. Populations from Australia and east Asia have white rump and tail (much as nominate *albifrons*).

### Measurements

In mm. Own measurements, BMNH, MN, NNH, NRK, UZM, ZMA, ZML, ZMO, ZMU, west Europe, Scandinavia and Siberia. Adults April-August, juveniles August-September.

**WING LENGTH**

| | | | |
|---|---|---|---|
| Ad ♂ | 168-187 | (177.2) | n = 65 |
| Ad ♀ | 167-183 | (175.1) | n = 45 |
| Juv | 151-171 | (167.6) | n = 48 |

• Birds from south Portugal, and North Africa to Middle East average smaller: ad ♂ 170-180 (175) (Cramp 1985). Birds from Russia: ad ♂ 165-187 (174.7, n = 32), ad ♀ 165-180 (171.5, n = 16) (Glutz *et al.* 1982). For Britain, Massey (1978) gives 160-179 (170.8, n = 41 ads).

**TAIL FORK**

| | | | |
|---|---|---|---|
| Ad ♂ | 25-49 | (40.7) | n = 64 |
| Ad ♀ | 25-43 | (33.3) | n = 45 |
| Juv | 12-21 | (16.2) | n = 44 |

**BILL**

| | | | |
|---|---|---|---|
| Ad ♂ | 27.4-34.0 | (30.2) | n = 64 |
| Ad ♀ | 26.2-32.3 | (28.9) | n = 45 |
| Juv | 20.0-29.2 | (25.1) | n = 48 |

• Massey (1978) gives 23.3-35.0 (29.7, n = 41 ads).

**BILL DEPTH AT GONYS**

| | | | |
|---|---|---|---|
| Ad ♂ | 4.8-6.2 | (5.5) | n = 65 |
| Ad ♀ | 4.7-5.8 | (5.0) | n = 45 |
| Juv | 4.1-5.4 | (4.8) | n = 49 |

**BILL DEPTH AT REAR EDGE OF NOSTRILS**

| | | | |
|---|---|---|---|
| Ad ♂ | 5.8-7.4 | (6.5) | n = 65 |
| Ad ♀ | 5.9-7.1 | (6.3) | n = 43 |
| Juv | 5.1-6.8 | (5.7) | n = 49 |

**TARSUS**

| | | | |
|---|---|---|---|
| Ad ♂ | 14.6-20.0 | (17.1) | n = 65 |
| Ad ♀ | 14.6-19.5 | (16.0) | n = 44 |
| Juv | 13.5-17.7 | (15.5) | n = 43 |

• Hario (1986) gives 14-20 (17, n = 157 ads).

**WEIGHT** (in grams)

Ad ♂ (Scotland and Netherlands) 50-63.

# Least Tern

*Sterna antillarum*

Photos **156-160**

### Identification in the field

The Least Tern is, generally speaking, identical with the Little Tern, but shows a grey rump and central part of tail concolorous with the back. Proportionately, it is a trifle smaller, with shorter legs, relatively slimmer bill and, on adults, generally longer tail streamers. T1-4 are grey, t5 grey or with white inner web, and t6 white with grey tinge to central and outer parts of inner web (sometimes white).

In **adult summer plumage** the majority have (1) 2 dark outer primaries, rarely 3 from end of May. Black loral stripe much as Little Tern's, but some (males) have broad black lores which are on average broader than Little's (male 3-4.5 mm at gape, female 2-3.5 mm), with narrower white wedge between lores and gape (1.5-2 mm). Upperpart coloration a shade more bluish-grey than on Little Tern. White forehead patch 12.5-18 (20) mm from bill base to above eye, normally shorter than on Little Tern, rarely extending behind eye. Some populations possibly show grey tinge to underbody more frequently than Little Tern (especially between south-central USA and Caribbean). The bill is yellow with (0) 1-8 (9) mm of black at tip. Legs reddish-orange (Massey 1978); sometimes a more greyish-yellow than on Little Tern (photographs, USA).

In **adult winter plumage** very like Little Tern, but tail and rump much as in adult summer plumage.

**Juvenile** much as juvenile Little, but dark V markings and spots generally more rounded (U-shaped), broader and browner, and dark bar on lesser coverts more distinct. Upperpart feathers have whitish to pale yellowish-brown edges in fresh plumage. Head rather like that of juvenile Little Tern; the mask can be pale-spotted on nape. Rump pale grey with narrow, pale yellow-brown edges. Underparts white with faint yellow-brown tinge. Tail band greyish-brown.

Legs black to pink, greyish-orange or pale-spotted (Massey 1978).

**First-winter plumage** much as Little Tern, but yellowish-brown and brown tinges may be retained until early winter. Legs black to orangey.

**First-summer plumage** as adult winter, but forehead and crown generally mottled paler and lesser coverts darker. Most of tail darker.

### Voice

Male's contact call is a hoarse *ki-dik*; this call is typically two-toned, similar in rhythm to call of European Oystercatcher *Haematopus ostralegus*. Other calls deeper and less sharp than Little Tern's, but several calls identical (Alström *et al.* 1992; K. Beylefeld & C. Wilds pers. comm.).

### Moult

Similar to that of Little Tern. Adults acquire summer plumage in late winter to early April (Massey 1978). Primary moult generally earlier than in Little Tern. Post-breeding moult may commence in late May (southern USA: Chandler & Wilds 1994); in summer, usually 1-2 (3) outer primaries are dark (2-3 on Little Tern). Most show winter head and bill in late August-September. Post-juvenile moult probably as that of Little Tern; in November, 1-3 inner primaries have been replaced. Subsequent, immature, moults identical with those of Little Tern.

***MAP 17*** Distribution of Least Tern
*Sterna antillarum.*

**SAUNDERS'S TERN** QUICK KEY TO IDENTIFICATION

1. **Forehead patch smaller, ending in rounded or square-cut rear edge in front of eye.**
2. **Upperparts paler grey than on Little Tern. No obvious contrast between back and rump/tail.**
3. **Rump and most of the tail pale grey; only t6 is predominantly white.**
4. **Legs darker, with brown tone.**
5. **Outermost 3 primaries deeper black than on Little Tern, with black shafts. Contrast accentuated by paler upperparts than on Little.**
6. **Tail streamers never as long as on long-tailed Little Terns.**

## Geographical variation

Validity of races dubious; to our eyes, only clinal variation exists.

Race *antillarum* (eastern North America) described above. Race *anthalassa* (inland USA and South Dakota) is said to be darker, more bluish-grey, a greater percentage showing grey tinge to underside, and with a larger number of (3 instead of 2) black outer primaries in summer (Oberholster 1974).

Race *browni* (Mexico, Pacific USA) seems to have on average shorter wings than other races, *browni* averaging 168.8 and *antillarum* 165.8 (Massey 1978). We failed to find any constant difference in wing measurements (skins, NMNH): *antillarum* (Caribbean) ♂ 163-180 (170.2, n = 26), ♀ 166-177 (169.9, n = 14); *antillarum* (eastern USA) ♂ 163-180 (170.8, n = 37), ♀ 160-172, (167.9, n = 19); *browni* (western USA, Mexico) ♂ 163-175 (170.9, n = 11), ♀ 165-175 (169.7, n = 7); *anthalassa* (southern USA) ♂ 167-173 (169.7, n = 7), ♀ 167 and 169 (n = 2). Wholly yellow bill tip most frequent in Caribbean populations, but regular also in other populations.

### Measurements

In mm. Own measurements, BMNH, NNH, ZMA, southern USA, West Indies.

**WING LENGTH**

| | | | |
|---|---|---|---|
| Ad ♂ | 160-180 | (169.9) | n = 113 |
| Ad ♀ | 154-177 | (168.1) | n = 59 |
| Juv | 146-165 | (156.8) | n = 8 |

• See Geographical Variation.

**TAIL FORK**

| | | | |
|---|---|---|---|
| Ad ♂ | 28-60 | (43.2) | n = 89 |
| Ad ♀ | 25-69 | (40.6) | n = 59 |
| Juv | 8-18 | (11.9) | n = 8 |

**BILL**

| | | | |
|---|---|---|---|
| Ad ♂ | 26.2-32.0 | (28.9) | n = 111 |
| Ad ♀ | 24.7-29.4 | (27.5) | n = 61 |
| Juv | 21.9-27.0 | (24.2) | n = 8 |

• average for *antillarum* ♂ 29.8, ♀ 28.0; for *browni* ♂ 28.2, ♀ 26.4.

**BILL DEPTH AT GONYS**

| | | | |
|---|---|---|---|
| Ad ♂ | 4.8-6.4 | (5.5) | n = 112 |
| Ad ♀ | 4.8-6.2 | (5.2) | n = 60 |
| Juv | 4.0-5.0 | (4.6) | n = 8 |

**BILL DEPTH AT REAR EDGE OF NOSTRILS**

| | | | |
|---|---|---|---|
| Ad ♂ | 5.8-7.3 | (6.3) | n = 112 |
| Ad ♀ | 5.6-7.0 | (6.2) | n = 60 |
| Juv | 5.1-6.2 | (5.7) | n = 8 |

**TARSUS**

| | | | |
|---|---|---|---|
| Ad ♂ | 13.8-17.2 | (15.4) | n = 114 |
| Ad ♀ | 13.2-16.6 | (15.4) | n = 62 |
| Juv | 12.8-16.4 | (14.8) | n = 8 |

**WEIGHT** (in grams)

30-45 (in breeding season, Netherlands Antilles)

# Saunders's Tern

*Sterna saundersi*

Photos **161-167**

### Identification in the field

The nearest breeding sites of Saunders's Tern are in the Persian Gulf. This species is very like Little Tern, and there is still great uncertainty surrounding its true status as a species. Many birds are intermediate between this species and Little Tern, and only those with a combination of all characters can be identified with certainty in the field – and only in adult summer plumage. Where the species breeds together with Little Tern, it prefers salt water whereas Little breeds inland.

In **adult summer plumage** the most important differences from Little Tern are: **1** The white forehead patch extends only to the eye, where it is rounded off or square-cut. Saunders's Tern lacks Little's suggestion of a white supercilium. Distance from bill base to rear edge of forehead patch above eye 9-14 mm (on Little, 15-20 mm). Up to 3 mm of black between eye and rear edge of forehead patch (patch normally reaches to eye on Little, or only 1 mm above). Black loral stripe 3-6 mm broad in front of eye, broadest on males (normally 3-4 mm on Little). See illustrations. **2** Legs are reddish-brown to mid-brown. Legs average shorter than on Little Tern. **3** Upperparts are pale grey, much as on adult Roseate Tern, with rump and tail concolorous; contrast between back and rump/tail is generally lacking. Little Tern has paler rump contrasting with darker back. This feature is aggravated by the fact that those Little Terns breeding within the range of Saunders's often have the central part of the tail grey; the rump, however, is normally paler and stands out more clearly against Little's darker grey upperparts. Furthermore, Little Tern normally shows paler bases to grey rump feathers, which may give mottled appearance to rump. On Saunders's, rump pale grey and tail pale grey; t1-4 pale grey, t6 white. In fresh plumage, rump and uppertail-coverts have white edges and then appear whiter. **4** Tail streamers are generally shorter, and never as long as on long-tailed Little Terns.

A much-debated character is that the outer 3 primaries are black (including black shafts) and form a broader, and purer black, leading edge to outer wing than on most Little Terns, this being accentuated by paler grey upperwing. This feature should, however, be used with caution owing to Little Tern's moult pattern. Birds studied in East Africa in winter did, nevertheless, appear to have more black on outermost primaries (normally 3-4 outer primaries black) than Little Terns. Beware, however, moulting Little Terns with up to 6-7 inner primaries moulted and contrasting with 3-4 outer unmoulted and dark ones, though Little Tern normally has paler shafts.

**Adult winter plumage** is almost identical with that of Little. The upperparts are darker grey than in the breeding season, and can be darker than on Little (Hollom *et al.* 1987). Uniform grey rump and back are difficult to use in the field, as many Little Terns within Saunders's range have equally grey rump and tail (see above). Black mask generally broader than on Little (mirrors the head pattern of summer plumage). Crown to nape dark.

**Juvenile** Probably identical with Little Tern. Some (Bahrain) have, however, shown a darker bar on secondaries.

***MAP 18*** Distribution of Saunders's Tern *Sterna saundersi.*

**SAUNDERS'S TERN** QUICK KEY TO IDENTIFICATION

1. **Forehead patch smaller, ending in rounded or square-cut rear edge in front of eye.**
2. **Upperparts paler grey than on Little Tern. No obvious contrast between back and rump/tail.**
3. **Rump and most of the tail pale grey; only t6 is predominantly white.**
4. **Legs darker, with brown tone.**
5. **Outermost 3 primaries deeper black than on Little Tern, with black shafts. Contrast accentuated by paler upperparts than on Little.**
6. **Tail streamers never as long as on long-tailed Little Terns.**

## Voice

A *kit-kit* or *kit-ir-kit*, as Little Tern's but possibly less sharp than latter's.

## Moult

Moults are generally later than those of Little.

**Adult** has a complete moult to **winter plumage** from August-September (about 30% bear summer plumage in September), later than Little Tern. First to be moulted are forehead and crown, together with some inner and central primaries. In September-October 6-8 inner primaries have been replaced. In November-January 2-3 inner primaries are normally renewed again, while 2-3 central ones are worn. The moult is arrested with 6-7 inner primaries replaced in January-April, simultaneously with moult to summer plumage. The tail is moulted in August-September, but the tail can be unchanged in February-March.

**Adult** has a partial moult to **summer plumage** in late February-April, probably generally later than Little Tern. Some, however, are largely in summer plumage in late February, apart from remnants of dark lesser-covert bar. The moult includes head, body, coverts, inner 3-4 primaries and any old outer primaries. Normally retains 3 outer primaries, which show good contrast with inners. The bill starts to turn yellow from base from late January to mid February. The tail is said normally to be moulted after the New Year. Some birds in February-March had a worn tail; those in April as a rule show fresh tail.

**Juvenile**'s moult probably much as that of Little Tern, but few birds studied. In March to late April, 4-5 inner primaries have been replaced and 3-4 outers are dark from wear.

## Geographical variation

Birds from the Persian Gulf and Arabia average longer-winged than those from Pakistan and East Africa (Cramp 1985). Differences, however, are small and intergrades occur.

### Measurements

In mm. Own measurements, BMNH, Red Sea, Indian Ocean.

WING LENGTH

| | | | |
|---|---|---|---|
| Ad ♂ | 163-178 | (168.1) | n = 15 |
| Ad ♀ | 161-172 | (167.1) | n = 21 |

• Birds from East Africa: ad ♂ 164-181 (174.8, n = 6), ad ♀ 164-180 (168.5, n = 7).

TAIL FORK

| | | | |
|---|---|---|---|
| Ad ♂ | 13-16 | (25.1) | n = 15 |
| Ad ♀ | 15-37 | (25.0) | n = 19 |

BILL

| | | | |
|---|---|---|---|
| Ad ♂ | 27.7-30.0 | (28.8) | n = 17 |
| Ad ♀ | 26.5-29.8 | (28.0) | n = 19 |

• Birds from East Africa: 28.6-30.7 (29.1, n = 10).

BILL DEPTH AT GONYS

| | | | |
|---|---|---|---|
| Ad ♂ | 4.9-6.1 | (5.5) | n = 17 |
| Ad ♀ | 4.9-5.5 | (5.2) | n = 23 |

BILL DEPTH AT REAR EDGE OF NOSTRILS

| | | | |
|---|---|---|---|
| Ad ♂ | 5.7-7.0 | (6.4) | n = 17 |
| Ad ♀ | 5.7-6.8 | (6.2) | n = 24 |

TARSUS

| | | | |
|---|---|---|---|
| Ad ♂ | 13.9-17.5 | (16.0) | n = 15 |
| Ad ♀ | 14.4-17.1 | (15.6) | n = 23 |

• Average for birds from East Africa: ad ♂ 16.3, ad ♀ 15.9.

# Whiskered Tern

Photos **168-178**

*Chlidonias hybridus*

## Identification in the field

The Whiskered Tern is the biggest *Chlidonias* tern. As its scientific name suggests, it looks like a mixture of Black Tern and *Sterna* terns. Compared with Black Tern, it has longer and more uniformly broad wings and a deeper tail fork, but its shape is always closer to that of Black Tern than to e.g. Common and Arctic Terns. The bill varies: large-billed males have a longer and broader bill than any Black Tern, whereas small-billed females can have a bill much as that of White-winged Black Tern.

Perched birds appear relatively short-bodied and long-legged. The short tail ends between the wingtip and the under-tail-coverts, a feature shared with other *Chlidonias* species. The legs are longer than on the latter, and show more 'knee'.

The flight resembles that of Black Tern, but is often more purposeful. Whiskered Terns forage like Black Terns by lunging towards the water surface, but the lunges are not normally so steep, and the species may also plunge-dive.

**Adult in summer plumage** has an obvious black *Sterna*-like cap with contrasting white cheeks. The cap extends down in front of the eye as on Common Tern, and only a narrow area of white is left between cap and gape. The underparts are coke-grey, usually blackest in the centre of the belly and showing good contrast with the white vent. The underparts give a dirty impression, like an oiled Arctic Tern! The pale grey underwings contrast well with the belly. The underwing markings and translucency are much as on Common Tern.

The upperparts are mid-grey with slightly darker mantle/back, and sometimes with secondaries and outer primaries darker. Rump and tail are grey. Bill and legs are dark red.

During the moult the cap becomes peppered white, like that of Gull-billed Tern.

Certain features of the plumage make confusion with, in particular, Arctic Tern theoretically possible, but in proportions the species is clearly closer to Black Tern. It lacks obvious tail streamers, has shorter and more uniformly broad wings and darker, uniform grey upperparts. In addition, the underparts are clearly darker, the legs distinctly longer and the bill darker red (Arctic Terns rarely have so dark a bill as Whiskered).

**Adult winter plumage** is very pale. The head is white with dark U-shaped band from eye to eye across the nape. The band slopes behind the eye towards the nape, and not drop down behind the lower edge of the eye as on Black and White-winged Black Terns. The crown is dark-streaked and merges diffusely into the mask. The cap is like that of winter-plumaged Common and Arctic Terns rather than that of Black and White-winged Black, but rarely can be reduced to a weak dark ear spot. The pale grey upperparts are the palest and most uniform among the *Chlidonias* species, and lack any obvious contrasts. The wings are normally uniform grey, but with dark alula and darker secondaries. Lesser coverts have at best a weak grey bar. Mantle, rump and tail are pale grey, as the back. The outer tail feathers have white outer webs as on White-winged Black Tern.

The underparts are white, often with a faint greyish 'Black Tern patch' on the breast sides. The bill is black, the legs red-brown.

Confusion is possible just as much with Common and Arctic Terns as with White-winged Black and Black. Black Tern proportions, uniform grey upperparts and normally weaker darker tips to the outer primaries below are important differences. Compared with Black and White-winged Black, Whiskered is paler above and has different head markings.

**Juvenile** has head and underparts much as adult winter, but newly fledged young can have darker (brown-toned) crown and lores. The darkest individuals appear at a distance to have a dark cap with pale blaze. Seen from behind, the nape is predominantly dark, without Black and White-winged Black's 'pony-tail' or whitish nape band. During autumn passage, the head is normally as in winter plumage.

The mantle is dark, contrasting with the pale wings. At a distance, the contrast recalls that of young White-winged Black Tern, but at closer range the feather markings are clearly different. Mantle/back and scapular feathers, together with tertials, have a yellow-brown base, black diagonal bar and broad sandy-coloured fringes which create a scaly pattern, most obvious on the tertials. Variation is, however, appreciable. Some have more uniform grey feathers, while darker individuals can approach juvenile White-winged Black Tern in 'darkness'. Rump and tail are grey; t6 has white outer web. More often than with the other two *Chlidonias* species, the tail has a dark terminal band.

The upperwing is pale grey. Lesser coverts can be somewhat darker, but an obvious dark covert bar as shown by White-winged Black Tern is unusual. Some have a triangular area of mid-grey on lesser and median coverts, and the inner coverts may have dark spots. The alula is dark, as on adult winter, and often stands out against paler surroundings.

The underparts are much as on adult

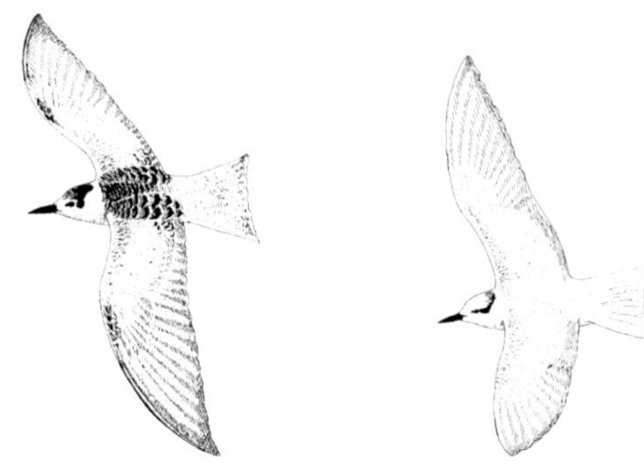

winter. Young Whiskered probably more often have a dark 'Black Tern patch' on the breast sides, but it is is generally weaker and paler than Black Tern's.

Juveniles moult early into **first-winter plumage**, and acquire grey upperpart feathers as soon as late summer. Black and White-winged Black Terns moult some back feathers no earlier than September, when the majority of Whiskered have pale grey upperparts. Some individuals examined in November had juvenile scapulars, like dark 'shoulder-straps' contrasting with pale grey back. Pure juvenile upperparts are on rare occasions retained until January.

**First-winter/first-summer plumage** is much as adult winter plumage, and after the last juvenile body feathers have been moulted cannot be distinguished from adults, apart from the fact that the primaries are renewed about two months later than on adults. Birds in March-May normally have 6-7 outer primaries worn.

**Second-summer plumage** is much as adult summer plumage, but with some white feathers in cap and underparts (latter may be almost pure white), and darker, relatively more worn 4-5 outer primaries.

## Voice

A hoarse *eirchk* or *kreerp*, rather like call of Black-winged Stilt *Himantopus himan-*

**PLATE 36**

**Whiskered Tern *Chlidonias hybridus***
The largest of the three species of marsh terns *Chlidonias*, in some plumages intermediate between *Chlidonias* and *Sterna*. Size and structure helpful. Whiskered Tern is only slightly longer-winged and longer-tailed than Black Tern. Perched birds appear long-legged and short-tailed. Tail reaches half way to wing tip.

1 **Juvenile.** Note checkered brown back showing good contrast with pale wings. Head pattern similar to that of Arctic Tern (see Black and White-winged Black Terns), in fresh plumage typically with strong brownish wash.
2 **Adult winter.** Note U-shaped head mask and dark-spotted crown.
3 **Adult summer (in early stages of moult to winter plumage).**
4 **Adult summer.** Note head pattern similar to that of Arctic Tern (including narrow white line between gape and cap), dark red bill, and white cheeks contrasting well with dark grey underparts.
5 **Adult moulting from summer to winter plumage (October).**
6 **Chick.**

*topus* (or Corncrake *Crex crex*), or thicker.

**Moult** *Chlidonias hybridus hybridus*

**Adult** has a complete moult to **winter plumage**. The moult begins in June-July with lores, crown, mantle and scapulars, followed by forehead, uppertail-coverts, underparts and tail (t1-t2-t3-t6-t4-t5) (Cramp 1985). The moult is normally limited to August, when the majority are predominantly in summer plumage (Thomas W. Johansen pers. comm.); usually some feathers in cap and breast have been renewed by early to mid August. In September the head is normally in winter plumage, but some belly feathers remain from summer plumage. The majority are in winter plumage from October-November. An adult from Denmark in October was in predominantly

**PLATE 37**

**Whiskered Tern *Chlidonias hybridus***

1 **Juvenile.** Clear contrast between dark, pale-checkered back and pale wings, the latter only infrequently showing darker lesser coverts. Head pattern similar to that of juvenile Arctic Tern. Frequently shows darker shading on sides of breast, but never so conspicuous as the similar marking on all Black Terns. Rump and tail pale grey. Outer tail feathers have whitish outer webs. Often shows traces of dark tail-band.

2 **Adult summer.** Upperparts grey with paler flight feathers.

3 **Juvenile moulting to first-winter.** During late summer/autumn, back shows mixture of juvenile and uniform grey feathers. Many moult early to first-winter (from end of July), whereas others bear juvenile plumage well into late autumn.

4 **Adult moulting from winter to summer plumage.** During moult (and in second-summer), underbody is a mixture of white and grey.

5 **Adult winter.** Upperparts almost uniform pale grey. Note U-shaped head marking and dark alula.

6 **Adult summer.** Superficially resembles well-marked adult summer Arctic Tern, but grey tail much shorter and belly sooty-grey. Bill and legs darker red than on average Arctic.

7 **Adult moulting from summer to winter plumage (September-October).** Note white-peppered black cap, similar to moulting Gull-billed Tern.

summer plumage (B. Bertel *in litt.*). The primary moult commences late July to late September. The birds leave the breeding sites with 3-7 (9) inner primaries replaced, and complete the primary moult in December-January, sometimes towards spring. A new moult series in the primaries may begin during late October to early February.

**Adult** has a partial moult to **summer plumage**. The moult begins in February-March, and includes head, body, coverts, tail (sometimes not t4-5) and to a varying extent the inner primaries. The moult can

**WHISKERED TERN** QUICK KEY TO IDENTIFICATION

1. **Flight and proportions much as those of Black Tern.**
2. **When perched, long-legged and short-tailed; wings clearly project beyond tail.**
3. **Summer-plumaged adult has black cap, white moustachial stripe and blackish-grey underparts. Upperparts grey.**
4. **In winter plumage, mask is like a dark U from eye to eye via nape.**
5. **Upperparts very pale and unmarked in winter plumage.**
6. **Can have faint dark breast-side patch in juvenile and winter plumages, weaker and more diffuse than on most Black Terns.**
7. **Juvenile plumage is retained for only a short period. Juveniles have dark saddle with broader and paler feather fringes than on White-winged Black Tern, forming speckled scaly pattern.**
8. **Tail grey with white sides. Tail streamers only slightly longer than Black Tern's.**

be completed by mid February, but normally summer plumage is not complete before early to mid April. A third series in the primaries commences late December to early March, but not if the second series starts late in the winter. In spring, the inner 6-7 have normally been replaced (from second series). Some may begin a third moult series in which 1-4 inner primaries are replaced at the same time as the outer primaries are being renewed. Variation is great and complex (Cramp 1985), and it is thought to be commoner than among other terns for occasional primaries to be leapfrogged in the moult sequence (several skins examined).

**Juvenile** has a complete moult to **first-winter plumage**. The moult starts from (June) July with mantle, t1 and possibly inner primary and scapulars. Birds in late July to mid September had replaced 40-60% of the back feathers. In August-September, the majority have a mainly uniform grey mantle/back, but some moult later, in October to early November. Scapulars and tertials are normally retained until mid November. The moult is completed in November-January, apart from secondaries and outermost primaries.

Juvenile upperparts have been observed on some birds in late autumn, these possibly originating from eastern populations with different moult (Kemp 1988). The primary moult probably begins from September-October. In March-May 3-4 inner primaries have normally been replaced, and in early June 6 inner primaries. A bird from 11 March, however, had not started the primary moult. A second moult series in the primaries may begin in January-April.

Subsequent moults largely unknown. Retained outer primaries are possibly changed in the second autumn.

Birds in **second-summer plumage** have acquired adult summer plumage, but with some white feathers in cap and underparts. They have replaced up to 4 inner primaries, and have 4-5 outer primaries worn (skins, BMNH).

Note: Breeding birds from southern Africa and other parts of the tropics have a moult contrary to that of northern populations owing to their different breeding season.

**Detailed description** *Chlidonias hybridus hybridus*

Length 23-25 cm, wingspan 74-78 cm.

**Adult summer plumage:** Cap black. White stripe between gape and cap 1-1.5 mm. White moustachial stripe to rear neck contrasts with grey throat and darker grey breast and belly. Throat sometimes whitish. Males can have blackish-grey belly, especially on central parts. Upperparts mid-grey. Remiges have narrow pale fringes. Fresh primaries whitish-grey, mid-grey when worn. Secondaries medium to dark grey. Tail grey; t6 has white outer web and grey tip. Axillaries grey, underwing-coverts and vent white. In worn plumage, underparts become whiter.

Bill dark red. Males have on average a longer and more powerful bill, with more obviously curved upper mandible and better-marked gonydeal angle. Legs carmine-red.

**Adult winter plumage:** Forehead, lores and crown white. Crown has dark streaks merging diffusely into dark mask from behind eye and through nape. Nape and upperparts uniform pale grey. T6 has white outer web. Lesser coverts sometimes slightly darker. Remiges as in summer plumage, but unmoulted primaries darker.

Underparts white, sometimes with grey patch on breast sides (more diffuse, paler and weaker than on Black Tern).

Bill black with variable red-brown tinge at base. Legs black, tinged red.

**Juvenile:** Head much as adult winter, but in

fresh plumage forehead and lores are dark-spotted (often with brown tinge), and forehead and crown may be tinged brown. Cap generally more distinct; some juveniles have almost complete cap, but always with paler blaze and some pale streaks in forehead and crown.

Upperparts show much contrast. Dark, vermiculated saddle contrasts with pale wings. Mantle/back, scapulars and tertials mid-grey with black to blackish-brown subterminal patches and pale yellow-brown fringes, latter normally as clear-cut pale sides. Rump and tail-coverts pale grey, sometimes with paler feather fringes. Tail feathers grey with narrow pale edges and darker outer part, latter forming dark tail band; t6 has white outer web.

Remiges darker grey than on adults, with narrow pale outer webs. Underparts white, as adult winter, but grey patches on breast sides generally more obvious.

Bill brownish-red with black tip; black from late summer. Legs brownish-red.

**First-winter plumage:** Much as adult winter plumage, but primary moult commences about two months later than with adults. Birds in March-May have moulted up to 4 inner primaries (own studies), but some have all primaries juvenile until March (Alström 1989; own studies).

**First-summer plumage:** Much as first-winter plumage, but cap generally darker (though always with element of white feathers). Belly white, often with some scattered dark grey feathers. In first summer, 4-6 inner primaries juvenile.

**Second-summer plumage:** Much as adult summer plumage, but cap can have white spots, underparts a few white feathers and upperparts some unmoulted grey-brown feathers. Up to 6 outer primaries worn.

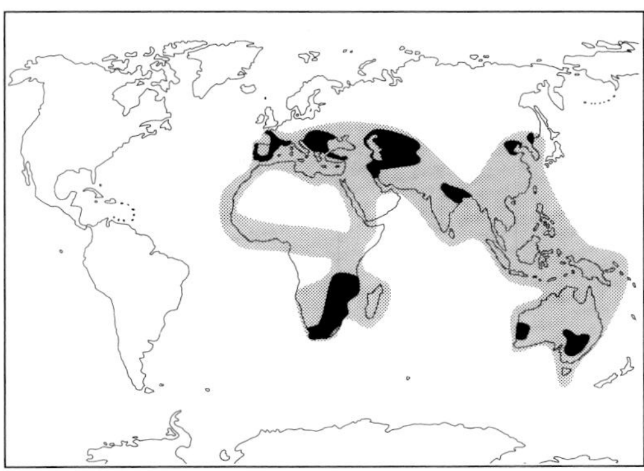

***MAP 19*** Distribution of Whiskered Tern *Chlidonias hybridus.*

## Geographical variation

Involves mostly size. Birds from Europe and North Africa have the largest bill. Race *delalandii* (East and southern Africa) are darker above and below and have a narrower moustachial stripe than the nominate form. Race *javanicus* (Java to Australia) has paler upperparts (colour tone rather as Common Tern), broader white cheek stripe and generally paler breast than nominate. The central belly is generally blacker than on nominate. Winter plumage paler than nominate, almost whitish-grey on upperparts.

### Measurements

In mm. Own measurements, BMNH, MN, NNM, NRK, UZM, ZMA, ZMO, ZML, Europe and North Africa. Adult March-July, juvenile/1st-winter July-January.

WING LENGTH

| | | | |
|---|---|---|---|
| Ad ♂ | 227-252 | (237.6) | n = 26 |
| Ad ♀ | 222-239 | (231.2) | n = 17 |
| Juv/1st-winter | 213-231 | (221.9) | n = 16 |

• East, Southeast and Central Asia: ad ♂ 214-237 (225.3, n = 21; average East Asia 228.9, average Java 221.2), ad ♀ 205-233 (218.7, n = 27) (own measurements). Persian Gulf: ad ♂ 214-235 (n = 12).

• Hario (1986) gives ad ♂ 224-245 (235, n = 13), ad ♀ 220-241 (229, n = 8).

• Glutz *et al.* (1982), for Europe and North Africa: ad ♂ 224-245 (234.9, n = 13), ad ♀ 220-241 (230.5, n = 13).

TAIL FORK

| | | | |
|---|---|---|---|
| Ad ♂ | 11-22 | (17.7) | n = 28 |
| Ad ♀ | 12-22 | (16.1) | n = 19 |
| Juv | 7-14 | (11.7) | n = 16 |

• *javanicus* (East and Southeast Asia): ad ♂ 14-19 (15.9, n = 10), ad ♀ 9-19 (14.1, n = 10), juv 10-16 (13.0, n = 8) (own measurements).

**BILL**

| | | | |
|---|---|---|---|
| Ad ♂ | 28.1-32.5 | (30.7) | n = 28 |
| Ad ♀ | 25.8-31.1 | (28.5) | n = 19 |
| Juv | 24.0-31.7 | (26.7) | n = 16 |

• Southeast, East and Central Asia: ad ♂ 25.5-33.1 (30.5, n = 22). Ad ♀ East and central Asia 27.5-32.9 (30.9, n = 7) (own measurements), Java 26.5-30.9 (28.1, n = 21).

**BILL DEPTH AT GONYS**

| | | | |
|---|---|---|---|
| Ad ♂ | 6.0-7.4 | (6.8) | n = 28 |
| Ad ♀ | 5.7-7.0 | (6.3) | n = 19 |
| Juv | 5.4-6.7 | (6.0) | n = 17 |

• Birds from East and Central Asia: ad ♂ 5.9-7.0 (6.7, n = 11), ad ♀ 5.6-6.5 (6.2, n = 7), juv 5.7-6.4 (6.1, n = 8) (own measurements, UZM, BMNH).

**BILL DEPTH AT REAR EDGE OF NOSTRILS**

| | | | |
|---|---|---|---|
| Ad ♂ | 7.4-9.3 | (8.2) | n = 28 |
| Ad ♀ | 7.1-8.5 | (7.9) | n = 19 |
| Juv | 6.4-8.4 | (7.3) | n = 17 |

• Birds from Southeast, East and Central Asia: ad ♂ 7.4-8.7 (8.3, n = 21), ad ♀ 6.6-8.2 (7.8, n = 17), juv 6.7-8.4 (7.4, n = 8) (own measurements, UZM, BMNH, NNH, ZMA).

**TARSUS**

| | | | |
|---|---|---|---|
| Ad ♂ | 20.9-23.4 | (22.2) | n = 26 |
| Ad ♀ | 20.0-23.6 | (21.8) | n = 18 |
| Juv | 19.4-23.6 | (21.7) | n = 17 |

• Cramp (1985) gives: ad ♂ 23-24 (23.3, n = 9), ad ♀ 21-24 (22.6, n = 11). Hario (1986) gives: ad 20.5-24.7 (22.5, n = 12).

• Birds from East and Central Asia: ad ♂ 19.9-23.3 (21.6, n = 11), ad ♀ 19.7-22.9 (21.0, n = 7).

**WEIGHT** (in grams)

• 7 ad ♂♂, northwest Iran, May, 83-91 (88.4) (Cramp 1985).

• One ♀ from Italy, May, 83 (Glutz *et al.* 1982).

# Black Tern

*Chlidonias niger*

Photos **179-188**

### Identification in the field

The Black Tern is a small compact tern which is easily identified in its dark summer plumage, but is less characteristic outside the breeding season. It is not, however, particularly difficult to identify. Compared with the *Sterna* species, the Black Tern is short-winged and short-tailed. The short tail is only slightly forked, and when held spread it is square-ended. The upperparts are always darker than those of other native terns. The proportions recall those of the other *Chlidonias* species (see below).

The Black Tern has a playful, pitching and erratic flight with frequent dips towards the water's surface, and when foraging often with yoyo-like movements for a couple of metres before snatching food from the surface. This flight, typical of *Chlidonias* species, recalls that of Little Gull *Larus minutus*, with which the Black Tern often associates. The flight appears buoyant but feeble – as if the wind could at any moment blow it away! The Black Tern does not, however, plunge-dive (though it is said to do so in salt water). Flocks may bathe in dense gatherings. The flight action and the dark plumage in summer give the species certain characteristics approaching storm-petrels or bats.

When perched, Black Terns are small and attenuated, almost submissive-looking with small delicate head and narrow 'effete' body. The tail ends roughly between vent and wingtips, which in typical *Chlidonias* fashion project several centimetres beyond the tail. The head is evenly rounded, with the highest point immediately behind the eye, but the forehead sometimes somewhat flatter. The slender, delicate bill has a barely downcurved tip. The legs are shorter than on the other *Chlidonias* species; the 'knee' appears to disappear directly into the body.

The greatest confusion risk is White-winged Black Tern, which because of its more rounded head and shorter bill looks more 'cute', and also has a somewhat shorter and broader body and wings, a less forked tail and longer legs.

The Nearctic race *surinamensis* differs somewhat in all plumages from the nominate form (see Geographical Variation). It has not yet been recorded in Europe, but is a possible vagrant or accidental.

**Adult in summer plumage** has greyish-black head and body contrasting well with grey underwings and white undertail-coverts. Males are darkest and normally have a uniformly dark head. Females have a paler grey throat and cheeks, giving rise to a certain 'capped effect' (rather like Yellow Wagtail *Motacilla flava* of the Balkan race *feldegg*). The dark head merges diffusely into mid-grey upperparts, on which the sides of the rump may be somewhat paler. Secondaries and outer primaries are slightly darker than the fresh inner primaries, but the contrast is never particularly obvious. Perched Black Terns show a certain contrast between paler leading edge of wing and dark body, but never so black-and-white as on White-winged Black Tern. Note, however, that backlighting makes the wings flash whitish-grey. The bill is dark. The legs are dark brown, sometimes with a dark red coloration.

In early summer (from late May, when the young are small), areas of the throat and around the eye are moulted. The throat becomes white and a white eye-ring appears. This happens so that the young are more easily able to pick out the bill in order to get food. Sometimes parts of the forehead and lores are also moulted, but a face as white-freckled as that typically acquired by White-winged Black during the same period cannot normally be expected before mid July. For a short period late in the spring moult and early in the autumn moult, individuals with dark cap and breast and paler, diffuse area on the cheeks are seen. Confusion with Whiskered Tern is then theoretically possible, but the upperparts are darker.

After midsummer the rest of the head and breast is moulted, with the belly normally last. Birds in Scandinavia in late summer (up to mid August) normally have a winter head and breast combined with at least 50% summer feathering on the belly, which therefore becomes variegated. Contrast between the now worn outer primaries and fresher inner ones becomes increasing obvious, and a dark secondary bar can be fairly distinct.

The winter plumage is acquired gradually during late summer and autumn (see Moult).

**Adult in winter plumage** has a uniform dark cap which broadens somewhat behind the eye towards the neck sides. A dark patch in front of the eye is generally bigger than on other *Chlidonias* terns and can reach the eye. The eye is surrounded by a white eye-ring, broadest above middle part of eye. A highly distinctive dark grey patch on the breast sides at the wing base creates, together with the dark cap, a dark 'double-mark' anteriorly. The breast patch is probably never completely lacking, but some have a weaker patch which can be rather like that of Whiskered Tern. The upperparts are pale brownish-grey with darker lesser coverts (most obvious with wear). Rump and tail are concolorous with the back, but the rump can be pale blue-grey. The outer tail feathers have a grey outer web. The underwing is pale grey.

**Juvenile** recalls adult winter plumage, but often has a brown-toned cap and generally bigger, darker and browner breast-side patches. The upperparts are both darker and browner than on adults. Darkest areas are the mantle and lesser coverts, which can form a continuous dark area from carpal to carpal that may continue down onto the back as a dark T shape. The contrast with the rest of the dark upperparts, however, is never striking. The upperpart feathers have pale

***PLATE 38***

**Black Tern *Chlidonias niger***

Small, dark tern with rather short tail and wings. Flight buoyant, often with yo-yo dips to surface to pick up food.

1 **Juvenile.** Upperparts show much less contrast between back and wings than on Whiskered and White-winged Black. Back greyish-brown with pale buff feather fringes. Solid black hood covers crown and ear-coverts. Broad dark patch at sides of breast together with dark hood produces dark double-patch'.

2 **Juvenile race *surinamensis*.** Identified by combination of white-streaked crown, darker and more uniform upperparts (especially rump), and broader dark breast patch merging together with grey flanks. Head pattern may look more similar to that of White-winged Black than to nominate Black Tern.

3 **First-summer/adult winter.** Upperparts medium grey, darker than on congeners.

4 **Adult moulting from summer to winter plumage (August-September).** Winter head combined with dark belly typical.

5 **Adult summer (June).** Starts moult to winter plumage with parts of throat and face as soon as young hatch.

6 **Adult male summer.** In early summer, head is sooty-black against blackish-grey body. Males normally have whole head black; females have dark grey throat and neck sides uniform with breast and belly, which makes black hood stand out.

7 **Adult summer race *surinamensis*.** Head and underparts a deeper black than in *niger*, thus closer in coloration to White-winged Black Tern.

fringes which are broadest and most distinct on scapulars and tertials, where, under good conditions, a narrow dark U-shaped mark can be detected inside the pale fringes. The rump is a trifle paler than the back, especially at the sides, but is never white. The tail is pale brownish-grey with pale grey sides, and sometimes has a faint dark terminal band.

The bill is dark, sometimes with paler base. The legs are orangey-grey.

Juvenile Black Terns are most easily distinguished from those of Whiskered and White-winged Black by a combination of dark breast patches, uniformly dark cap separated from the characteristic breast

patches by a white indentation, dark brown upperparts rather lacking in contrast, broad pale fringes to dark scapulars and tertials (create scaly pattern on the best-marked individuals), and pure grey outer tail feathers. Alström (1989) demonstrates, in a series of pictures, a clear contrast between back and upperwing-coverts, but the contrast has never been seen to be so striking in the field. Lighting conditions and printing of photographs come in here: in prolonged observations the true appearance will be revealed.

**First-winter/first-summer plumage** is much as adult winter plumage. It is acquired after the New Year and is carried through into the summer of the second calendar-year. It is distinguished from adult winter by grey-brown and worn retained juvenile remiges (4-6 outer primaries in summer), and normally a more obvious dark bar on the lesser coverts. A few dark feathers may be present in the head and underparts. The plumage appears washed out and untidy, quite unlike the juvenile's fresh plumage and the adult's variegated transitional plumage.

The ensuing **second-winter plumage** is identical with adult winter plumage, but some juvenile outer primaries are likely to be present until the middle of winter.

**Second-summer plumage** is much as adult summer plumage, but with a variable element of white feathering on the head and body, sometimes like a 'winter head' on an otherwise greyish-black body. After midsummer the plumage cannot be distinguished from transitional plumages of adults, but possibly has darker and relatively more worn outer primaries.

## Voice

A short and sharp, nasal *kja*, sounding clipped. Also a sharp *klitt*, conversational (Bruun *et al.* 1987).

## Moult

**Adult** has a complete moult to **winter plumage**. The moult begins with throat and parts of lores and around the eye in late May to early June (while the young are still small) and is followed by the rest of the head, which is fully moulted mid June to late July. Last to be moulted are the feathers around the bill base. The breast is moulted from early July and is normally fully moulted by early August. The belly is moulted later: in Scandinavia, the majority have had over half the underparts in summer plumage in July to mid August. Last moulted are lower belly and some flank feathers (mid to late September). Birds in the Netherlands can have head and body in winter plumage from early August, but as a rule have plumage development much as Scandinavian birds up to early September. A largish percentage (20-25%), however, bear pure winter plumage in late August to early September. Greater coverts together with some mantle and scapular feathers may be retained longer. Greater coverts may be moulted all at once.

A few retain full summer plumage for longer. Of those studied in the Netherlands in late September, 2% had pure summer plumage (pers. obs.). A bird from Denmark in early November was still in summer plumage (J. Frimer Andersen *in litt.*).

Upperparts and wing-coverts are moulted simultaneously with breast and

belly. First to be moulted are lesser coverts (which can be fresh in early August), and last the greater coverts, which can be moulted in one go in mid August to late September. The upperparts are normally renewed in early September, apart from some greater coverts.

The primary moult is similar to that of Common Tern. Cramp (1985) states that the inner primaries are moulted only once annually, unlike the situation with White-winged Black and Whiskered Terns. In spring/summer, (1-2) 4-5 (6) inner primaries have been replaced. The moult is arrested in summer, and resumed during the autumn, normally when head and breast have been renewed. A number of skins from Scandinavia and north Europe in May to early August showed no active moult in summer; one bird had primary 3 in growth. Some have three generations of primaries in summer, the central feathers darkest and most worn. Cramp (1985) states that primary moult commences early July to mid August (England and the Netherlands). This discrepancy can be explained by the fact that the birds do not begin the moult until reaching stop-over sites farther south in Europe, especially in the Netherlands, where active moult of central primaries is the rule. In the Netherlands, normally the inner primaries 2-4 are replaced during August. The moult is arrested with (3-4) 5 (6) inners new before the migration in September (Walters 1987; pers. obs.). Birds with delayed moult of head and body feathers also have delayed primary moult (pers. obs., Netherlands). At the same time as the autumn primary moult parts of the secondaries are moulted, though normally not the central 30-40% (skins, UZM, NNH), which are moulted at the same time as the outer primary in the winter quarters. Primary moult terminates from January-March; fresh winter-plumaged birds normally have outer 3-5 primaries worn, but in January-March only the outer primary is worn. During the moult of the greater coverts, pale bases of the flight feathers are revealed.

Tail moult begins at the earliest in July, with t1. In European breeding populations about 25% had replaced t1(2) in late July, and one individual t1-4. In September-October t1-4 have normally been replaced, but some have not started the tail moult (skins, NNH, ZMA, BMNH). T5-6 are probably renewed in winter quarters, with t4-5 last (Cramp 1985; pers. obs.).

**Adult** has a partial moult to **summer plumage**. The moult includes head, body, coverts, tail and up to 6 inner primaries. Occasionally parts of the tail (especially t4-5) and also some lesser and median coverts are not moulted. The inner primaries are moulted from late November, often before the previous moult series has ended. In January-February up to 4 inner primaries have been replaced.

3
2
1
5
4
7
6
8

**PLATE 39**

**Black Tern *Chlidonias niger***

1 **Juvenile *niger*.** Note medium-dark, rather uniform upperparts and dark double-patch created by hood and breast patches. Rump slightly paler than back.

2 **Juvenile *surinamensis*.** Upperparts darker than in *niger*; note especially darker rump. Dark breast patch extends to grey flanks. Outer web of outer tail feathers darker grey than medium grey of *niger*.

3 **Juvenile *niger*.**

4 **First-summer *niger*.** Similar to adult winter (not illustrated). Note contrast between old and new feathers.

5 **Adult summer *niger* moulting to winter (late August-September).**

6 **Adult summer male *niger*.** Adult has blackish head and body in slight contrast to paler grey upperparts and underwing. Vent white. In strong sunlight, upperwing may appear pale, but never strikingly white as on White-winged Black.

7 **Adult summer *surinamensis*.** Head and underbody deep black, similar to White-winged Black Tern, but underwing-coverts whitish and upperparts similar to *niger*.

8 **Adult summer *niger* moulting into winter plumage (June-July).** In early moult, throat becomes whitish. May for a short period look similar to Whiskered Tern, but never shows full white cheek stripe in combination with black cap and sooty-grey underparts. Bill and legs are dark, not red.

(1) 4-6 inner primaries are changed during spring; the moult is suspended in March and resumed in late summer and autumn (see above). Odd outer and inner secondaries may be replaced in February-March.

Body, tail and coverts are moulted in January-February. Summer plumage is acquired in early to late March (early April); some tail feathers (most commonly t3-5) later.

**Juvenile** has a complete moult to **first-winter plumage** in the winter quarters. The moult begins in October-November with head, mantle and scapulars, together with t1. Primary moult commences in December-January and finishes in June-August; in November-December 3 inners are replaced, and in May-August (3) 4-5 (6) inner primaries have been replaced. A bird from Öland on 2 July had changed the inner 6 primaries. Primary moult is suspended during the summer and resumed the following autumn. Body and tail moult is normally completed in March, but some juvenile tertials, coverts and tail feathers are not replaced in the first summer, when they are worn and contrast well with fresh feathers. T4-5 are often worn in May-June; t6 may be renewed in May.

A new moult series in the primaries may commence in May-June.

This plumage is replaced directly by **second-winter plumage**. The last juvenile primaries are moulted in the second winter, sometimes after the New Year. Birds from Liberia (NNH) had outer primary growing in mid August.

**Detailed description** *Chlidonias niger niger*

Length 22-24 cm, wingspan 64-88 cm.

**Adult ♂ summer plumage:** Head and nape black, in fresh plumage with green gloss on forehead, crown and nape. Upperparts blackish-grey, in fresh plumage tinged bluish and with some feathers having narrow pale edges. Uppertail-coverts, rump sides and tail may be slightly paler grey. With wear, plumage becomes duller and acquires a brown tinge. Tail grey, any retained old rectrices grey-brown; t6 has pale grey outer web.

Underparts from throat to lower belly blackish-grey to greyish-black, rarely with grey spots/patches. Worn underparts may be paler. Underwing mid-grey (rarely, whiter), undertail-coverts white.

Remiges blackish-grey, on fresh birds silver-tinted, becoming gradually darker from wear during the summer. Up to 6 inner primaries blackish-grey, contrasting slightly with worn brownish-black outers. Inner webs of primaries dark grey.

Bill black, rarely dark reddish-brown; cutting edges red. Legs dark brown to red-brown, more rarely black (a few per cent) or bright red (Steinhaus 1980; Brichetti 1986).

**Adult ♀ summer plumage:** As adult male, but underparts and sometimes mantle/back paler blackish-grey. Dark cap (as that of Yellow Wagtail of race *feldegg*) stands out against paler cheeks.

**BLACK TERN** QUICK KEY TO IDENTIFICATION

1 **In summer plumage, blackish-grey with uniformly mid-grey upperside, grey underwing and white vent.**
2 **From late May, throat and areas around eye are moulted.**
3 **Dark patches on breast sides always present in juvenile and winter plumages.**
4 **In winter and immature plumages, the uniformly dark upperside is the darkest of all the** *Chlidonias* **terns.**
5 **In juvenile and winter plumages, the cap is all dark from crown to nape and upper ear-coverts.**
6 **Juvenile is the darkest and most uniformly patterned young** *Chlidonias* **and lacks obvious contrast between back and wings. A dark brown coloration is evident.**
7 **Juvenile has a broad dark band across the upper mantle from carpal to carpal and often somewhat darker lower mantle/upper back.**
8 **Rump concolorous with back or a shade paler – never pure white.**

Some males can have female-like cap, which in such cases is broader and contrasts with paler chin.

**Adult winter plumage:** Face and eye-ring white. Mask (crown to nape and ear-coverts) black. Fresh feathers may have narrow white fringes, though these are soon abraded.

Upperparts mid-grey with darker mantle and lesser coverts. Fresh feathers on upperparts have narrow pale grey tips. With wear, dark bars on lesser coverts and secondaries become more obvious.

Underparts white with dark oval patch on breast side. The patch varies, and can be black, but is more often grey and somewhat diffusely outlined, but is probably never lacking altogether. Underwings pale grey to greyish-white. Fresh remiges silvery in tone, darker when worn. In spring and summer 3-7 outer primaries are darker and contrast slightly with paler inners, which can form weak pale wedge in hand. Bill and legs black to dark brown.

**Juvenile:** Head as adult winter plumage, but on recently fledged birds the face is tinged grey-brown or yellowish-brown and cap has narrow pale feather tips. White eye-ring often more distinct, especially in front of eye.

Upperparts mid-grey to mid-brown, darkest on mantle and lesser coverts and sometimes on central back (creating dark T or band from carpal to carpal). The feathers have blackish-grey U-shaped subterminal spots and pale sandy-coloured to warm brown tips, most distinct on scapulars and tertials; some have more uniformly coloured feathers. Brown tinges normally disappear in August. Wing-coverts have narrow black shaft streaks. Rump and tail-coverts sometimes paler than back and with narrow grey to white fringes, broadest on tail-coverts. Tail feathers dark grey with white edges; t6 has grey outer web. May have darker tail band. Remiges dark grey with narrow ( mm) white edges and tips to secondaries and inner 6-8 primaries.

Underparts white; breast may have pink to yellow-brown tinge. Dark patch on breast side dark grey to blackish-brown, generally more distinct than on adult winter. Rarely, upper flanks have dark elements (see *surinamensis* under Geographical Variation).

Bill dark grey-brown to black; base of lower mandible blue-grey to greyish-yellow. Legs brown to yellow-brown, sometimes with tinge of red.

**First-winter/first-summer plumage:** Much as adult winter plumage, but may acquire some dark feathers on head and underparts (less than 20%). Some median coverts paler grey. Normally, outer 4-5 primaries are worn in summer and show better contrast with new inners than on adults. Tail can be worn in summer.

**Second-winter plumage:** Much as adult winter plumage.

**Second-summer plumage:** Much as adult summer, but with some white areas in head (especially forehead, throat and foreneck) and underparts. Outer 4-5 primaries generally darker than on adults.

Some second-summer-plumage types are possibly 'advanced' first-summers, or failed breeders which have started the moult to winter plumage early. Cramp (1985) mentions seven out of 20 from the Netherlands in July-August in such plumage, none of them from breeding sites.

## Geographical variation

The race *surinamensis* (North America) generally has shorter wings and longer legs than *niger*, but measurements overlap (see Measurements).

**Adult summer plumage** has a velvety-black head and underbody (as summer-plumaged White-winged Black Tern) contrasting more clearly with the upperparts than on *niger*. Black of head extends to mantle, and rest of upperparts are a shade darker than on *niger*. Leading edge of wing can be almost white. Males have a deeper black head than females, which can have a slightly paler throat (normally not so obvious as on *niger*). Leading edge of wing and underwing-coverts white. Tail grey; rarely (<1%), t6 has a white outer web. Legs and bill black, sometimes tinged reddish-brown. Plumage brown-tinged with wear.

Generally moults to winter plumage later than *niger*. Earliest in winter plumage mid August, but many are still in summer plumage in September. Moulted first (mid June to mid August) are rear lores, throat and areas beneath eye. During autumn moult, head and breast are normally as pale-mottled as on White-winged Black Tern. Tail moult similar to that of *niger*; t1 moulted in early to mid August. Up to 5 inner primaries moulted in autumn (to December).

**Adult winter plumage** is distinguished from *niger* by broader dark patches on breast sides which merge directly into grey flanks, unlike on *niger*. The facial mask is paler, as crown is dark grey with pale streaks and feather fringes contrasting with black ear-coverts and broad white eye-ring. Head on palest-marked individuals is similar to that of White-winged Black, but the dark extension down the nape is broader (as on *niger*, but frequently reaching mantle). Upperparts rather uniform dark grey, with blackish-grey lesser coverts and upper mantle, and dark grey rump and tail concolorous with back. Nominate *niger* has more solid black mask and normally somewhat paler rump.

**Juvenile** is distinguished from *niger* by darker, less contrastingly patterned upperparts. As on adults, the broad dark breast patches merge into grey flanks (may even penetrate to breast), and crown has pale streaks on grey ground colour, contrasting with black ear-coverts. Frequently, mask reaches to mantle. Upperparts dark brown with grey-brown feather bases and narrow mid-brown feather fringes. Dark brown subterminal spots generally broader and more conspicuous than on *niger*, especially on scapulars and tertials; tertials have the most distinct dark subterminal spots and the palest (yellow to yellow-brown) fringes, though these are narrower and darker

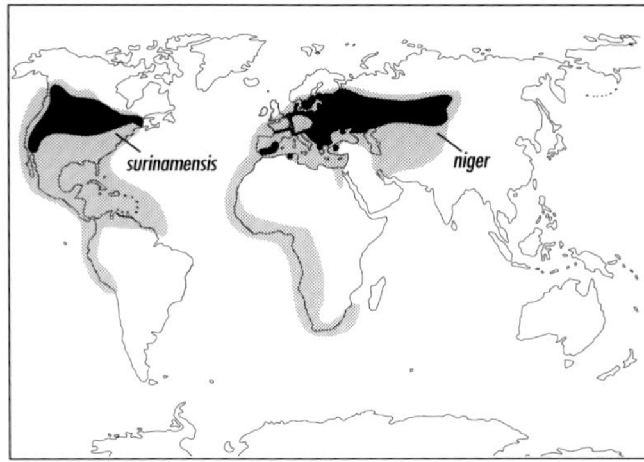


***MAP 20*** Distribution of Black Tern *Chlidonias niger.*

than on *niger* (less than 1 mm broad). Rarely, upperparts lack pale feather fringes. Rump and tail dark grey to dark grey-brown, at best slightly paler than back (especially rump, which can rarely have pale feather fringes; 10-15% may be similar to *niger*). The tail feathers have narrow pale edges. Upperparts lacking in contrast, having only slight suggestion of darker leading edge to wing.

**First-summer plumage** much as adult winter. Crown is white-spotted; some have more complete dark cap to mantle. Rump paler than tail, especially in fresh plumage (April-June). Upperparts dark grey with darker mantle and lesser coverts. In summer, 5-6 (9) inner primaries and t1-3 (6) have been replaced; all primaries may be new around August. Contrast between worn and new feathers on upperparts common. Moult similar to that of *niger*, although tends to moult larger number of primaries in spring.

**Second-summer plumage** much as adult summer, but can have an element of white on underparts.

### Measurements

In mm. Own measurements, BMNH, MN, NMNH, NNH, NRK, UZM, ZMA, ZMH, ZML, ZMO, ZMU. Nominate *niger*, north and central Europe and Siberia: April-September, juvenile August-September. Race *surinamensis*, North and Central America: adult May-August, juvenile August-September.

**WING LENGTH**

| | | | |
|---|---|---|---|
| *niger* | | | |
| Ad ♂ | 205-230 | (216.5) | n = 170 |
| Ad ♀ | 200-224 | (211.8) | n = 108 |
| Juv | 190-221 | (204.9) | n = 101 |
| *surinamensis* | | | |
| Ad ♂ | 200-225 | (211.2) | n = 103 |
| Ad ♀ | 196-223 | (208.8) | n = 54 |
| Juv | 193-213 | (200.8) | n = 61 |

**TAIL FORK**

| | | | |
|---|---|---|---|
| *niger* | | | |
| Ad ♂ | 11-26 | (16.6) | n = 170 |
| Ad ♀ | 11-23 | (16.1) | n = 113 |
| Juv | 8-19 | (12.8) | n = 92 |
| *surinamensis* | | | |
| Ad ♂ | 12-27 | (18.0) | n = 97 |
| Ad ♀ | 11-22 | (16.9) | n = 53 |
| Juv | 7-20 | (11.8) | n = 62 |

• Cramp (1985): *niger* Ad ♂ 15-25 (18.8, n = 38), Ad ♀ 13-21 (17.2, n = 31).
• Three *niger* in 1st summer: 14, 14 and 17; ten *surinamensis* 11-19.

**BILL**

| | | | |
|---|---|---|---|
| *niger* | | | |
| Ad ♂ | 25.0-30.0 | (27.5) | n = 171 |
| Ad ♀ | 23.8-28.7 | (26.5) | n = 107 |
| Juv | 20.7-27.0 | (24.2) | n = 95 |
| *surinamensis* | | | |
| Ad ♂ | 23.7-29.0 | (27.3) | n = 99 |
| Ad ♀ | 23.8-29.3 | (26.4) | n = 54 |
| Juv | 20.9-27.0 | (24.1) | n = 61 |

**BILL DEPTH AT GONYS**

| | | | |
|---|---|---|---|
| *niger* | | | |
| Ad ♂ | 4.8-6.1 | (5.2) | n = 171 |
| Ad ♀ | 4.6-5.8 | (5.1) | n = 107 |
| Juv | 4.3-5.8 | (4.8) | n = 94 |
| *surinamensis* | | | |
| Ad ♂ | 4.6-5.8 | (5.1) | n = 100 |
| Ad ♀ | 4.6-5.7 | (4.9) | n = 54 |
| Juv | 4.3-5.2 | (4.9) | n = 61 |

**BILL DEPTH AT REAR EDGE OF NOSTRILS**

| | | | |
|---|---|---|---|
| *niger* | | | |
| Ad ♂ | 5.5-7.1 | (6.2) | n = 171 |
| Ad ♀ | 5.4-7.2 | (5.9) | n = 110 |
| Juv | 4.9-6.5 | (5.6) | n = 95 |
| *surinamensis* | | | |
| Ad ♂ | 5.5-6.9 | (6.0) | n = 103 |
| Ad ♀ | 5.2-6.5 | (5.8) | n = 54 |
| Juv | 4.9-6.3 | (5.6) | n = 60 |

**TARSUS**

| | | | |
|---|---|---|---|
| *niger* | | | |
| Ad ♂ | 13.4-17.4 | (15.7) | n = 171 |
| Ad ♀ | 13.7-17.8 | (15.5) | n = 111 |
| Juv | 13.8-17.8 | (15.3) | n = 95 |
| *surinamensis* | | | |
| Ad ♂ | 15.0-17.9 | (16.4) | n = 103 |
| Ad ♀ | 13.8-17.7 | (16.0) | n = 54 |
| Juv | 14.5-17.7 | (15.9) | n = 61 |

• Cramp (1985) gives, for *niger*: Ad ♂ 15-18 (16.2, n = 39), Ad ♀ 15-17 (16.3, n = 38), juv 14.8-17.0 (16.2, n = 12).

**WEIGHT** (in grams)

Netherlands, August: Ad 60-86 (73.5, n = 28), juv 56-88 (71.9, n = 50) (Cramp 1985), lighter on average in May-July.
• Glutz *et al.* (1982) give, for breeding birds from Czechoslovakia: Ad ♂ 56.3-71.0 (61.7, n = 10), Ad ♀ 52.8-64.0 (57.4, n = 4).
• Two juvs from Denmark, late August, weighed 55 and 69.

# White-winged Black Tern

*Chlidonias leucopterus*

Photos **189-201**

### Identification in the field

The White-winged Black Tern is the smallest of the *Chlidonias* terns. It is a trifle shorter- and blunter-winged and shorter-tailed than Black Tern. The more rounded head and more delicate bill give it a 'good-natured', childlike appearance. The bill is clearly shorter than the length of the head. The highest point of the head is immediately above the eye. The tail fork is shallower, and the species shows an evenly squared-off tail more often than Black Tern. The legs are longer than Black Tern's, with visible 'knee' on upper 30%.

The flight recalls that of Black Tern, but is generally steadier and more direct, rather like that of Little Gull *Larus minutus*. The body seems to move less than Black Tern's in flight, which includes periods of gliding. It flies in dense flocks, e.g. when catching insects, the flocks showing more synchronised reactions than those of Black Tern. The Little Gull impression becomes more obvious in winter plumage, when the head has some features approaching those of Little Gull.

Proportions are of greatest value when identifying individuals in immature and winter plumages.

**Adult in summer plumage** is so striking that the proportions are largely overlooked: few other birds have such a contrasting and characteristic plumage, like a fancy-dress costume or a flying black-and-white patchwork.

Head, body and underwing-coverts are a deep velvety-black, with highly contrasting whitish leading edge of wing, white rump and tail and pale remiges. Particularly striking is the razor-sharp contrast between mantle and lesser coverts, while further back the contrast is somewhat less, especially on birds with a dark secondary bar and greyer areas on inner median and greater coverts. These areas can create a diffuse grey triangle on the inner wing, which is broadest at the rear. Rump and tail are white. The outer 2-3 (4) primaries are blackish and contrast with the otherwise very pale outer part of the wing. The bill is black, and the legs blood-red.

Perched birds, too, show conspicuous contrast between black body and white leading edge of wing.

The contrasts in summer plumage are extremely striking in direct lighting, but against the light, when pale areas become darker, the differences between pale and dark colours are reduced.

As with Black Tern, parts of the face are moulted in late May to early June while the young are small. Unlike Black, however, areas around bill and throat are moulted simultaneously so that the face becomes white-freckled. Typically, the throat does not become white before the rest of the head. The body is moulted progressively during the autumn. Usually the black underwing-coverts are moulted last, and black elements can be present in otherwise pure winter plumage. Most commonly these are also the areas which are moulted first into summer plumage, which of course facilitates identification.

**Adult winter plumage** is paler than that of Black Tern, especially on the foreparts. Most important is that the species lacks Black Tern's dark patches on the breast sides, but the head is also whiter, having only black ear-coverts and dark-streaked crown, normally separated from each other by a white supercilium. Some can be white-headed apart from dark ear-coverts. The nape, seen from behind, is white with a narrow dark central stripe which broadens somewhat downwards (like a 'pony-tail'). The white neck sides extend farther up into the nape than on Black Tern.

The upperparts are pale grey, with narrow dark bars on lesser coverts and secondaries. In late winter, the bars stand out clearly against faded median and greater coverts. The rump is even paler and sometimes contrasts clearly with grey back and tail, but in late winter pale feather tips are often abraded and the contrast diminishes. The outer tail feathers have white outer webs, which can be conspicuous on the spread tail. Black tips to the greater coverts often form a diagnostic black bar across the white underwing. The legs are red.

Head markings combined with delicate black bill give the winter plumage a character approaching that of Little Gull.

The moult to summer plumage takes place in March-April, when every conceivable type of transitional plumage is seen. Normally at least 50-70% of the underwing-coverts are black. From April, bears summer plumage (many birds studied during final stages of spring passage in North Africa, Israel and Greece).

**Juvenile** is contrastingly marked – upperparts in fact mirror adult's pattern. The head may be Black Tern-like in early autumn, but with narrower dark stripe in nape centre as white neck sides reach farther up than on Black Tern. Seen from behind, shows a distinct 'pony-tail' as dark coloration broadens downwards. A white supercilium soon appears and the head becomes similar to that of winter plumage.

The underparts are white, very rarely with faint brown breast-side patches as on a poorly marked Black Tern. Dark brownish-black mantle, back, scapulars and tertials form a distinct dark saddle, striking both in flight and when perched. The feathers are dark brownish-black with mid-grey bases, but some feathers (especially tertials and scapulars) may have paler fringes, though these are narrower than on Black Tern. Rarely, the upperparts are paler grey, but always clearly contrasting with wings and rump.

The upperwing is contrastingly marked, with white leading edge (broader than Black Tern's), dark lesser-covert bar and pale grey central area contrasting with darker remiges. The rump is white, while the tail-coverts are grey and slightly paler than the grey tail. T6 has a white outer web; occasionally, a narrow dark terminal band is visible on the tail.

Juvenile is distinguished from Black Tern by more contrasting upperparts with darker saddle/paler wings, white rump and white outer web to outermost tail feathers. The head from autumn is paler and the breast sides white without Black Tern's distinct dark patches. Bill and legs are of same colour as Black Tern's, but respectively shorter and longer.

Juvenile plumage is largely retained during autumn migration, but scattered pale grey feathers can appear from September, and exceptionally the species is in first-winter plumage in September (Cramp 1985).

**First-winter/first-summer plumage** is acquired in winter quarters, and is generally speaking retained into the first summer, when the plumage is washed out and worn. The plumage is much as adult winter, with similar head and underparts. The upperparts are pale grey-brown to grey with dark bars on lesser coverts and secondaries. Sometimes the mantle is somewhat darker than the scapulars and back. Retained juvenile mantle, back, scapulars and tertials may be present.

During the summer the inner 2-5 primaries are normally replaced by new pale grey ones, contrasting with the worn, grey-brown outer primaries. A few have replaced all primaries in June-July.

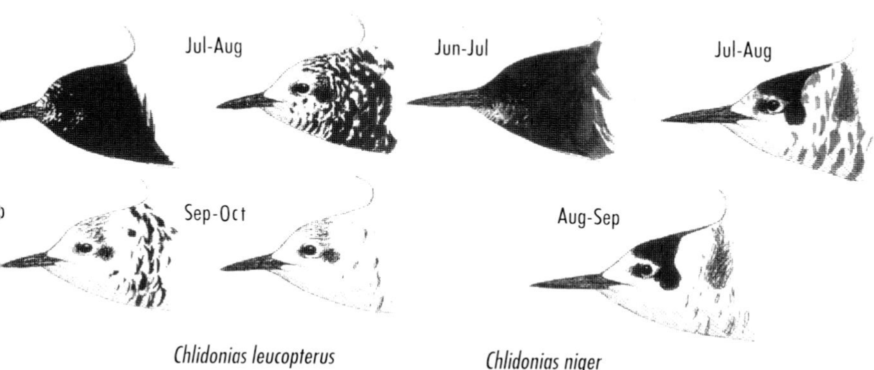


**FIGURE 7** Development from summer to winter head in White-winged Tern and nominate Black Tern. The normal development in White-winged Black is an equal spread of pale feathers in face, thus making face white-mottled in early stages of moult (from end of May to middle of June). In Black Tern, throat and cheeks normally are moulted earliest, followed by feathers around eye. There is some variation, but the development shown holds good for the majority. Note, however, that in the Nearctic race of Black Tern (*surinamensis*) the moult is in most cases similar to that of White-winged Black.

The legs are greyish-red, sometimes red as on adults.

Underparts and underwing-coverts are normally white, but some may acquire small areas of black.

**Second-summer plumage** is much as adult summer plumage, but is dull black rather than velvety-black, and sometimes brown-tinged. Normally elements of white are present on body and, especially, underwing-coverts, which then become blotchy. Alula and primary coverts are dark-patterned (white on adult). Outer 4 primaries are often darker and browner than on adults. The secondaries usually have a dark bar across inner half. The tail can be greyer than on adults, and often worn, with several generations of rectrices.

It should be borne in mind that some adults probably do not moult completely into summer plumage (Schmidt 1991). The safest subadult characters are dull black head and body, dark alula and primary coverts, spotted underwing-coverts and often 4 dark outer primaries.

## Voice

A hoarse and dry *kersch*, deeper and harsher than Black Tern's, can recall that of Little Tern. Also a short *kett* or *kreck*.

## Moult

**Adult** has a complete moult to **winter plumage**. The moult begins in late May to early June on the breeding grounds. First to be moulted are feathers around bill base, in forehead and lores. During brood-feeding period the face becomes white-freckled, rarely with white throat. In July the rest of the head is moulted, while the body is normally moulted in August, with belly last. Many have completed the head and body moult in early September. At the same time the primary moult commences, though inner primaries may be renewed in early June. Primary moult is arrested during autumn migration with 1-5 new. In skin series, up to 7 inners have been replaced. Primary moult is normally completed in Decem-

1
2
5
3
4
6
8
7
7
7
12
9
10
11

**PLATE 40**

**White-winged Black Tern *Chlidonias leucopterus.***

The smallest marsh tern, with proportionally shorter and weaker bill, more rounded head and least forked tail. Flight action as congeners.

1 **Juvenile.** In fresh plumage, head pattern is similar to that of Black Tern, but with traces of white supercilium and broader white extension on neck sides. Mantle dark brown, showing rather good contrast with paler wings (compared with Black Tern).

2 **Juvenile.** Brightly coloured individual. Crown in juveniles soon becomes white-streaked, isolating dark ear coverts.

3 **Juvenile.** In flight, note good contrast between back and wings. Breast sides white, lacking dark patch of Black and some Whiskered Terns. White rump is in good contrast to brown back and in less contrast to pale grey tail. Outer tail feathers have white outer webs.

4 **Juvenile.** Exceptionally, a small brown patch is visible on breast sides. Whole plumage juvenile into at least beginning of September, when some grey feathers may appear on mantle.

5 **First-summer/adult winter.** In first summer, as adult winter (see text). Head predominantly white, with dark ear-coverts and dark-streaked crown. Some appear mostly white-headed.

6 **First-summer/adult winter.** Similar to Whiskered Tern, but note reduced dark head markings, darker lesser-covert bar, lack of dark patches at sides of breast and whitish rump.

7 **Adult summer.** Striking black and white plumage makes adult summers among the most beautiful and easy-to-identify terns. Note deep velvety-black body and underwing-coverts contrasting with whitish wings. On upperparts, contrast is very strong between black mantle and white lesser coverts. Bill black or reddish-brown, legs bright red.

8 **Adult summer moulting into winter plumage (June-July).** Moult starts when young hatch. Face then becomes white-freckled.

9 **Adult moulting into winter plumage (August to mid September).** During early autumn gradually whiter. Normally, black underwing-coverts are moulted last, thus standing out against predominantly pale plumage.

10 **Adult in almost complete winter plumage (late September/October to March).** Very pale. Many show diagnostic black bar across underwing in winter.

11 **Adult summer.** Strikingly black and white even when perched.

12 **Second-summer.** Matt black. Broader dark outer hand. White mottling on underwing-coverts.

ber-February. T1 may be moulted before the autumn migration; rarely, the entire tail is moulted before migration.

The rest of the moult takes place during autumn migration. Last to be moulted are underwing-coverts, tertials, and parts of median and greater coverts. Some greater underwing-coverts may be retained, or have black tips in winter.

A second moult series in the primaries may begin in late November to early January, and is suspended in late April to early May with 6-8 (9) inner primaries new. At the same time a new moult series begins in the tail. A second moult series of the secondaries (outers) begins in May.

**Adult** has a partial moult to **summer plumage**. The moult includes head, body, tail, wing-coverts and inner primaries (see above). The moult commences in early February to early March with lesser and median upperwing-coverts, tertials and the longest scapulars, followed by underwing-coverts. Several hundred individuals scrutinised in the Gambia in late March to mid April were very variable, but at least 50-70% of the underwing-coverts had been moulted, and 5-10% were in full summer plumage. Cramp (1985) states that the majority have replaced the wing feathers, body, tail and most of the upperparts, while the head can still be in winter plumage in mid April. On arrival in the West Palearctic (from mid April), more or less all are in summer plumage (all birds examined in

**WHITE-WINGED BLACK TERN** QUICK KEY TO IDENTIFICATION

1 **Summer-plumaged adult highly characteristic. Black head/body and underwing-coverts contrast sharply with pale wing and undertail-coverts.**
2 **Razor-sharp contrast between mantle and lesser coverts, gradually diminishing towards lower back.**
3 **Rump white.**
4 **Bill shorter but legs longer than Black Tern's.**
5 **In winter/immature plumages, head is white with black ear-coverts and grey-streaked crown.**
6 **Apart from exceptional cases, lacks dark patch on breast sides.**
7 **Juvenile's upperparts mirror those of adult: good contrast between dark saddle and pale wings, both on flying and on perched birds.**
8 **Juveniles soon develop adult head markings.**
9 **Juveniles have pale upperwings with narrow dark bar on lesser coverts.**
10 **In winter plumage pale, but often with traces of dark bar on greater underwing-coverts.**

North Africa, Middle East and Greece mid April to mid May).

Some begin a third series in the primaries in early February to mid April, which is arrested in May with inner 3 (4) replaced. About 20% are said not to replace the inner primaries at this time (Cramp 1985). The percentage is likely sometimes to be greater: a few observed in Greece in early to mid May had a moult limit in the inner primaries.

**Juvenile** has a complete moult to **first-winter plumage**. The moult may begin in September with a few upperpart feathers, but it is likely that the plumage is mostly moulted quite rapidly after arrival in the winter quarters, from November. In mid to late November, head, parts of the body and upperwing-coverts together with t1-2 have been moulted, but upperparts on the whole juvenile. Areas of mantle, back, scapulars and tertials (especially tertials) and also lesser coverts may be juvenile up to late January. The moult normally terminates in February, but odd upperpart feathers, wing-coverts and outer tail feathers may be retained until May-June (pers. obs.). The primary moult begins in late November to early February, when inner 3-5 primaries are replaced, and ends in June-August (commonest with birds which oversummer in winter quarters). Some change only 2-4 inner primaries during the winter and presumably moult the rest in late summer and autumn (when up to 4 outer primaries can be worn). Rarely, all primaries are juvenile until late January (skins, BMNH).

In **first summer** head and body are retained from first winter, but a minor element of black may be acquired in head and body. A second primary moult series begins in May-June, at the same as the plumage is replaced by **second-winter plumage**. In December-January, 1-2 outer primaries and central tail feathers are in moult.

Moult to **second-summer plumage** much as that of adult, but some probably change only part of the plumage in the second summer. Some birds in May had renewed the inner 6 primaries and the tail, apart from t2-4.

#### Detailed description

Length 20-23 cm, wingspan 63-67 cm.

**Adult summer plumage:** Head, body and underwing-coverts velvety-black, with slight green tinge to crown, neck sides and nape. Scapulars dull black to blackish-grey; may retain odd scapulars from winter plumage. Greater underwing-coverts rarely pale. Rump to tail and undertail-coverts white. Uppertail-coverts sometimes pale grey. T1, more rarely also t2-5, pale grey. Outer (1) 2-3 (4) primaries blackish (tinged silvery-grey in spring, brownish in summer and autumn). Remaining primaries silver-grey, any fresh inners paler silver-grey. Secondaries and tertials mid-grey. Inner secondaries (up to 50%) generally darkest. Some have pale grey secondaries, but usually the inners are darker. Lesser upperwing-coverts white, median coverts pale grey, greater coverts mid-grey. Primary coverts and some greater coverts pale grey or white. Inner median and greater coverts are often darkest, and together with dark inner secondaries form a dark triangle on rear inner wing.

Underwing bicoloured. Pale flight-feather bases contrast well with black underwing-coverts. Primary coverts and greater coverts can be paler grey.

In July-August variable. The majority have head and forebody in winter plumage, while the rest of the body is in transitional plumage. Underwing-coverts normally black.

Sexes more or less identical. Males generally the cleanest, most contrastingly marked; the tail is white, but often has some grey feathers (especially t3-5). Females are generally duller black, with grey-toned body and scapulars; tail white to grey (grey tail commoner on females than on males).

Bill black to dark red, with carmine-red base in breeding season. Legs blood-red to orange-red.

**Adult winter plumage:** Forehead, forecrown and supercilium white. Crown white with variable blackish streaking. Ear-coverts and central parts of crown black, broadest at rear of nape. Nape sides and underparts white; greater underwing-coverts may have black tips. Mantle and lesser coverts dark grey. Back, median coverts and greater coverts together with scapulars pale grey. May retain scattered body feathers from summer plumage.

Rump and uppertail-coverts white. Tail pale grey; t6 has white outer web.

Secondaries and outer primaries black to blackish-grey before the moult in September-December. Fresh feathers mid-grey with silvery tinge.

In worn plumage (winter and early spring), upperpart contrasts are most distinct: dark lesser-covert and secondary bars stand out against pale, washed-out coverts.

Bill black. Legs dark red with grey or black tinge.

**Juvenile:** Head rather as adult winter, but crown is blacker (resembling Black Tern) and forehead to crown in fresh plumage are tinged yellowish-brown. From September, head becomes much as that of adult winter. Mantle, back, scapulars and tertials dark brownish-black with grey bases and narrow pale fringes. Scapulars and tertials may have broader pale bases, and rarely mantle and back are dark grey. Tertials can have dark subterminal spot. Rump white (rarely, grey-toned). Uppertail-coverts mid-grey with pale fringes. Lesser upperwing-coverts and primary coverts blackish-grey with variable pale fringes. Median and greater coverts pale grey. Tail feathers grey with white outer webs; t6 has white outer web, perhaps with grey tinge near tip. Remiges dark grey with slight silvery coloration. Primaries have narrow white fringes, broadest on inner primaries.

Underparts white. Rarely (<1%) with diffuse mid-brown patch on breast sides (always weaker than Black Tern's).

Bill blackish-brown with paler red to greyish-yellow base. Legs red, red-brown or greyish-orange.

**First-winter/first-summer plumage** (and **second-winter plumage**): Much as adult winter plumage. In first summer like worn adult winter, but outer primaries (up to 5) grey-brown from wear. Head and body normally in winter plumage, but elements of black may be present on body and underwing-coverts. Some juvenile wing-coverts may be retained. Moults to winter plumage later than adults. Worn outer primaries can be present up to December-January in second winter.

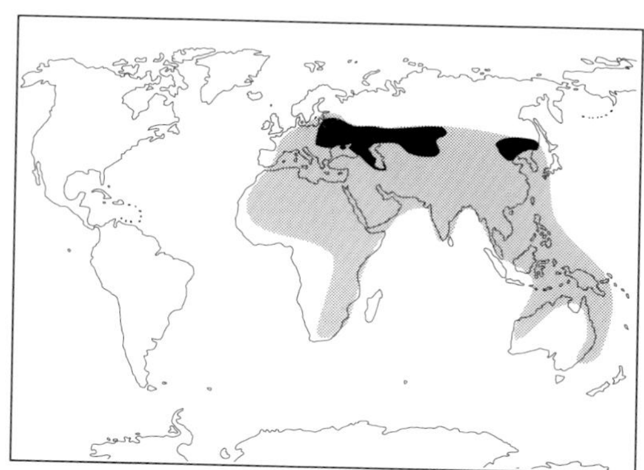

***MAP 21*** **Distribution of White-winged Black Tern *Chlidonias leucopterus*.**

**Second-summer plumage:** Much as adult summer, but head and body dull black (brown-toned). Underparts and especially underwing-coverts have variable element of white feathering. Outer 3-5 primaries worn and brownish. Secondaries generally darker than in adult summer plumage. Primary coverts and alula dark. Tail grey, or white with some old grey rectrices (especially t3-5).

## Geographical variation

Slight. Birds from Southeast Asia have on average longer and deeper bill than West Palearctic birds: ad ♂ 23.9-28.0 (25.9, n = 18), ad ♀ 23.9-25.8 (24.8, n = 13); bill depth at gonys, ad 5.7-7.1 (6.3, n = 10).

## Hybrids

Interbreeding between Black Tern and White-winged Black Tern has been described from Sweden (Alexandersson 1979) and the Netherlands (van IJzendoorn 1980). In both cases, the Black Tern was a male. The literature contains a couple of descriptions of presumed juvenile Black x White-winged Black Tern hybrids (Vinicombe 1980; Davis 1982).

*Individual 1* (Davis 1982, September): Shape and flight as Black Tern. Plumage much as juvenile White-winged Black, but saddle paler brown. Rear edge of head dark. Rear scapulars with broad pale fringes. Dark breast-side patches as on Black Tern, but browner. Underwing as juvenile Black Tern.

*Individual 2* (Vinicombe 1980, September): Shape and flight as Black Tern, but plumage much as juvenile White-winged Black. Cap paler brown than on both species. Saddle darkest on mantle, less distinct than on White-winged Black and with pale fringes. Leading edge of wing white (as winter-plumaged White-winged Black), but inner lesser coverts dark. Some median coverts dark. Narrow dark bar across greater primary coverts and central greater coverts. Rump white, tinged grey. Dark breast-side patches as on Black Tern, but paler brown. Bill black with red base. Legs very short and reddish-brown.

### Measurements

In mm. Own measurements, BMNH, MN, NNH, NRK, UZM, ZMA, ZML, ZMO, ZMU. Central Europe (May-August) and Africa (November-April); juveniles/1st-winters August-March.

WING LENGTH

| | | | |
|---|---|---|---|
| Ad ♂ | 205-221 | (208.6) | n = 50 |
| Ad ♀ | 190-218 | (206.5) | n = 51 |
| Juv | 193-216 | (203.7) | n = 69 |

• Hario (1986) gives: Ad 193-218 (202, n = 8), juv 186-208 (198, n = 12). Glutz *et al.* (1982) give, for east European birds: Ad ♂ 205-221 (215.3, n = 9), Ad ♀ 201-218 (210.5, n = 7).

TAIL FORK

| | | | |
|---|---|---|---|
| Ad ♂ | 5-12 | (8.2) | n = 51 |
| Ad ♀ | 4-13 | (7.9) | n = 43 |
| Juv | 4-12 | (7.3) | n = 66 |

BILL

| | | | |
|---|---|---|---|
| Ad ♂ | 21.0-27.9 | (23.9) | n = 50 |
| Ad ♀ | 21.2-26.4 | (23.3) | n = 51 |
| Juv | 20.0-26.0 | (23.2) | n = 66 |

• Hario (1986) gives: Ad 20.9-24.1 (22.6, n = 8), juv 20.0-24.3 (21.9, n = 12). Cramp (1985) gives: Ad ♂ 25-28 (25.9, n = 28), Ad ♀ 23-26 (24.7, n = 34).

BILL DEPTH AT GONYS

| | | | |
|---|---|---|---|
| Ad ♂ | 4.9-5.9 | (5.3) | n = 50 |
| Ad ♀ | 4.7-5.9 | (5.2) | n = 51 |
| Juv | 4.7-5.6 | (5.1) | n = 66 |

BILL DEPTH AT REAR EDGE OF NOSTRILS

| | | | |
|---|---|---|---|
| Ad ♂ | 5.8-7.0 | (6.5) | n = 50 |
| Ad ♀ | 5.5-7.0 | (6.1) | n = 51 |
| Juv | 5.3-6.8 | (6.0) | n = 66 |

TARSUS

| | | | |
|---|---|---|---|
| Ad ♂ | 17.9-20.8 | (18.9) | n = 51 |
| Ad ♀ | 17.3-20.6 | (18.9) | n = 51 |
| Juv | 17.3-20.6 | (18.9) | n = 66 |

• Hario (1986) gives: Ad 22.7-26.2 (23.7, n = 9), juv 22.2-25.1 (23.6, n = 7). Cramp (1985) gives: Ad ♂ 19-21 (20.0, n = 21), Ad ♀ 18-21 (19.6, n = 28).

WEIGHT (in grams)

Ad ♂♂ from Kazakhstan and Mongolia, June-July, 60-80 (68.7, n = 11); Lake Baikal, Ad ♂ 65.2-76.8, Ad ♀ 61.6-76.8 (Glutz *et al.* 1982). Ad ♂, Netherlands, 4 September, 58 (skin, ZMA 35701).

# Brown Noddy

*Anous stolidus*

Photos **202-206**

### Identification in the field

Unlike other terns, the Brown Noddy is dark throughout the year and has a long, wedge-shaped tail. It is thus distinctive and can hardly be confused with other terns apart from other *Anous* species. Brown Noddy is the largest of these. It is almost as big as Sandwich Tern, but, compared with other terns, has relatively shorter and broader wings. Dark plumage and wedge-shaped tail (appears pointed when closed) make this species most likely to be confused with certain shearwaters and skuas. The purposeful flight, however, is more direct, with almost plover (*Pluvialis*)-like wingbeats (can also be compared with those of Sooty Tern or smaller gulls). It often rests for long periods on sandbanks, rocks and posts and the like. It does not plunge-dive, but snatches food direct from the water's surface.

The plumage is brownish-black, but with paler forehead and somewhat darker primaries. The median underwing-coverts are paler than the body. The wedge-shaped tail is normally very obvious, but when the central tail feathers are in moult the tail becomes forked for a brief period. The 'streamers', however, never look long, narrow and pointed – instead it appears as if the central part is missing. The shape of the fork can also look rather like that of Leach's Storm-petrel *Oceanodroma leucorhoa*. Brown Noddy is dark grey-brown with slightly darker remiges and pale forehead. Only in good lighting does it become slightly two-toned, with darker flight feathers and a shade paler upperparts.

The bill is the most powerful of that of all *Anous* species. The upper mandible has a clearly curved tip.

**Adult** has whitish-grey forehead merging into violet-grey crown. The pale forehead contrasts well with the black loral stripe, which normally has curved edges. Broad white crescents above and below the eye give a 'spectacled' appearance. The black loral stripe normally continues into a narrow black band across the lower forehead. The plumage is otherwise blackish-brown, slightly paler (especially on belly) when worn. The blacker flight feathers, however, show only poor contrast with the rest of the plumage. The long black bill is quite powerful and distinctive. The legs are dark red-brown. The plumage is fairly similar throughout the year.

**Juvenile** is much as adult, but is duller blackish-brown with more poorly demarcated grey-brown forehead and crown, though clearly whitish on the forehead. Forehead and crown normally have dark spots. Coverts and upperparts have narrow pale feather fringes (though these are visible only at close range). The outline of the black loral stripe varies in shape, and is often straight; on the other hand, it is common for the loral stripe not to continue across the forehead.

**Subadults** are adult-like, and probably cannot be separated in the field once the head has been moulted.

### Voice

A harsh *kark*.

### Moult

**Adult** has a complete moult after the breeding season. Primary moult begins with the inner primary during or immedi-

**BROWN NODDY** QUICK KEY TO IDENTIFICATION

1. **Compact, dark tern with wedge-shaped tail.**
2. **Forehead is pale, merging gradually into crown.**
3. **Can be taken for a shearwater in flight, but has longer tail, more obviously wedge-shaped than on any shearwater.**
4. **Differs from skuas in lacking pale areas on inner hand.**
5. **Central parts of underwing are paler than belly and fore- and hindwing.**
6. **Bill is more powerful than that of similar species, with clearly curved tip to upper mandible; bill never looks disproportionately thin. It is as long as the head.**
7. **Juvenile much as adult, but forehead often whiter and slightly scaly.**

ately following the brood-feeding period, and is completed after 6-7 months (Cramp 1985). Outer primaries often worn in October-December. Tail moult commences when inner 1-4 primaries have been renewed. Moult sequence normally t1-t6-t3-t2-t4-t5, sometimes asymmetrical. Body feathers are moulted at same time as tail moult begins. South Atlantic populations are said to have a different moult, beginning primary moult a few months before the breeding season and finishing it during brood-feeding, when a new moult series may begin. A partial moult takes place before the breeding season, when head, body feathers and tail are renewed (at least among populations with a 12-month breeding cycle: Cramp 1985). Sometimes the inner 1-3 primaries are also moulted.

**Juveniles** have a complete moult within their first year. After 7-11 months the primary moult commences.

**Detailed description** *Anous stolidus stolidus*

**Adult:** Forehead pale grey to greyish-white, merging diffusely into darker, often lilac-grey to blue-grey crown. Narrow white line between forehead and lores. Lores black (may continue as a narrow black area above bill base). Eyelids white. Rest of head, body and wing-coverts sooty-brown, but face and undertail-coverts grey-toned. Lesser underwing-coverts darker. Flight and tail feathers together with primary coverts and alula black. With wear, the plumage becomes more uniformly dark, and pale forehead stands out conspicuously. Central part of upperwing then becomes paler, contrasting with darker lesser coverts and remiges. In winter, many individuals have grey spots in central forehead and crown. Bill black. Legs are black, sometimes with brown tinge to tarsus.

Adult males generally have cleaner and paler forehead and also deeper blue-grey to violet-grey tinge to neck sides. Females often have dark-spotted central forehead and crown and generally have browner and duller head than males.

**Juvenile:** Much as adult, but in fresh plumage darker and without grey coloration. Forehead is greyish with white feather fringes, most obvious towards lores (appears slightly scaly). Crown darker than adult's. Often lacks black area over bill base (Malling Olsen 1989). Upperparts have narrow pale feather fringes. With wear, crown becomes concolorous with rest of head, and pale forehead is then smaller than on adults, and can disappear when heavily worn; upperpart feathers can fade to mid-brown.

**Immatures:** Similar to adults, but may have less distinct, grey-toned crown.

## Geographical variation

Slight. Race *pileatus* (Red Sea, Indian Ocean and Pacific Ocean) in fresh plumage has more distinctly blue-toned forehead and crown, darker than *stolidus*. Ear-coverts (and also head and body) have plum-coloured tinge. Seems generally to have darker head than *stolidus*. Nominate *stolidus* generally has longer wings than *pileatus* (see Measurements). In addition, the front part of the forehead is often whiter (whitish-grey) and the crown sides tinged violet-grey. A larger percentage than of *pileatus* lack the black line above the bill base. Populations from Western Australia are the darkest (Cramp 1985).

**Measurements**

In mm. Own measurements, NNH, UZM, ZMA, ZML, ZMO. Race *pileatus*, Indian Ocean, Fiji, Tahiti and Samoa; *stolidus*, Caribbean and Surinam.

WING LENGTH

| | | | |
|---|---|---|---|
| *pileatus* | | | |
| Ad ♂ | 275-299 | (287.7) | n = 15 |
| Ad ♀ | 265-290 | (275.8) | n = 15 |
| Juv | 249-264 | (259.6) | n = 6 |
| *stolidus* | | | |
| Ad ♂ | 268-277 | (272.0) | n = 10 |
| Ad ♀ | 254-273 | (262.5) | n = 16 |

• Two juv *stolidus* 258 and 269.

BILL

| | | | |
|---|---|---|---|
| *pileatus* | | | |
| Ad ♂ | 40.1-45.6 | (43.3) | n = 17 |
| Ad ♀ | 37.5-44.5 | (40.9) | n = 19 |
| Juv | 34.8-41.3 | (38.3) | n = 6 |
| *stolidus* | | | |
| Ad ♂ | 40.0-48.0 | (44.3) | n = 10 |
| Ad ♀ | 37.8-42.9 | (41.5) | n = 16 |

BILL DEPTH AT GONYS

| | | | |
|---|---|---|---|
| *pileatus* | | | |
| Ad ♂ | 7.7-8.7 | (8.2) | n = 15 |
| Ad ♀ | 7.0-8.3 | (7.6) | n = 19 |
| Juv | 6.4-7.0 | (6.8) | n = 6 |
| *stolidus* | | | |
| Ad ♂ | 7.2-8.8 | (8.1) | n = 11 |
| Ad ♀ | 6.5-8.1 | (7.1) | n = 15 |

BILL DEPTH AT REAR EDGE OF NOSTRILS

| | | | |
|---|---|---|---|
| *pileatus* | | | |
| Ad ♂ | 8.9-10.0 | (9.5) | n = 15 |
| Ad ♀ | 8.0-10.0 | (9.1) | n = 17 |
| Juv | 6.5-8.2 | (7.8) | n = 6 |
| *stolidus* | | | |
| Ad ♂ | 8.5-10.1 | (9.3) | n = 11 |
| Ad ♀ | 7.9-9.6 | (8.7) | n = 15 |

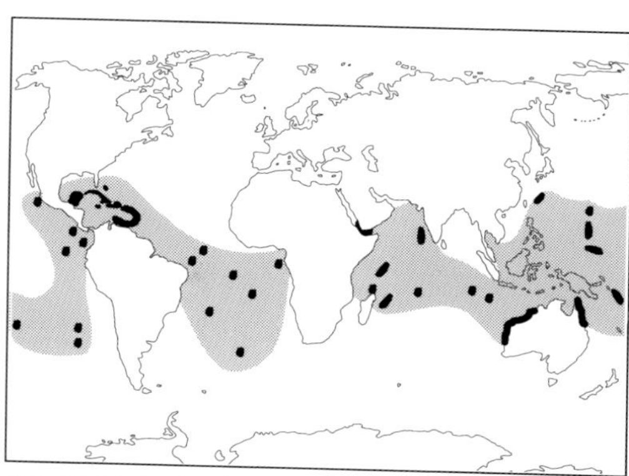

***MAP 22*** Distribution of Brown Noddy *Anous stolidus.*

TARSUS

| | | | |
|---|---|---|---|
| *pileatus* | | | |
| Ad ♂ | 22.8-27.9 | (24.9) | n = 15 |
| Ad ♀ | 22.2-26.5 | (20.8) | n = 18 |
| Juv | 20.5-23.8 | (23.0) | n = 6 |
| *stolidus* | | | |
| Ad ♂ | 21.9-25.2 | (23.6) | n = 11 |
| Ad ♀ | 21.5-23.9 | (22.5) | n = 11 |

• Two juv *stolidus* 21.8 and 24.2. Cramp (1985) gives, for *pileatus*: ad ♂ 25-27 (25.7, n = 9), ad ♀ 25-26 (25.6, n = 5).

WEIGHT (in grams)

Nominate *stolidus*, breeding ad 160-205, generally lighter after breeding season (Cramp 1985). Race *pileatus*, breeding ad 177-204.

# Black Noddy

Photos **207-208**

*Anous minutus*

### Identification in the field

The Black Noddy breeds in tropical waters, in Oceania, the Caribbean and in central parts of the Atlantic at the same places as Brown Noddy. Compared with the latter, it is smaller and slimmer, and looks all black in the field, including on the underwing-coverts. Most important is the fact that the bill is much thinner and relatively longer – clearly longer than the head (equal in length on Brown Noddy). The bill has only a slightly curved tip. The head markings recall those of Brown Noddy with the latter's pale forehead, but the forehead is often whiter and in the black plumage stands out more conspicuously on the face. The border of the lores with the forehead is often straight, and the lower forehead is white and lacks the black band over the bill base shown by many Brown Noddies, but this feature is of less value than the bill, since the border can be curved as on most Brown Noddies. Note in addition that Brown Noddy (especially juveniles) can have a straighter edge to the loral stripe.

The thinness of the bill is accentuated by its shape. The sides are convex, so that the outer part when seen head-on appears strikingly thin. In this respect, the bill shape is rather like that of Roseate Tern.

**Adult** has a white forehead and crown sharply demarcated from black lores but more poorly so from the greyish, often silver-toned nape. The plumage is otherwise entirely blackish-brown; the slightly blacker flight feathers and the sometimes grey-toned breast are not normally detectable in the field. The tail has been reported as greyer than that of Brown Noddy (Harrison 1983). With wear, the plumage becomes brown-tinged, but is

***PLATE 41***

**Brown Noddy *Anous stolidus* and Black Noddy *Anous minutus***

Noddies are brown, unusual terns with wedge-shaped tails, from tropical waters.

1 **Brown Noddy, adult.** Fresh adult plumage is dark brown, but with wear paler. Note pale covert bar. Underwing paler than body. Not, that moulting noddies may show forked tail (when central tail feathers are missing), but tail shape always appears different from that of other terns.

2 **Black Noddy, adult.** Smaller and blacker than Brown Noddy, with uniform dark upper- and underwings. Bill much more slender than on Brown, often looking disproportionally slim. White cap extends further through crown than on most Brown Noddies.

3 **Brown Noddy, juvenile.** Similar to adult, but in fresh plumage with pale edges to upperpart feathers and mottled cap.

4 **Brown Noddy, adult.** Fresh plumage. Note dark bar across base of upper mandible and grey tinge to neck sides (in some populations lavender-coloured).

5 **Brown Noddy, juvenile.** Some birds show whiter cap, often with some dark feathers. Best separated from worn (thus brown-tinged) Black Noddy by shape and relative length of bill.

6 **Black Noddy, juvenile.** Generally darker than Brown Noddy, with narrower pale feather fringes to upperparts.

7 **Black Noddy, adult.** In fresh plumage sooty-black, but with wear brown-tinged, although always darker than Brown Noddy. Note very slender bill and broader, more contrasting whitish cap than on Brown Noddy. Black edge of lores normally straighter than the curved shape on Brown Noddy.

1
2
4
5
7

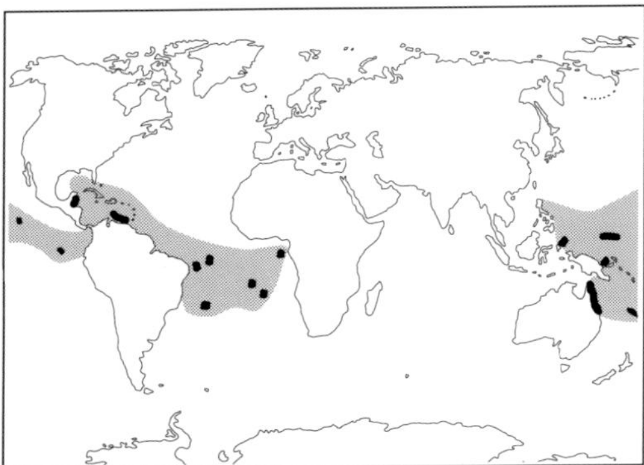

**MAP 23** Distribution of Black Noddy *Anous minutus.*

always darker than Brown Noddy's.

**Juvenile** differs from adult in having the white forehead and crown sharply demarcated from the nape. Upperparts and upperwing-coverts also have narrow yellowish-brown fringes. The entire plumage is a duller brownish-black than adult's.

## Moult

Probably much as that of Brown Noddy.

**BLACK NODDY** QUICK KEY TO IDENTIFICATION

1. **Smaller and slimmer than Brown Noddy and with all-black plumage.**
2. **Bill very thin and long, longer than head length.**
3. **Forehead often whiter than Brown Noddy's.**
4. **Underwing-coverts dark, as rest of underparts.**

### Measurements

In mm. Own measurements, NNH, UZM. Race *minutus*, Kermadec, Australia and Micronesia.

**WING LENGTH**

Ad 218-238 (228.8) n = 21
• ♂ 225-234 (229.1, n = 6), ♀ 218-230 (223.9, n = 6).
• Five *americanus* ads 220-222 (Caribbean, NNH).

**BILL**

Ad 39.0-45.8 (42.2) n = 23
• ♂ 39-45 (41.8, n = 5), ♀ 39.5-43.3 (41.6, n = 5).
• Two *americanus* ads 41.3 and 43.2 (Caribbean, NNH).

**BILL DEPTH AT GONYS**

Ad 5.3-7.0 (6.0) n = 23
• ♂ 5.6-7.0 (6.0, n = 5), ♀ 5.3-6.6 (5.9, n = 6).
• Two *americanus* ads 6.0 and 6.5 (Caribbean, NNH).

**BILL DEPTH AT REAR EDGE OF NOSTRILS**

Ad 6.6-7.8 (7.3) n = 23
• ♂ 6.6-7.8 (7.1, n = 5), ♀ 6.8-8.4 (7.4, n = 5).
• Two *americanus* ads 6.9 and 7.6 (Caribbean, NNH).

**TARSUS**

Ad 18.5-22.3 (20.5) n = 21
• ♂ 20.2-22.0 (21.1, n = 5), ♀ 20.0-22.3 (21.04, n = 5).
• Two *americanus* ads 19.9 and 21.0 (Caribbean, NNH).

**WEIGHT** (in grams)

Three ads 95-110 (NNH, UZM).

# References

*Includes works cited and consulted.*


Alexandersson, H. 1979. En hybridisering mellan vitvingad tärna *Chlidonias leucopterus* och svarttärna *Chlidonias niger* på Öland 1978. *Calidris* 8:151-3.

Alström, P. 1989. Identification of marsh terns in juvenile and winter plumage. *Brit. Birds* 82: 296-319.

– 1991. Fältbestämning av *Chlidonias*-tärnor. *Vår Fågelvärld* 51, 5: 56-9.

–, P. Colston & I. Lewington. 1992. *En fälthandbok över sällsynta fåglar i Europa*. Domino Books, Jersey.

Andersen, F.S. 1959. Bills, eggs and nests of captured Arctic terns *Sterna paradisaea* and Common Terns *Sterna hirundo*. *Dansk Orn. Foren. Tidsskr.* 53.

Austin, O. 1938. Some results from adult tern trapping at the Cape Cod colonies. *Bird Banding* 9: 12-25.

Bacetti, N. 1986. Leg colour in Black Tern. *Dutch Birding* 4: 141.

Baker, K. 1993. *Identification guide to European Non-Passerines*. BTO Field Guide No. 24. Norfolk.

Baker, N.E. 1984. Lesser Crested Tern in Benghazi, Libya. *OSME Bull.* 12, spring 1984.

Barthel, P.H. 1989. Mystery photographs 33: Whiskered tern. *Dutch Birding* 11: 168-9.

– 1991. Die Unterscheidung von Fluß- *Sterna hirundo* und Küstenseeschwalbe *S. paradisaea* mit Anmerkungen zur Forsters- *S. forsteri* und Rosenseeschwalbe *S. dougallii*. *Limicola* 5: 1-32.

Bijersbergen, R. 1988. Dougalls Stern hybridiserend met Visdief op Hoogen Platen in 1982. *Dutch Birding* 10: 121-4.

Blidberg, G. 1982. Massuppträdande av mellanåriga tärnor. *Fåglar i Södra Halland.*

– 1983. Silvertärna eller fisktärna? *Calidris* 12: 204-5.

Boesman, P. 1992. Sierlijke Stern te Zeebrugge in juni-juli 1988. *Dutch Birding* 14: 161-70.

Bacetti, N. 1986. Leg colour in Black Tern. *Dutch Birding* 4: 141.

Breife, B., N. Holmström & L. Blomquist. 1993. Sjöfågelboken. Fältbestämning av sträckande sjöfåglar. *Vår Fågelvärld*, special supplement 18. Stenåsa.

Brichetti, P. & U.G. Foschi. 1987. The Lesser Crested Tern in the Western Mediterranean and Europe. *Brit. Birds* 80: 276-80.

Britton, D. 180. Mystery photographs 44: Caspian Tern. *Brit. Birds* 73: 348-9.

Britton, P.L. (ed.) 1980. *Birds of East Africa: their habitat, status and distribution*. East Africa Nat. Hist. Soc., Nairobi.

– 1982. Identification of White-cheeked Tern. *Dutch Birding* 4: 55-7.

Brouwer, E. 1990. Royal Terns in Spain in September 1989. *Dutch Birding* 12: 186.

Bruun, B., H. Delin & L. Svensson, 1987. *Alla Europas fåglar in färg*. Bonniers.

Bruun, J.B. 1971. Unge terner. *Feltornitologen* 13: 138-40.

– 1973. Unge terner. *Feltornitologen* 15: 182-4.

Buccetti, N. 1986. Leg colour of Black Tern. *Dutch Birding* 8: 141.

Bundy, G. 1982. Field characters of first-year White-winged Black Terns. *Brit. Birds* 75: 129-31.

– 1986. Notes on seabirds in South Eastern Arabia. *Sandgrouse* 7: 29-42.

Burggraeve, G. 1977. Waarnemingen bij een vermoedelijk gemengd broedpaar Dougalls Stern *Sterna dougalli* x Visdief *Sterna hirundo* te Knokke. *Gierfalk* 67: 75-80.

Cave, B. 1982. Forster's Tern in Cornwall: new to Britain and Ireland. *Brit. Birds* 75: 55-60.

Chamberlain, E.B. 1939. Leg colour in Royal Terns. *Auk* 56: 64-7.

Chandler, R.J., & C. Wilds. 1994. Little, Least and Saunders's Terns. *Brit. Birds* 87: 60-7.

Christie, D.A. 1982. Common Tern feeding by wading. *Brit. Birds* 75: 129.

Clement, P., & L. Batten 1989. The identification of large terns. *Brit. Birds* 82: 411-413.

– L. Batten & C.D.R. Heard. 1989. The identification of large terns. *Brit. Birds* 82: 411-14.

Colenutt, S.R. Mystery photographs 176: Crested Tern. *Brit. Birds* 85: 112-14.

Cormons, G.D. 1976. Roseate Tern bill colour changes in relation to nesting status and food supply. *Wilson Bull.* 88: 377-89.

Cramp, S. (ed.) 1985. *The Birds of the Western Palearctic*, vol. 5. Oxford University Press.

Cullen, J.M. 1957. Plumage, age and mortality in the Arctic Tern. *Bird Study* 4: 197-207.

Darling, P. 1985. Leg-length of Black and White-winged Black Terns. *Brit. Birds* 78: 238.

Davenport, M., & J.N. Hollyer. 1982. Royal Tern in Kent. **In** Sharrock, J.T.R., & P.J. Grant: *Birds new to Britain and Ireland*. T. & A.D.Poyser.

Davis, A.H. 1982. Terns showing mixed characters of Black and White-winged Black Terns. *Brit. Birds* 75: 579-80.

— & K. Vinicombe. 1978. Field identification of Gull-billed Terns. *Brit. Birds* 71: 466-8.

Delin, H., & L. Svensson. 1988. *Photographic guide to the birds of Britain and Europe*. Hamlyn.

Dementiev, G.P., & H.P. Gladkov. 1951. *The birds of the Soviet Union*. Moscow.

Dennis, M. 1993. A first-summer Roseate Tern. *Birding World* 6: 125.

de Schauensee, R.M., W.H. Phelps & G. Tudor. 1978. *A guide to the birds of Venezuela*. Princeton University Press.

Devillers, P. 1978. Illustration du plumage juvénile des Sternes arctique *Sterna paradisaea* et pierregarin *Sterna hirundo*. Gerfaut 68: 91-6.

Dixey, A.E., A. Ferguson, R. Hegwood & A.R. Taylor. 1983. Aleutian Tern on the Farne Islands. **In** Sharrock, J.T.R., & P.J. Grant: *Birds new to Britain and Ireland*. T. & A.D. Poyser.

Doherty, P. 1989. Solution to quizbird photograph. *Birding World* 2: 106-7.

— 1989. Ageing of White-winged Black terns. *Birding World* 2: 328-9.

— 1989. Solution to quizbird photograph. *Birding World* 2: 149-50.

Donaldson, G. 1968. Bill colour changes in adult Roseate Terns. *Auk* 85: 662-8.

— 1971. Roseate Tern breeds during the second year. *Bird-Banding* 42: 300.

Dubois, P.J. 1991. Identification forum: Royal, Lesser Crested and Elegant Terns. *Birding World* 4: 120-3.

Dunn, E.K. 1984. Common Tern feeding while walking. *Brit. Birds* 77: 485-6.

Dwight, J. 1901. The sequence of moult and plumages of the Laridae (gulls and terns). *Auk* 18: 49-63.

Eigenhuis, K.J. 1980. Meer over de Dougalls Stern *Sterna dougalli* in het Zwin in 1979. *Dutch Birding* 1: 59-60.

Etchécopar, R.D., & F. Hüe. 1967. *The birds of North Africa from the Canary Islands to the Red Sea*. Oliver & Boyd, Edinburgh.

ffrench, R. 1973. *A guide to the birds of Trinidad and Tobago*. Livingston Publishing Company, Wynnewood, Pennsylvania.

Forsberg, M. 1991. Skäggtärna på Getterön. *Vår Fågelvärld* 51, 5: 54-5.

Gantlett, S.J.M. 1988. Lesser Crested Tern in Norfolk. *Brit. Birds* 81: 282-3.

— & A. Harris. 1987. Identification of large terns. *Brit. Birds* 80: 256-76.

— & — 1988. Identification of large terns. *Brit. Birds* 211-22.

Ginn, H.B., & D.S. Melville. 1983. *Moult in birds*. BTO Guide No. 19.

Glutz von Blotzheim, U.N., & K.M. Bauer (eds.). 1982. *Handbuch der Vögel Mitteleuropas*, vol. 8/II Charadriiformes (part 3). Akademische Verlagsgesellschaft, Wiesbaden.

Grant, P.J. 1978. Upperwing pattern of adult Gull-billed and Sandwich Terns. *Brit. Birds* 71: 468-9.

— 1984. Orange-billed large terns. *Brit. Birds* 77: 372-7.

— & R.E. Scott. 1980. Further notes on the 'portlandica' plumage phases of terns. **In** Sharrock, J.T.R. (ed.), *The frontiers of bird identification*. Macmillan, London.

— & — 1980. Field identification of juvenile Common, Arctic and Roseate Terns. **In** Sharrock, J.T.R. (ed.), *The frontiers of bird identification*. Macmillan, London.

Greenwood, J. 1986. Sandwich Tern feeding over fresh water. *Brit. Birds* 79: 42-3.

Gudow, P.R., I. Andrews, A. Brown & A.J. Kilgour. 1986. Arctic Tern with head-pattern resembling that of Forster's tern. *Brit. Birds* 79: 504-6.

Hario, N. 1986. *Itamären lokkilinnut*. Lintutieto.

Harris, A. 1988. Identification of adult Sooty and Bridled Terns. *Brit. Birds* 81: 525-30.

—, K. Vinicombe & L. Tucker. 1989. *The Macmillan guide to bird identification*. Macmillan.

Harrison, C.J.O. 1983. The occurrence of Saunders's Little Tern in the Upper Arabian Gulf. *Sandgrouse* 5: 100-1.

Harrison, P. 1983. *Seabirds; an identification guide*. Croom Helm.

— 1987. *Seabirds of the world: a photographic guide*. Christopher Helm.

Haverschmidt, F. 1972. Further evidence of the 'portlandica' plumage phase of terns. *Brit. Birds* 65: 117-19.

Hays, H. 1975. Probable Common x Roseate Tern hybrids. *Auk* 92: 219-34.

Hirschfeld, E. 1990. White-cheeked Tern identification. *Birding World* 3: 234-236.

Hirschfeld, E. 1991. Winter plumage of Gull-billed Tern. *Brit. Birds* 84: 168.

Hodgson, I., T. Wyatt & T. Wyatt. 1983. Dark breast-side marks on adult Whiskered Terns. *Brit. Birds* 76: 454.

Hollom, P.A.D., R.F. Porter, S. Christensen & I. Willis. 1987. *The birds of the Middle East and North Africa*. T. & A.D. Poyser.

Holman, D.J. 1982. Mystery photographs 69: Bridled Tern. *Brit. Birds* 75: 422-3.
Hume, R.A. 1979. Mystery photographs 28: Common Tern. *Brit. Birds* 72: 218.
– 1981. Mystery photographs 57: Arctic Tern. *Brit. Birds* 74: 394-6.
– 1982. Mystery photographs 65: Little Tern. *Brit. Birds* 75: 224.
– 1993. Common, Arctic and Roseate Terns: an identification review. *Brit. Birds* 86: 210-17.
– 1993. *The Common Tern*. Hamlyn.
– & P.J. Grant. 1980. The upperwing patterns of Common and Arctic Terns. **In** Sharrock, J.T.R. (ed.), *The frontiers of bird identification*. Macmillan.
– & R.F. Porter. 1981. Identification of a Whiskered Tern in first-winter plumage. *Brit. Birds* 74: 43-5.
Hurford, C. 1989. Lesser Crested Tern: new to Britain and Ireland. *Brit. Birds* 82: 396-8.

Jacobsen, J.R. 1961. Bestemmelse af Havterne *Sterna paradisaea* og Fjordterne *Sterna hirundo* i naturen. *Dansk Orn. Foren. Tidsskr.* 55: 89-96.
Jonsson, L. 1976. *Fåglar i naturen: hav och kust.* Stockholm.
– 1992. *Birds of Europe with North Africa and the Middle East.* A. & C. Black, London.
Jukema, J. 1984a. Visdieven in eerste wisselkleed te Harlingen. *Dutch Birding* 6: 132-3.
– 1984b. Visdief met geheel rode snavel in mei. *Dutch Birding* 6: 133-4.
– 1987. Noordse Stern in onvolwassen kleed te Harlingen. *Dutch Birding* 9: 122-3.

Kaufmann, K. 1983. Tail moult of Forster's tern. *Brit. Birds* 76: 357.
– 1987. The practiced eye. Terns overhead. *American Birds* 41: 184-7.
– 1990. *A field guide to advanced birding*. Houghton Mifflin Company, Boston.
Kemp, J.B. 1982. Identification of juvenile Common, Arctic and Roseate Terns. *Brit. Birds* 75: 127.
Kemp, J. 1988. Whiskered Tern in Norfolk. *Birding World* 1: 398-9.
Kennedy, P.G. 1982. Royal Tern in Co. Dublin. **In** Sharrock, J.T.R., & P.J. Grant (eds.), *Birds new to Britain and Ireland.* T. & A.D. Poyser.
Kennerley. P.R., P.J. Leader & M.R. Leven. 1993. Aleutian Tern: the first record for Hong Kong. *Hong Kong Bird Report* 1992: 1-7-13.
King, B. 1973. Probable Sandwich Tern showing runt and albinistic characters. *Brit. Birds* 66: 538-9.
– & R.M. Curber. 1984. White-winged Black Tern feeding by wading. *Brit. Birds* 77: 486.
Kirkham, I.R., & I.C.T. Nisbet. 1987. Feeding techniques and field identification of Arctic, Common and Roseate Terns. *Brit. Birds* 80: 41-7.
Kjellén, N. 1992. *Argentina november 1991*. SOF.
Kollberg, B., B. Kollberg & N. Eriksson. 1983. Sottärna *Sterna fuscata* på Hallands Väderö i juli 1977 ett fynd av en för landet ny fågelart. *Vår Fågelvärld* 42: 21-2.
Koppejan, T. 1990. Reuzenstern met rode poten. *Dutch Birding* 10: 241.
Krabbe, N. 1980. *Checklist of the birds of Eilat.* Copenhagen.

Lee, D.S. 1992. Specimen records of Aleutian Tern from the Philippines. *Condor* 94: 276-9.
Lewington, I., P. Alström & P. Colston 1991. *A field guide to the rare birds of Britain and Europe.* HarperCollins.
Lewis, A., & D. Pomeroy. 1989. *A bird atlas of Kenya*. A.A. Balkema, Rotterdam/Brookfield.
Lithner, S. 1983. Identification of Sooty and Bridled Terns. *Brit. Birds* 73: 348-9.
Lorentson, B. 1984. Identifiering av fisk- och silvertärna i olika åldrar. *Vår Fågelvärld* 43: 81-3.
Lundberg, B. 1983. Svarttärna en bildserie. *Calidris* 12: 179-81.

Maasen, E.J., & H. van der Meulen. 1983. Visdief te IJmuiden in februari 1983. *Dutch Birding* 5: 74.
Madge, S.C. 1982. April records of White-cheeked Tern in Sinai. *Dutch Birding* 4: 104-5.
– & P.S. Madge. 1983. Forster's Tern in Cornwall. **In** Sharrock, J.T.R., & P.J. Grant (eds.), *Birds new to Britain and Ireland.* T. & A.D. Poyser.
Magnusson, A., & E. Hansson. 1990. Andra fyndet av rosentärna i Sverige. *Vår Fågelvärld* 49: 147.
Malling Olsen, K. 1982. Lär att bestemme hav- og fjordterne. *Fugle* 2, 3: 18-19.
– 1987. Moseterner, del 1: gamle (adulte) fugle. *Fugle* 7, 5: 18-20.
– 1988. Moseterner, del 2: ungfugle om efteråret. *Fugle* 8, 1: 26-7.
– 1989a. Terner. **In** Meltofte, H., & J. Fjeldså (eds.), *Fuglene i Danmark*, vol. 2: 47-63. Gyldendal, Copenhagen.
– 1989b. Head pattern of brown Noddy. *Dutch Birding* 11: 126-7.
– 1989c. Art- och åldersbestämning av *Chlidonias*-tärnor. Del 1: gamla (adulta) fåglar. *Calidris* 18: 11-20.
– 1989d. Art- och åldersbestämning av *Chlidonias*-tärnor. Del 2: ungfåglar på hösten. *Calidris* 18: 163-9.
– 1992. Hav- och fjordterne et af de evigtunge problemer. *Pica* 4, 1: 18-21.
– 1992. Unge hav- og fjordterner feltbestem-

melse. *Pica* 4, 2: 28-31.

– 1993. Fisktärna och silvertärna. *Vår Fågelvärld* 52, 3: 36-7.

– 1993. Sandtärna och kentsk tärna i sommardräkt en liten fältbestämningsguide. *Anser* 32: 50-1.

– 1993. Portlandicatärnor. *Fåglar i Stockholmstrakten* 18: 55-60.

– 1993. Sträcket av måsar och tärnor vid Falsterbo sommaren och hösten 1991 och 1992. *Anser* 32: 253-62.

– & R. Danielsen. 1989. Juvenile Arctic Tern with aberrantly coloured bare parts and abnormally patterned primaries. *Dutch Birding* 11: 123.

Massey, B.W. 1976. Vocal differences between American Least Tern and the European Little Tern. *Auk* 93: 760-73.

– & J.K. Atwood. 1978. Plumages of the Least Tern. *Bird-Banding* 49: 360-71.

Mauer, K.A. 1984. Verenkleed van juveniele Reuzenstern. *Dutch Birding* 6: 100-1.

Meininger, P.L., P.A. Wolf, D.A. Hadoud & M.F.A. Enghaier. 1994. Rediscovery of Lesser Crested Terns breeding in Libya. *Brit. Birds* 87: 160-70.

Mitchell, D. 1989. Sandwich Tern with all-yellow bill. *Brit. Birds* 82: 414.

Moon, S.J. 1983. The eventual identification of a Royal Tern in Mid Glamorgan. *Brit. Birds* 76: 335-40.

Morin, J., & N. Thenell. 1993. Fältbestämning av tärnor (del 1). *Milvus* 23, 2: 24-36.

–, – & J. Sandström. 1993. Fältbestämning av tärnor (del 2). *Milvus* 23, 3: 20-28.

Mullarney, K. 1987. Identification of Roseate Tern in juvenile plumage. *International Bird Identification. Proceedings from the 4th International Identification Meeting*. IBC, Eilat.

– 1988a. Identification of Roseate Tern in juvenile plumage. *Dutch Birding* 10: 109-20.

– 1988b. Identification of adult Roseate Tern. *Dutch Birding* 10: 136-7.

Oberholster, H.C. 1974. *The bird life of Texas*. University of Texas Press, Austin & London.

Oreel, G.J. 1974. Identification of Roseate Tern. *Brit. Birds* 68: 167-8.

– 1981. On field identification of Common and Arctic Tern. *Dutch Birding* 3: 18.

– 1981. On field identification of White-capped Noddy. *Dutch Birding* 3: 140.

Ouweneel, G.L. 1989. Wintering of Sandwich Tern in the Netherlands. *Dutch Birding* 11: 172-4.

Ovaa, A.H. 1987. Forsters Stern bij Ritthem in november 1986. *Dutch Birding* 9: 158-61.

Palmer, R.S. 1941. 'White-faced' terns. *Auk* 58: 164-78.

Parkes, K.C. 1985. Several 'adult' Common Terns attempting to feed juvenile. *Brit. Birds* 78: 147-8.

Pizzey, G. 1980. *A Field Guide to the Birds of Australia*. Collins, London.

Pringle, J.D. 1987. *The shorebirds of Australia*. The national Photographic Index of Australian Wildlife. Angus Publishers.

Reid, K. 1988. Early acquisition of first-winter plumages by White-winged Black Terns. *Brit. Birds* 81: 398.

Richardson, R.A. 1953. A distinction in flight between Arctic and Common Tern. *Brit. Birds* 46: 411-412.

Robbins, C.S. 1974. Probable interbreeding of Common and Roseate Terns. *Brit. Birds* 68: 168-73.

Roberts, T.J. 1991. *The birds of Pakistan*, vol. 1. Oxford University Press.

Robinson, H.W. 1940. The Sandwich Tern breeding in winter plumage and in immature plumages. *Ibis* 14: 150-1.

Scharringa, J. 1980. American Sandwich Tern *Sterna sandvicensis acuflavida* in the Netherlands. *Dutch Birding* 1: 60.

Schekkerman, H., & P.L. Meininger. 1990. Brilsterns in Nederland en Belgie in juni-augustus 1989. *Dutch Birding* 5: 233-8.

Schmidt, C. 1988. Rätselvogel 8. Küstenseeschwalbe. *Limicola* 2: 222-4.

– 1991. Die Bestimmung der Sumpfseeschwalben *Chlidonias*. *Limicola* 5: 93-124.

Scott, R.E., & P.J. Grant. 1980. Uncompleted moult in *Sterna* terns and the problem of identification. **In** Sharrock, J.T.R. (ed.), *The frontiers of bird identification*. Macmillan.

Serra, L. 1993. Juvenile Little Tern starting primary moult in Europe. *Ringing and Migration* 14: 148.

Serventy, D.L., V. Serventy & J. Warham. 1971. *The handbook of Australian seabirds*. A.H. & A.W. Reed.

Slater, P., & R. Slater. 1986. *The Slater field guide to Australian birds*. Rugby.

Smart, M. 1984. Identification of Lesser Crested Tern and its status in the western Mediterranean. *Brit. Birds* 77: 371-2.

Stallcup, R.W. 1976. Pelagic birds of Monterey Bay, California. *Western Birds* 7: 113-36.

Steele, J., & C. McGuigan. 1989. Plumage features of a hybrid juvenile Lesser Crested x Sandwich Tern. *Birding World* 2: 391-2.

Steinbacher, G., & F. Goethe. 1935. Schnabelfärbung bei der Flußseeschwalbe *Sterna hirundo* und Küstenseeschwalbe *Sterna paradisaea*.

*Vogelzug* 6.
Steinhaus, G.H. 1980. Black Tern with bright red legs. *Dutch Birding* 2: 59.
Stern, M.A., & R.L. Jarvis. 1991. Sexual dimorphism and assortive mating in Black Terns. *Wilson Bull.* 103: 266-271.
Stewart, B. 1984. Roseate Tern in first-summer plumage. *Brit. Birds* 77: 359-60.
Stiles, F.G., A.F. Skutch & D. Gardner. 1989. *A guide to the birds of Costa Rica.* Christopher Helm.
Sundberg, J., & K. Söderberg. 1983. Fältbestämning av fisktärna *Sterna hirundo* och silvertärna *Sterna paradisaea. Fåglar i Stockholmstrakten* 12: 86-97.

Thompson, P., N. Lethaby & A. Silcocks. 1985. Identification of large terns. *Brit. Birds* 78: 236-7.
Tostain, O., & J.L. Dujardin. 1987. Black Tern in French Guiana. *Dutch Birding* 9: 68-9.
Trotignon, J. 1988. Les pays d'étangs partie de la guifette moustac. *L'Oiseaux* 11: 50-4.

Ullman, M. 1989. Wing patterns of Common and Arctic Terns. *Brit. Birds* 82: 414-16.
— 1992. Mörka vingteckningar hos tärnor. *Vår Fågelvärld* 51, 2: 22-3.
Urban, E.K., C.H. Fry & S. Keith. 1986. *The birds of Africa*, vol. 2. Academic Press.

van Aalst, G.W.N. 1989. Caspian tern with bright red legs. *Dutch Birding* 11: 27.
van den Berg, A.B. 1979. Witwangstern *Chlidonias hybridus* bij Almere. *Dutch Birding* 1: 22-3.
— 1980. Dougalls Stern *Sterna dougalli* broedend een kilometer buiten Nederland. *Dutch Birding* 2: 21.
— & J.W. de Roever. 1982. Dougalls Stern te IJmuiden in juli 1982. *Dutch Birding* 4: 93-5.
— & J.W. de Roever. 1983. Dougalls Stern te IJmuiden in juli 1982. *Dutch Birding* 5: 103-4.
Vanderbilcke, P. 1979. Velddeterminatie van Visdief, Noordse en Dougall's Stern. *Veldornitologisch Tijdschrift* 2: 93-8.
van Halewijn, R. 1990. Voous' Antilliaanse favoriet: Geelsnavelsterns. *Het Vogeljaar* 38: 127-33.
van IJzendoorn, E.J. 1980. Broedgeval van Zwarte *Chlidonias niger* x Witvleugelstern *C. leucopterus. Dutch Birding* 2: 62-5.
— & F. de Miranda. 1980a. Onvolledig zomerkleed bij Witvleugelstern *Chlidonias leucopterus. Dutch Birding* 1: 108.
— & — 1980b. Over verenkleden van Witvleugelstern in september. *Dutch Birding* 2: 62-5.
Verroken, L. 1990. Presumed hybrid Sandwich x Lesser Crested Tern. *Birding World* 3: 418-19.
Vinicombe, K.E. 1980. Tern showing mixed characters of Black Tern and White-winged Black Tern. *Brit. Birds* 73: 223-5.
— 1985. Mystery photographs 104: Black Tern. *Brit. Birds* 78: 378-80.
— 1989. Field identification of Gull-billed Tern. *Brit. Birds* 82: 3-13.
Voous, K.H. 1983. *The birds of the Netherlands Antilles* (2nd edition). De Walburg Press.

Walhout, J. 1988. Dougalls Stern met hybride juveniel de Vlissingen in september-oktober 1984. *Dutch Birding* 10: 124-7.
Walker, D., & R. Turley. 1989. White-cheeked Tern in Kent. *Birding World* 2: 173-5.
Walker, F.J. 1981a. Notes on the birds of northern Oman. *Sandgrouse* 2: 33-55.
— 1981b. Notes on the birds of Dhofar, Oman. *Sandgrouse* 2: 56-85.
Wallace, D.I.M. 1973. Identification of some scarce or difficult west Palearctic birds. *Brit. Birds* 66: 376-89.
—, D. Reese, J. Busby, P. Parkington & R. Hume. 1990. *Birds by character: the field guide to jizz identification.* Macmillan.
Wassink, A. 1982. April records of White-cheeked Tern in Israel. *Dutch Birding* 4: 62.
Weir, D. 1983. The Northumberland Aleutian Tern. *Brit. Birds* 76: 459-60.
Wheeler, P. 1989. Geographical variation in Royal Terns. *Birding World* 2: 326-7.
Wilds, C. 1985. Elegant Tern at Chintoteaque National Wildlife Refuge. *The Raven* 56: 38-9.
— 1993. The identification and ageing of Forster's and Common Terns. *Birding* 20: 94-108.
Williamson, K. 1980. Juvenile and winter plumages of the marsh terns. **In** Sharrock, J.T.R. (ed.), *The frontiers of bird identification.* Macmillan.

Yates, B., & H. Taffs. 1990. Least Tern in East Sussex a new Western Palearctic bird. *Birding World* 3: 197-8.

# Index

Figures in **bold** refer to the photos, *italic* figures refer to the plates.

**Gull-billed Tern** *Gelochelidon nilotica*

1 Adult summer plumage. Note heavy, black bill and all-grey upperparts. North Carolina, USA, 19 May 1993. *Arnoud B. van den Berg.*

2 Adult summer plumage. Typical but rather short-billed individual. Note underwing pattern compared with Sandwich Tern. Outer tail feathers worn. Abu Simbel, Egypt, April 1993. *Magnus Ullman.*

3 Adult's summer plumage. Note rounded head, heavy bill and long, black legs. North Carolina, USA, 19 May 1993. *Arnoud B. van den Berg.*

4 Winter plumage. Note grey rump and dark trailing edge to primaries, gradually broadening towards tip. Oman. *Hanne & Jens Eriksen.*

**Gull-billed Tern** *Gelochelidon nilotica*

5 Adult winter plumage. Note white head with black 'highwayman's mask'. Malindi, Kenya, January 1985. *Klaus Malling Olsen.*

6 Second-summer. Note winter-plumaged head and very worn 4 outer primaries and primary coverts, as well as dark secondary bar. Bahrain, July 1990. *Erik Hirschfeld.*

7 Second-summer. As adult summer, but note darker outer primaries. North Carolina, USA, 19 May 1993. *Arnoud B. van den Berg.*

8 Juvenile. Note pale-based bill. Faint buff wash to poorly marked upperparts typical for fresh juveniles. Head pattern similar to adult winter. Schleswig-Holstein, Germany, July 1990. *Thorsten Stegmann.*

9 Juvenile. Same individual as in photo 8. Schleswig-Holstein, Germany, July 1990. *Thorsten Stegmann.*

12

14

**Caspian Tern** *Sterna caspia*

**10** Adult summer plumage. Typical individual showing large, red bill and short crest. Turku, Finland, July 1988. *Henry Lehto.*

**11** Adult summer plumage. Note typical front-heavy shape and uniform pale grey upperwing. Finland, May 1988. *Pekka J. Nikander.*

**12** Mostly adults in summer plumage (or nearly complete moult to summer plumage). As early as February, the majority develop summer plumage. Saloum-Delta, Senegal, 4 February 1990. *Anders Tvevad.*

**13** Adult summer. Note solid dark undersurface to primaries (recalling Northern Gannet *Morus bassanus*) and very short tail. Israel, 5 April 1994. *Klaus Malling Olsen.*

**14** Winter plumage. Note dark-spotted, pale forehead. Texas, USA, 26 February 1982. *Arnoud B. van den Berg.*

**Caspian Tern** *Sterna caspia*

**15** First-summer. Similar to adult winter. Note darker outer primaries and dark tips to tail. Oman. *Hanne & Jens Eriksen.*

**16** Juvenile. Dark-centred feathers on upperparts, shorter and more orange-tinged bill than on adults and pale legs are most important characters ditinguishing juvenile from adult (see 10). Finland, July 1988. *Henry Lehto.*

**17** Juvenile. Heavily marked individual. Finland, 21 July 1988. *Tom Lindroos.*

**18** Juvenile in flight. Note orange-tinged bill, dark-tipped tail and winter head. USA, September 1973. *Markku Huhta-Koivisto.*

**19** Flock, with Forster's Terns. Note size, and also difference in stage of head moult, some birds being in winter plumage and others mainly in summer plumage. Texas, USA, early October 1993. *Knud Larsen.*

**Royal Tern** *Sterna maxima*

20 Two adult summer *maxima* and one immature (probably first-winter). Note entirely orange-red bill. Texas, USA, 24 March 1983. *Arnoud B. van den Berg.*

21 Adult summer (or second-summer) *maxima*. Note slender shape. Compare pattern of primaries with that of Caspian Tern. North Carolina, USA, 19 May 1993. *Arnoud B. van den Berg.*

22 Adult winter *maxima*. Compare with Caspian Tern: note much whiter head, isolated dark eye, narrow black mask and all-orange bill. Texas, USA, early October 1993. *Knud Larsen.*

**Royal Tern** *Sterna maxima*

23 Second-winter *maxima* (as adult, but note dark primary coverts). Note slightly uptilted bill, typical of the species. Compare size with that of accompanying Forster's Terns and Laughing Gulls *Larus atricilla*. New Jersey, USA, 29 September 1989. *Klaus Malling Olsen.*

24 Adult winter *albididorsalis*. Note more yellow-tinged bill than in *maxima*. On many fresh birds, primaries show the darker areas obvious on this photo. Second-outermost primary growing, outer primary much worn and faded. The Gambia, mid November 1993. *Hans Larsson.*

25 Adult winter and first-winter *albididorsalis,* with Sandwich Terns. Compare shape and coloration of bill with 23, and size with Sandwich Terns. The Gambia, November 1986. *Hadoram Shirihai.*

26 Adult winter *maxima*. Note contrast between outer worn primaries and paler inners. New Jersey, USA, 3 October 1989. *Thure Wikberg.*

27 Second-winter *maxima*. Unusually red-billed individual. Note worn outer primaries and dark-patterned tail feathers, indicating second-winter. New Jersey, USA, 2 October 1989. *Thure Wikberg.*

**Royal Tern** *Sterna maxima*

**28** First-winter *maxima*. Like adult winter, but with dark secondary bar, dark-patterned tail, and much more worn outer primaries and primary coverts. Florida, USA, May 1992. *Lars-Erik Nygren.*

**29** Juvenile moulting to first-winter. Note pale legs, dark-centred tertials and dark covert bars. Bill typically shorter than on adult. New Jersey, USA, 31 August 1989. *Henry Lehto.*

**30** First-winter. Best distinguished from adult by dark-centred tertials. USA, September 1991. *Peter de Knijff.*

**31** First-winter. Note juvenile-patterned wing and dark-tipped tail. Texas, USA, September. *Harry Lehto.*

32

**Crested Tern** *Sterna bergii*

32 Adult *velox* breeding plumage, with Lesser Crested Terns. Note larger size, heavier, colder yellow bill (like ripe grapefruit) and white forehead compared with Lesser Crested Tern. Karan, Saudi Arabia, 5 June 1991. *Arnoud B. van den Berg.*

33 Adult and juvenile/1. winter *velox*. Note dark grey upperparts and diffusely marked, pale-spotted mask i winter plumages. First-winter worn and mottled. Malindi, Kenya, 1983. *Arie de Knijff.*

34 Winter plumage *velox*. Black mask unusually well defined, but note bill coloration, dark grey upperwing (visible at bend) and - from below - grey flight feather Hurghada, Egypt, April 1993. *Magnus Ullman.*

**Crested Tern** *Sterna bergii*

35 Second-winter *velox*. Oman, January. *Hanne & Jens Eriksen.*

36 Second-winter *velox*. Note worn outer primaries, dark secondary bar and dark-patterned tail. Malindi, Kenya, January. *Markku Huhta-Koivisto.*

37 First-winter *velox*. Note mixture of worn and new (dark grey) feathers, dark lesser- and greater-covert bars, and dark-centred tertials. Kenya, December 1983. *Arie de Knijff.*

38 Second-summer (or older) *velox*. Note very broad and dark tips to all but central pair of tail feathers. Dark trailing edge on hand - as on Lesser Crested Tern - broad and prominent. Karan, Saudi Arabia, 1 June 1991. *Arnoud B. van den Berg.*

39 Adult winter *cristata*. Upperparts much paler than in *velox*, but not so striking as in East African *thalassina*. Victoria, Australia, 24 September 1988. *Klaus Malling Olsen.*

40 Adult winter *velox*. Oman, September 1990. *Hanne & Jens Eriksen.*

**Lesser Crested Tern** *Sterna bengalensis*

41 Adults in summer plumage. Note growing white feathers in forehead from middle of breeding season (as in Sandwich Tern). Karan, Saudi Arabia, 4 June 1991. *Arnoud B. van den Berg.*

42 Adult breeding plumage. Note Sandwich Tern-like jizz. Karan, Saudi Arabia, 3 June 1991. *Arnoud B. van den Berg.*

43 Adults in breeding plumage, with Crested Tern *velox*. Compare size, darkness of upperparts, bill shape and coloration, and forehead pattern of the two species. Bill coloration like that of orange. Abu Ali, Saudi Arabia, 26 April 1991. *Arnoud B. van den Berg.*

44 Adult winter plumage. Note dark, worn outer primaries and secondary bar. All-white tail and pale grey primary coverts indicate this age. Yemen, November 1993. *Magnus Ullman.*

**Lesser Crested Tern** *Sterna bengalensis*

**45** First-winter. Note all-dark primaries and primary coverts, dark-tipped tail and dark bars across lesser coverts and secondaries (the latter broader and more conspicuous than in 44). The Gambia, November 1989. *Magnus Ullman.*

**46** Adult winter plumage, with Common and Caspian Terns. Note similarity to Sandwich Tern, but orange bill. Malindi, Kenya, January. *Markku Huhta-Koivisto.*

**47** Juvenile. Whole plumage seemingly in juvenile stage, although mantle feathers not visible. Bill shorter than on adult. Yemen, November 1993. *Magnus Ullman.*

**48** Second-winter. Similar to adult winter, but note darker-centred tertials. Oman, September. *Hanne & Jens Eriksen.*

**Sandwich Tern** *Sterna sandvicensis*

49 Adult summer, in start of moult to winter plumage. First white feathers to appear in head are normally in upper and middle part of lores. Scania, Sweden, early September 1985. *Åse Mielow.*

50 Adult winter plumage. Note contrast between outer and inner primaries. United Arab Emirates, December 1991. *Tom Lindroos.*

51 Adult winter *sandvicensis*. A very pale-headed individual. Netherlands, 11 February 1989. *Arie de Knijff.*

52 Adult *sandvicensis* moulting from winter to summer plumage. Note fresh primaries, in *sandvicensis* with broad, pale line to inner webs and conspicuous pale primary tips. Netherlands, 10 March 1990. *Arie de Knijff.*

53 Adult winter *acuflavida*. Like *sandvicensis*, but with much narrower pale areas on inner webs and tips of primaries. Florida, USA, December 1987. *Pekka J. Nikander.*

54 Juvenile in moult to first-winter. Note dark-tipped tail, typical of juvenile. United Arab Emirates, December 1991. *Tom Lindroos.*

**Sandwich Tern** *Sterna sandvicensis*

5 Juvenile moulting to first-winter. More advanced stage than in 56. Best aged by dark-centred tertials. Netherlands, September 1988. *René Pop.*

6 Juvenile moulting to first-winter. Note mixture of juvenile and adult-type (uniform grey) feathers on mantle and scapulars. Forehead starting to whiten. Netherlands, 1 August 1987. *Arnoud B. van den Berg.*

7 Adult summer Cayenne Tern (*S.(s.) eurygnatha*). Like Sandwich Tern (*acuflavida*), but bill yellow or orange (varying, usually with some grey, or yellow with orange basal part). Aruba, Lesser Antilles, May 1993. *Karel Beylevelt.*

**58** Adult summer Cayenne Tern. A red-billed individual; note, however, that bill is never as 'ripe-orange-coloured' as on Lesser Crested and Elegant Terns. Bird in background shows bill similar to that of Sandwich Tern. Aruba, Lesser Antilles, May 1993. *Karel Beylevelt.*

**59** Cayenne Tern. Note variation in bill coloration, some showing almost red bill. Also note Roseate Terns in background (adult summer plus one first-summer). Aruba, May 1993. *Karel Beylevelt.*

62

**Elegant Tern** *Sterna elegans*

**60** Adult breeding plumage, with Bonaparte's Gull *Larus Philadelphia* and Forster's Tern. Note long, ruffed crest (depending on alertness) and slender bill, latter red at base and yellower near tip. Many males have red colour at base of bill recalling colour of ripe tomato. California, USA, 14 April 1992. *Jonathan Alderfer.*

**61** Winter plumage. Tail pattern on middle bird indicat second-winter. California, USA, August 1992. *Hans Roersma.*

**62** Adult and probably second-winter(flying). Dark secondary bar on left bird indicates second-winter. California, USA, 14 April 1992. *Jonathan Alderfer.*

**Elegant Tern** *Sterna elegans*

**63** Adult winter. Note complete black mask covering eye. Long, drooping bill visible. California, USA, 24 September 1986. *Jonathan Alderfer.*

**64** Second-winter in flight. Note dark secondary bar, and very dark outer primaries and primary coverts. California, USA, August 1987. *Jonathan Alderfer.*

**65** Second-winter (in flight); basically adult, but note dark-tipped outer rectrices. Lower bird to the left juvenile; note dark upper mandible. California, USA, 24 September 1986. *Jonathan Alderfer.*

**66** Juvenile moulting to first-winter. Note plumage pattern and, compared with adults, shorter and paler bill. Legs pale. California, USA, 24 September 1986. *Jonathan Alderfer.*

**Roseate Tern** *Sterna dougallii*

67 Adult summer plumage. Note all-dark bill (red at base on left bird), orange-reddish legs and very pale, pearly-grey upperparts. White inner webs of primaries create broad, white line on folded wing. Aruba, Lesser Antilles, May 1993. *Karel Beylevelt.*

68 Adult summer plumage with juvenile. At time of feeding young, bill is at its reddest; note more dark on lower than on upper mandible (opposite to e.g. Common Tern). Very long outer tail feathers, and more elegant look than Common Tern owing to longer and more slender bill and longer legs. Rockabill, Republic of Ireland, 9 August 1986. *Killian Mullarney.*

69 Adult moulting to winter plumage. Note darker lesser coverts. Outer worn primaries in very sharp contrast to paler inner primaries. Vlissingen, Netherlands, October 1984. *René Pop.*

70 Adults moulting from winter to summer plumage, with Cayenne Terns. Note very pale, pearly-grey upperparts (v only faint contrast between tail/rump and back/wings). V long outer tail feathers always obvious in adults. Aruba, L Antilles, May 1993. *Karel Beylevelt.*

71 Adult summer plumage, with Cayenne Terns. Note unde pattern and very long outer tail feathers. Aruba, Lesser A May 1993. *Karel Beylevelt.*

72 First-summer with adults. Combination of white foreheac dark lesser-covert bar indicates this age. USA, Septembe *Jonsson.*

**Roseate Tern** *Sterna dougallii*

73 Juveniles. Note differences in upperpart pattern, typical head coloration (with pale spot on upper part of lores), dark legs and overall appearance resembling small juvenile Sandwich Terns. Rockabill, Republic of Ireland, 12 August 1984. *Killian Mullarney.*

74 Juvenile. An unusually pale-headed individual. Rockabill, Republic of Ireland, 12 August 1984. *Killian Mullarney.*

75 Juvenile in flight. Note upperpart pattern intermediate between Common and Arctic Terns. Rockabill, Republic of Ireland, 19 August 1984. *Killian Mullarney.*

76 Juvenile in flight. Note underwing-pattern differences from Common and Arctic Terns. Rockabill, Republic of Ireland, 19 August 1984. *Killian Mullarney.*

77 Juvenile hybrid Roseate X Common Tern. Upperpart coloration similar to juvenile Roseate, but note reddish legs, amount of white on forehead (and, atypically for both species, even pale tips to head feathers) and primary pattern typical of Common Tern. Vlissingen, Netherlands, October 1989. *René Pop.*

**Common Tern** *Sterna hirundo*

**78** Adult summer and juvenile. Juvenile unusually heavily marked. Netherlands, early August 1992. *Karel Beylevelt.*

**79** Adult summer plumage with juvenile. Note typical shape of adult (long legs, somewhat angular head with highest point well behind eye), as well as dark-tipped bill. Finland, August 1987. *Pekka J. Nikander.*

**80** Adult summer. Note dark-tipped bill, pale breast and amount of white in lores. This individual shows larger amount of black on bill tip than most western European birds. Finland, August 1987. *Pekka J. Nikander.*

**81** Adult in fresh summer plumage. In early summer underparts may appear greyer through wear, thus recalling Arctic Tern. Maryland, USA, 17 May 1994. *Klaus Malling Olsen.*

**82** Adult moulting to winter plumage. Note brown-tinge cap when worn, and contrast between outer and inner primaries. Netherlands, August 1989. *Hans Gebuis.*

84

85

87

**Common Tern** *Sterna hirundo*

Adult summer. Note typical, deep-bellied jizz, rather long and slender head and bill and dark outer primaries. Compare translucency of wings with that of Arctic Tern. Camargue, France, June 1983. *Klaus Malling Olsen.*

Adult summer. Note broadness and contrast of dark trailing edge to outer primaries, and compare with Arctic Tern. North Carolina, USA, 19 May 1993. *Arnoud B. van den Berg.*

Adult summer. A worn individual, in late summer typically showing dark secondaries and white-mottled underparts. Pas-de-Calais, France, 29 August 1993. *Klaus Malling Olsen.*

Adult moulting from summer to winter plumage. Very similar to subadult, this stage is common from middle of September. Black bill (with extreme tip pale), winter head and body, and dark lesser-covert bar are all typical of winter plumage; note dark outer primaries and primary coverts, bearing resemblance especially to second-year birds. Netherlands, 18 September 1993. *Klaus Malling Olsen.*

**87** Adult summer *longipennis* (or intermediate). Note darker bill and greyer underparts than on bird in background. Israel, May. *Hadoram Shirihai.*

**88** (Adult) moulting into winter plumage. It is unusual for a bird in such an early stage of moult to show all-dark bill. This and very dark outer primaries may be characters of subadult. Netherlands, September 1988. *Arie de Knijff.*

**89** Winter plumage. Very similar to first-summer. United Arab Emirates, December 1991. *Tom Lindroos.*

**Common Tern** *Sterna hirundo*

90 First-summer. A typical individual, looking like a worn, pale-backed juvenile. Washington, USA, September 1987. *Henry Lehto.*

91 Second-summer (type). Basically like adult, but with pale forehead, traces of dark lesser-covert bar and very dark outer primaries. Washington, USA, August 1987. *Harry Lehto.*

92 Juvenile. A coarsely patterned individual, showing the typical pale brown tinge on upperparts of fresh birds. Netherlands, 1 August 1987. *Arnoud B. van den Berg.*

93 Juvenile. Upperparts grey with white bars when more worn. Note pale upper and lower eyelids and grey, pale-fringed coverts in good contrast to dark lesser coverts. Netherlands, August 1987. *René Pop.*

94 Juvenile. Note darker secondary bar (the most important single character compared with Arctic Tern and grey-tinged rump. Skagen, Denmark, early September 1985. *Klaus Malling Olsen.*

95 Juvenile. Typical individual. Pas-de-Calais, France, 28 August 1993. *Klaus Malling Olsen.*

96 Juvenile. With wear, upperparts turn grey. Note unusually contrasting dark trailing edge to inner wing. Bill often turning dark later in autumn. Netherlands, August 1992. *René Pop.*

**Arctic Tern** *Sterna paradisaea*

97 Adult summer. Note blood-red bill and legs, white cheeks in contrast to silvery-grey breast, and upperpart coloration approaching that of underside. Iceland, July 1985. *René Pop.*

98 Adult summer. Note very long tail streamers, rounded head and short, red bill. Primaries typically appear paler than rest of upperwing; note atypically dark secondaries (may be effect of light conditions). Netherlands, May 1978. *René Pop.*

99 Adult summer. Note typical outline of slim body (deepest at breast) and narrow, but well-defined dark trailing edge to 7-8 outer primaries (less well demarcated on innermost dark). Grey body is always in good contrast to white underwing. Öland, Sweden, 28 May 1993. *Klaus Malling Olsen.*

100 Second-summer. Basically like adult summer, but with varying amount of pale in forehead, white-mottled underparts and (not visible, but present on the actual bird) darker lesser-covert bar. Note translucency of primaries typical of Arctic Tern. Zealand, Denmark, 1 August 1993. *Peter Kock.*

**Arctic Tern** *Sterna paradisaea*

**101** Second-summer. Note dark leading edge of wing, white-spotted forehead, white-mottled breast and shorter streamers than on adult. Västerbotten, Sweden, July 1980. *Knud Larsen.*

**102** First-summer. Note similarities to juvenile, but with all-grey back and whiter crown. On this individual crown is dark-spotted, but many birds show all-white crown, making black mask appear as a dark triangle behind the eye, much narrower than on congeners. Iceland, August. *Lars Jonsson.*

**103** Juvenile in flight. Many juveniles show a shorter dark trailing edge to the wing, exceptionally covering just 4-5 outer primary tips. Note black mask and all-white underparts compared with adult. Zealand, Denmark, July/August. *Knud Falk.*

**104** Juvenile. Unusually coarsely dark-marked individual. Note short legs (compared with Common) and trace of dark spots on median coverts, thus causing dark lesser-coverts not to stand out so clearly as on Common. Netherlands, 20 November 1991. *Arie de Knijff.*

**Arctic Tern** *Sterna paradisaea*

**105** Juvenile. An average-patterned individual. Note that brown tinge to upperparts is a colder greyish-brown coloration than on Common. Note, too, lack of pale eyelids. Netherlands, 11 September 1988. *Arie de Knijff.*

**106** Juvenile. Typical grey, white and black individual. Note rounded shape, short legs and characters mentioned above (104-105). Netherlands, August 1987. *René Pop.*

**107** Juvenile. Note wholly pale secondaries. Netherlands, 22 September 1990. *Arnoud B. van den Berg.*

108

**Aleutian Tern** *Sterna aleutica*

**108** Adult summer. Combination of Bridled Tern-like head and pale grey upperparts typical. Note Common Tern-like contrast between outer and inner primaries. Homer, Alaska, June 1992. *Karel Beylevelt.*

**109** Adult summer. Note pale grey underparts similar to those of Arctic Tern and *longipennis* Common Tern. Sakhalin, June 1991. *Magnus Ullman.*

**110** Adult summer. Note white rump and tail contrasting with grey upperparts. Sakhalin, June 1991. *Magnus Ullman.*

**111** Adult summer. Note dark trailing edge to wing with white gap on inner primaries. Sakhalin, June 1991. *Magnus Ullman.*

**Forster's Tern** *Sterna forsteri*

**112** Adult summer. Note tail pattern and very pale primaries, pale underparts and heavy bill and legs. Virginia, USA, 17 May 1994. *Klaus Malling Olsen.*

**113** Adult summer. Note very pale upperside of primaries. Virginia, USA, 17 May 1994. *Klaus Malling Olsen.*

**114** Adult winter. White head with black 'highwayman's mask' combined with slender, dark bill and brown legs makes winter plumage most characteristic. USA, September 1991. *Peter de Knijff.*

**115** Adults winter plumage. Note contrasting whitish rump and (on left bird) dark inner wedge on tail. New Jersey, USA, 29 September 1989. *Klaus Malling Olsen.*

**Forster's Tern** *Sterna forsteri*

**116** Adult almost completing moult to winter plumage. Note fainter dark trailing edge to primaries than on Common Tern and dark inner webs to outermost rectrices. Adults in September-October are normally i complete winter plumage apart from old, outer 1(2) primaries. New Jersey, USA, 29 September 1989. *Thu Wikberg.*

**117** First-summer. Basically similar to adult winter, but not paler legs and darker lesser coverts. Florida, USA, 6 April 1992. *Björn Hillarp.*

**118** Juvenile. A very fresh bird showing pale brown fringe to upperpart feathers (coloration similar to juvenile Common, but on average paler and more sandy-tinged). Brown tinge is quickly lost. USA, September 1991. *Peter de Knijff.*

**119** Juvenile, average autumn bird. Basically like adult winter, but note dark-centred tertials and darker primaries. USA, September 1991. *Peter de Knijff.*

**120** Second-summer. As adult summer, but note darker outer primaries. Delaware, USA, 16 May 1994. *Klaus Malling Olsen.*

124

**White-cheeked Tern** *Sterna repressa*

**121** Adult summer. Basically like dark Common Tern, but with well-defined white cheek, thus also recalling adult summer Whiskered Tern. Karan, Saudi Arabia, 2 June 1991. *Arnoud B. van den Berg.*

**122** Adult summer. Note dark trailing edge to whole underwing. Above, fresh primaries paler than rest of upperparts. Karan, Saudi Arabia, 3 June 1991. *Arnoud B. van den Berg.*

**123** Adult summer. See caption 118, as well as tendency to paler mid-wing panel. Karan, Saudi Arabia, 5 June 1991. *Arnoud B. van den Berg.*

**124** Adult summer. Note dark grey upperparts. Outer, worn primaries darker than inners. Bahrain, late summer. *Erik Hirschfeld.*

**125** Second-summer type (or adult moulting from winter to summer plumage). Second-summer types show a mixture of dark grey and white feathers on underparts, as well as narrow white bar over base of bill. Israel, early March 1983. *Karel Beylevelt.*

**White-cheeked Tern** *Sterna repressa*

**126** First-winter. Like adult winter, but with retained juvenile greater coverts and one tertial. Head pattern close to that of Common Tern, but dark mask broader, reaching eye level. Yemen, November 1992. *Magnus Ullman.*

**127** First-winter/summer. Note retained, bleached outer primaries and winter-looking head pattern. Karan, Saudi Arabia, 4 June 1991. *Arnoud B. van den Berg.*

**128** First-summer. Similar to Common Tern, but with darker upperparts. Sinai, September 1990. *Hadoram Shirihai.*

**129** Juvenile. Superficially like dark Common Tern, but with darker-centred feathers on mantle and tertials and often stronger cinnamon tinge. Sinai, September 1990. *Hadoram Shirihai.*

**Bridled Tern** *Sterna anaethetus*

**30** Adult summer *antarctica*. Compare head pattern with that of Sooty Tern. Note contrast between black head pattern and brownish mantle. Karan, Saudi Arabia, 3 June 1991. *Arnoud B. van den Berg.*

**31** Adult summer *antarctica*. Note pale collar; compare Sooty Tern in photo 141. Aride, Seychelles, October 1987. *Henrik Kisbye.*

**32** Adult summer *melanoptera*. Note broader nape band and whiter outer tail than in 139. Aruba, May 1993. *Karel Beylevelt.*

**133** Adult summer *antarctica*. Compare underwing pattern with that of Sooty Tern (140). The eastern race have white areas in tail restricted to t6. Karan, Saudi Arabia, 4 June 1991. *Arnoud B. van den Berg.*

**134** Adult summer *melanoptera*. Note larger amount of white in tail than in *antarctica*. Aruba, Lesser Antilles, May 1993. *Karel Beylevelt.*

**Bridled Tern** *Sterna anaethetus*

**135** Race *antarctica*, probably worn adult. Note dark lesser coverts, occurring in worn plumage. Yemen, 13 June 1984. *Arnoud B. van den Berg.*

**136** Juvenile *antarctica*. Note head pattern resembling that of pale adult. Aride, Seychelles, 9 October 1987. *Henrik Kisbye.*

**137** Juvenile *anaethetus*. Rather dark individual. Red Sea, September 1992. *Hadoram Shirihai.*

**138** Juvenile. Note wing pattern. Aride, Seychelles, 9 October 1987. *Henrik Kisbye.*

**Sooty Tern** *Sterna fuscata*

**139** Adult summer. Note uniform dark upperparts and more rounded forehead patch not tapering behind eye. Aruba, Lesser Antilles, May 1994. *Karel Beylevelt.*

**140** Adult summer. Compare underwing pattern with that of Bridled Tern, the solid dark primaries being in good contrast to white coverts. Queensland, Australia, 12 September 1988. *Klaus Malling Olsen.*

**141** Adult summer. Compare collar with that of Bridled Tern (132). Aruba, Lesser Antilles, May 1994. *Karel Beylevelt.*

**142** Adult summer, worn individual. Note (when worn) darker lesser coverts. Queensland, Australia, 12 September 1988. *Klaus Malling Olsen.*

**Sooty Tern** *Sterna fuscata*

**143** Subadult (probably second or third year). Basically as adult, but with dark-spotted underparts. Cousin, Seychelles, October 1987. *Henrik Kisbye*.

**144** Juvenile. Note dark brown, pale-spotted plumage. Queensland, Australia, 13 September 1988. *Klaus Malling Olsen*.

**145** Juvenile. Bearing some similarity to a large, long-winged Black Tern, but easily identified by pale belly patch and underwings (normally palest in middle parts). Queensland, Australia, 12 September 1988. *Klaus Malling Olsen*.

**146** Juvenile. Plumage variable, this individual darker than 145, especially on lesser coverts and axillaries. Aride, Seychelles, October 1987. *Henrik Kisbye*.

**Little Tern** *Sterna albifrons*

**147** Adult male summer. Note pointed extension of white forehead to just over eye, and white rump. Ebro delta, Spain, June. *Karel Beylevelt.*

**148** Adult summer. Note 2 dark outer primaries and white rump. Note that oil pollution causes unusual wing markings. Israel, 3 April 1994. *Klaus Malling Olsen.*

**149** Adult moulting into winter plumage. Note growing white feathers in forehead and bill darkening from base. Three different generations of primaries visible. Flevoland, Netherlands, 28 September 1993. *Ger Meesters.*

**150** Adult summer *sinensis.* Note long tail of this race. China, May 1993. *Tom Lindroos.*

**151** Adult summer. Note white underparts and tail. Netherlands, June 1979. *René Pop.*

**Little Tern** *Sterna albifrons*

**152** Adults moulting into winter plumage. Note differences in bill coloration, some being all dark-billed. Netherlands, September 1990. *Hans Gebuis.*

**153** Juvenile. Note juvenile-patterned upperparts and narrow dark leading edge to wing. Turkey, August. *Markku Huhta-Koivisto.*

**154** Juvenile moulting into first-winter. Note retained juvenile feathers with narrow dark Vs. Netherlands. August 1987. *René Pop.*

**155** First-summer. Similar to adult winter. Sinai, Septembe 1990. *Hadoram Shirihai.*

**Least Tern** *Sterna antillarum*

**156** Adult summer. Aruba, Lesser Antilles, May 1994. *Karel Beylevelt.*

**157** Adult summer. White outer rectrices contrast with grey rump and rest of tail. North Carolina, USA, 19 May 1993. *Arnoud B. van den Berg.*

**158** Adult summer. Almost identical to Little Tern, but note grey tinge to tail feathers. USA, May. *Karel Beylevelt.*

**159** First-summer. Superficially like adult winter. Probably indistinguishable from Little Tern, but with on average broader leading edge to wing. North Carolina, USA, 19 May 1993. *Arnoud B. van den Berg.*

**160** Adult summer. Note grey rump and tail (and just single dark outermost primary, probably more frequent on Least than on Little Tern). Grey tinge to breast sides visible. USA, spring. *Karel Beylevelt.*

**Saunders's Tern** *Sterna saundersi*

**161** Adult summer. Compare shape of white forehead with that of Little and Least Terns, not reaching eye. In summer plumage, upperparts paler pearly-grey than on Little Tern, uniform with rump and central pair of tail feathers. Oman, May 1993. *Hanne & Jens Eriksen.*

**162** Winter plumage. Note grey centres of rump and tail in contrast to white sides of rump. In winter plumage, averages darker than Little Tern (opposite to summer plumage!). Bahrain, autumn 1990. *Erik Hirschfeld.*

**163** Winter plumage. Probably indistinguishable from Little Tern, but in direct comparison darker. Note grey rump on left individual. Yemen, November 1993. *Magnus Ullman.*

**Saunders's Tern** *Sterna saundersi*

**164** Winter plumage. See caption to 163. Yemen, November 1993. *Magnus Ullman.*

**165** Adult moulting into winter plumage. Note moult (delayed compared with Little Tern). Bahrain, autumn 1990. *Erik Hirschfeld.*

**166** Juvenile. Probably identical to Little Tern (apart from rump and tail pattern); probably more individuals shows darker secondaries than in Little Tern. Bahrain, August 1990. *Erik Hirschfeld.*

**167** Adult moulting from summer to winter plumage. Note 3 dark outer primaries and darker grey upperparts than on Little Tern. Oman, October. *Hanne & Jens Eriksen.*

**Whiskered Tern** *Chlidonias hybridus*

**168** Adult summer. Note dark belly, long legs and head pattern, recalling Arctic Tern. Israel, April. *Hadoram Shirihai.*

**169** Adult summer. Note dark grey belly, dark red bill and broad dark trailing edge to primaries. May look similar to some Arctic Terns (but note features above), but never shows deeply forked, white tail. Ebro delta, Spain, May 1987. *René Pop.*

**170** Adult summer. Note uniform grey upperparts and short tail compared with *Sterna* species. Crete, Greece, May. *Knud Falk.*

**171** Adult summer moulting to winter plumage. Note white-peppered head, indicating head moult similar to that of Gull-billed Tern. Sweden, October 1992. *Hans Larsson.*

**172** Adult winter and individuals moulting into summer (probably first- and second-summers). A very pale-headed bird with head pattern recalling White-winged Black Tern. Oman, May. *Hanne & Jens Eriksen.*

**Whiskered Tern** *Chlidonias hybridus*

**173** Adult winter. Note head pattern similar to that of Common Tern rather than to Black and White-winged Black Terns. Thailand, January 1994. *Terje Axelsen.*

**174** First-winter. Many birds are in first-winter from late July. Aged by lack of moult, dark secondaries and dark-tipped tail. Note that lesser coverts may be conspicuously darker than rest of inner wing. Turkey, September 1981. *Markku Huhta-Koivisto.*

**175** Juvenile, with Common Tern. Note checkered upperparts. Israel, September. *Hadoram Shirihai.*

**176** Moulting from juvenile to first-winter. Note retained juvenile scapulars and tertials. The species often looks long-legged, reinforced by the short tail which, typically for *Chlidonias* terns, ends well before wingtips. Israel, 4 December 1986. *Pekka J. Nikander.*

**177** Juvenile. Note checkered mantle and stronger bill than on other *Chlidonias* terns. Israel, early August 1992. *Thomas W. Johansen.*

**178** Juvenile/first-winter. Note dark sides of breast (normally much less prominent than on Black Tern, but sometimes as strong as on poorly marked Black). Dark breast sides are, however, frequently lacking. Israel, December 1986. *Markku Huhta-Koivisto.*

179

**Black Tern** *Chlidonias niger*

**179** Adult breeding *niger*. Bird feeding young has started moult, in Black Tern typically beginning with chin and throat. Dark-hooded bird probably male. Netherlands, June 1978. *René Pop.*

**180** Adult *niger*, moulting from summer to winter plumage. Belly and hind-body are moulted last. In August, most have winter head combined with black belly. Zealand, Denmark, late August 1982. *Knud Larsen.*

**181** Adult *surinamensis* moulting into winter plumage. Most moult forehead and throat at the same time, and become white-freckled as in White-winged Black Tern. Note similarities in head pattern to latter species. California, USA, 23 July 1985. *Harry Lehto.*

**Black Tern** *Chlidonias niger*

**182** Adult *niger* winter with juvenile. Adults have black head pattern and uniform grey upperpart; juveniles are browner-tinged on head and show brown, pale-fringed feathers on mantle and scapulars. Note dark patch on side of breast, on average stronger on juvenile. Netherlands, 1 September 1987. *Arnoud B. van den Berg.*

**183** Adult *surinamensis* moulting into winter plumage. Upperparts average darker than in *niger*, especially rump, which is at most a shade paler than tail. California, 28 July 1987. *Harry Lehto.*

**184** Adult *niger* near end of moult to winter plumage. Note dark patches on sides of breast. Netherlands, September 1987. *Hans Gebuis.*

**Black Tern** *Chlidonias niger*

**185** Juvenile *niger*. Note solid dark hood (compared with White-winged Black and Whiskered Terns), delicately scaled brown upperparts and dark patches on sides of breast. Netherlands, August 1992. *René Pop.*

**186** Juvenile *niger*. Note weak upperparts contrast compared with White-winged Black and Whiskered Terns, somewhat paler grey rump and typical, slender head shape compared with White-winged Black. Note shape and extent of breast patches. The Gambia, November 1993. *Hans Larsson.*

**187** Juvenile *surinamensis*. Compare head and breast patterns with 185. Race *surinamensis* typically shows blackish ear-coverts contrasting with pale-streaked crown, giving a superficial resemblance to White-winged Black. Note, however, much darker and more uniform upperparts and distinct broad dark patches on sides of breast, typically penetrating to flanks. North Carolina, 2 September 1989. *Henry Lehto.*

**188** Juvenile *surinamensis*. Note much larger amount of dark on breast sides and flanks than in *niger*, as well as pale-streaked crown. North Carolina, USA, 20 August 1988. *Harry Lehto.*

**White-winged Black Tern** *Chlidonias leucopterus*

**189** Adult summer. Note velvet-black head and body, white lesser coverts and long, reddish legs. Oman, May 1991. *Hanne & Jens Eriksen.*

**190** Adult summer starting moult while feeding young. Face becomes white-freckled at start of breeding season. Yakutsk, Siberia, June 1993. *Hanne & Jens Eriksen.*

**191** Adults summer, with Black Terns. Note black body and underwing-coverts of White-winged Black and compare with Black. Compare also upperparts, differing clearly between the two species. Poland, April 1992. *Hans Gebuis.*

**192** Adult near end of moult to winter plumage. Note white head, with just faint dark markings, and retained dark summer feathers (especially greater coverts). Compare head and bill shape with Black Tern. Netherlands, 1 September 1987. *Arnoud B. van den Berg.*

**193** Adult moulting to winter plumage. Note retained black greater coverts in good contrast to rest of underwing. Such dark lines may be retained during winter, and are then diagnostic for White-winged Black. Turkey, September. *Markku Huhta-Koivisto.*

**White-winged Black Tern** *Chlidonias leucopterus*

**194** Adult summer plumage. A typical individual; some birds show pale greater coverts and/or reddish bill. Kazakhstan, late May 1989. *Magnus Ullman.*

**195** Second-summer. Note dull black plumage, white feathers in underparts and larger amount of dark primaries than on adult. Kazakhstan, late May 1989. *Magnus Ullman.*

**196** First-summer. Basically like abraded juvenile, but with uniform grey mantle and moult in inner primaries. Scania, Sweden, late August 1986. *Jan Abramowitc.*

**197** Juvenile. Note dark saddle in clear contrast to pale wings (contrast recalling adult summer). Head with much white. less black than on other *Chlidonias* species; dark ear patch typically isolated from dark hood by white supercilium. Eilat, Israel, 29 August 1986. *Pekka J. Nikander.*

**White-winged Black Tern** *Chlidonias leucopterus*

**198** Juveniles and first-winter. Note fuller cap and darker saddle of juveniles. Oman, October. *Hanne & Jens Eriksen.*

**199** Juveniles. Oman, October. *Hanne & Jens Eriksen.*

**200** Juvenile, with Common Tern juvenile. Note larger amount of dark on head compared to 196. Breast lacks dark marking of Black (and some Whiskered) Terns. Netherlands, 1 October 1990. *René Pop.*

**201** Juvenile. A very few show a diffuse, brown patch on sides of breast, thus recalling Black Tern, but patch both smaller and browner. Note typical head pattern; dark ear patches look like head-phones. Turkey, September. *Markku Huhta-Koivisto.*

**Brown Noddy** *Anous stolidus*

**202** Adults. Note variation in black extension over base of bill, as well as intenseness of pale forehead. Queensland, Australia, 12 September 1988. *Klaus Malling Olsen.*

**203** Adult *stolidus*. Compared with *pileatus*, on average whiter-fronted with violet-grey tinge to sides of head. Saba, Lesser Antilles, May 1993. *Karel Beylevelt.*

**Brown Noddy** *Anous stolidus*

**204** Adult *stolidus*. Aruba, Lesser Antilles, May 1993. *Karel Beylevelt.*

**205** Adult *stolidus*. Note contrast between dark secondaries and paler coverts, pale underwing-coverts and long, graduated tail. Florida, USA, 9 May 1990. *Henry Lehto.*

**206** Juvenile *pileatus*. Note dark-mottled white forehead, shorter bill than on adults and faint pale fringes to upperparts. Queensland, Australia, 12 September 1988. *Klaus Malling Olsen.*

208

**Black Noddy** *Anous minutus*

**207** Black Noddy (centre) and Brown Noddies. Note the whiter cap of Black Noddy. Aruba, Lesser Antilles, August. *Dick Meijer.*

**208** Black Noddy. Note very worn plumage. Aruba, Lesser Antilles, May 1994. *Karel Beylevelt.*